The Portrayal of Breastfeeding in Literature

The Portrayal of Breastfeeding in Literature

B. J. Woodstein

ANTHEM PRESS

Anthem Press
An imprint of Wimbledon Publishing Company
www.anthempress.com

This edition first published in UK and USA 2024
by ANTHEM PRESS
75–76 Blackfriars Road, London SE1 8HA, UK
or PO Box 9779, London SW19 7ZG, UK
and
244 Madison Ave #116, New York, NY 10016, USA

First published in the UK and USA by Anthem Press in 2022

Copyright © B. J. Woodstein 2024

The author asserts the moral right to be identified as the author of this work.

All rights reserved. Without limiting the rights under copyright reserved above,
no part of this publication may be reproduced, stored or introduced into
a retrieval system, or transmitted, in any form or by any means
(electronic, mechanical, photocopying, recording or otherwise),
without the prior written permission of both the copyright
owner and the above publisher of this book.

British Library Cataloguing-in-Publication Data
A catalogue record for this book is available from the British Library.

Library of Congress Control Number: 2024939487

ISBN-13: 978-1-83999-309-1 (Pbk)
ISBN-10: 1-83999-309-X (Pbk)

Cover image: Baby and mother. Low poly wireframe breastfeeding. Vector polygonal image in the form of a starry sky or space, consisting of points, lines, and shapes in the form of stars with struct shapes by anttonart / Shutterstock.com

This title is also available as an e-book.

For Fi, Esther and Tovah, with all my love

CONTENTS

List of Tables — ix

Acknowledgements — xi

Introduction — 1

1. Background on Breasts and Breastfeeding — 13
2. Literature for Children — 29
3. Literature for Adults — 59
4. Analysis of Differences — 107

Conclusion — 127

References — 137

Index — 149

TABLES

1 The results from English-language picturebooks that show feeding in the images   33
2 The results from English-language original picturebooks that show feeding in the images   33
3 The results from Swedish-language picturebooks that show feeding in the images   44

ACKNOWLEDGEMENTS

I would like to gratefully acknowledge a number of people and organisations that helped me with this book.

First, in 2016, I received a grant from Svenska Barnboksinstitutet (the Swedish Institute for Children's Books (SBI)) in Stockholm, Sweden, to carry out research there. This enabled me to access Swedish-language picturebooks that feature breastfeeding, and it led to my first academic publication on the subject. That article, 'Breast versus Bottle: The Feeding of Babies in English and Swedish Picturebooks', was published in 2017 in *Barnboken, tidskrift för barnlitteraturforskning (Journal of Children's Literature Research*; Epstein 2017), and that forms the basis of the chapter on children's literature here. Thank you to everyone at SBI for being so welcoming and helpful, including Dr. Åsa Warnqvist, Lillemor Torstensson, Karin Mossed, Simon Springare and Hanna Liljeqvist. Thank you as well for the permission to revise my article from *Barnboken* for this book.

In 2020, I received a grant from Norsk Barneboksinstitutt (the Norwegian Children's Books Institute (NBI)) through the Kari Skjønsbergs Fond in order to research in Oslo, in Norway. While I have not included my findings on breastfeeding in Norwegian-language picturebooks in this book, I want to express my gratitude to those at NBI and at the National Library of Norway, including Kristin Ørjasæter, Anne Kristin Lande and Sofie Arneberg, who helped me find works to analyse.

Saskia Vogel, a fellow translator from Swedish to English, directed me to Karolina Ramqvist's work, which was very important to my understanding of contemporary literature for adults, and so I am grateful to Saskia.

I would also like to thank Swedish author Kristina Sandberg for her friendship and for her insightful literary analyses. Thank you to Kristina and to her family, Mats, Elsa and Estrid, for all the lovely times we have shared.

Two organisations aimed at supporting breastfeeding provided me with information and statistics. Thank you to Fliss Lambert from the National Breastfeeding Helpline in the United Kingdom, where I am a volunteer breastfeeding counsellor, for the information and encouragement. And in

Sweden, thank you to Yamina Hamidi, the administrator of Amningshjälpen (Breastfeeding Help), who was incredibly helpful, first by collating suggestions of breastfeeding-related literature for me to read and then by giving me statistics to use in my analysis. Thank you as well to Amningshjälpen's peer supporters for their reading recommendations.

Thank you to Anthem Press and especially to Megan Greiving for your belief in the subject of this book. I also gratefully acknowledge the useful feedback from the peer reviewers, whose ideas have strengthened the work here.

I also want to thank Professor Amy Brown for her encouragement and for her work, which helped inspire me to write a research-based book on this topic that is accessible to a wide audience.

And, of course, thank you to those of you who are interested in breastfeeding and who are reading this book, or who breastfeed, support other people with breastfeeding, write about breastfeeding or otherwise care about breastfeeding. As this book shows, we have much work still to do, but our efforts should not be undervalued.

Finally, I wish to wholeheartedly thank my wife, Fi Woodstein, and our daughters, Esther and Tovah. Without Fi's support and encouragement, I would not have been able to continue on my own breastfeeding journey, which is what led to my academic interest in the depictions of mothers and breastfeeding in literature. Esther and Tovah are my champion breastfeeders and they have helped me to become a better person and mother. Fi, Esther and Tovah bring love, joy and laughter to every day, and I am grateful more than I can say for their presence in my life. Thank you to my three beloveds for being who you are.

Once again, thank you to all who have supported me with this project.

INTRODUCTION

Breastfeeding: the evolutionary normal means for humans, as mammals, to nourish and nurture babies. Or is it in fact something disgusting, something that gets in the way of heterosexual relationships or that keeps fathers from developing close relationships with their children? Or is it perhaps a way of determining whether someone is a 'good' mother? Or, on the other hand, is it a feminist activity, a challenge to the patriarchy? Does a breastfeeding woman use her body how she likes, turning away from the male gaze? Must breastfeeding be kept to private, darkened rooms, or can it be done anywhere, any time? Is it part of women's work, and how should it be valued? How much does it contribute to society? What messages does a given society send to women about what their breasts are for, and how does literature embody this? And is this different across cultures? Finally, but not less importantly, why does any of this matter? Why is it worth discussing?

These are some of the issues I explore in this book. *The Portrayal of Breastfeeding in Literature* is a work that sits at the intersection of literary studies, cultural theory, sociology, politics and feminist theory, with a few other fields appearing as relevant, such as health, religion, history, art history, somatics and translation studies. The aim here is to understand how literature influences and is influenced by societal views of gender and how fiction for adults and children both shapes and is shaped by expectations for girls and women in a given society. With this analysis, I hope to raise fresh awareness of the power of literature to influence how readers see their own and other people's bodies, and also to illuminate cultural, political and historical differences that affect what writers describe and illustrators depict in literature when it comes to breasts and breastfeeding. I will explore the currently prevailing ways of depicting female bodies in English- and Swedish-language literature and discuss how societal norms influence the writing and illustrating of literature. My perspective is feminist and political, as are my aims. I hope raising awareness of literary depictions of breastfeeding can help lead to changing perceptions of breastfeeding and women's bodies.

In society today, women's bodies are only acceptable and bearable – or bareable – if they are sexy and sexual. Bare breasts are welcome if they are used to sell objects, including women's own bodies, but not if there are babies or children attached to them.

The apparent fear of, or disgust with, the bare breast is obvious not only when it comes to social media, advertisements and public spaces; in this book, I argue that we are uncomfortable with the depiction of breasts, especially in regard to breastfeeding, in literature too, at least in English-language texts. The question this leaves us with is what we can do to change this limited understanding of breastfeeding and of women, and the concomitant detrimental treatment and lack of respect accorded to women and their children.

While this is a book supported by academic evidence and analysis, it is also meant to be accessible and activist, something that anyone can read and use to further their own explorations of breastfeeding in the media. I use a feminist lens to critique the way that one form of popular culture and media – literature – represents the female body, and the messages that this can send, and then, furthermore, to suggest that we need to challenge prevailing notions of what breasts are for and what they can do, what breastfeeding is and what it means to mother. The body is a private space, but it is also a public and political one. In the era of #MeToo, when more women are speaking honestly about the ways in which others have treated their bodies as objects and tried to control them mentally and physically, it is essential that we analyse how we can ensure that women feel able and supported to use their bodies as they wish. We must advocate for women's rights and we must change the way societies around the world treat and value women. This book, then, can be seen as a call to arms or, perhaps, a call to breasts.

The Academic Study of Breastfeeding

Perhaps not surprisingly, given the male-dominated norm in our society, there are very few books or articles that discuss the depiction of women's bodies in literature[1] and even fewer that focus specifically on breasts, despite the obvious need for such material. This book attempts to fill a bit of the gap, and to do so in a cross-cultural way, thereby comparing different cultures and why their representations of breasts and breastfeeding are different.

The academic study of breastfeeding is a relatively new one (see Stearns 1999). Of course, lactation has been and continues to be studied in terms of anatomy, biology, anthropology and breastfeeding support work (e.g.

---

1. There are some works that explore aspects of women's bodies in general, such as Karín Lesnik-Oberstein (2006), on body hair (her book has one chapter on hair in the English literary tradition, by Carolyn D. Williams (2006)), or Kate Lister (2020) on various sex-related topics, such as the vulva, but not many on the female body in literature.

Wambach and Riordan 2016), and recent work has also explored it in regard to topics such as child and maternal health, policy, support and breastfeeding trauma, among others (e.g. Brown 2019, which is a popular book based on the author's scholarly work). Ann Marie A. Short writes:

> Since 1995, when Patricia Stuart Macadam and Katherine A. Dettwyler published *Breastfeeding: Biocultural Perspectives*, the body of scholarship on breastfeeding and culture has steadily grown, including, most recently, books by Joan B. Wolf, Bernice L. Hausmann, and Katherine Foss. In addition, such books as *Lactivism* (Jung) and *Bottled Up* (Barston), and Hanna Rosin's Atlantic article 'The Case against Breastfeeding', alongside the rise of digital connectedness and social media, have all invited more public engagement with debates around infant feeding and motherhood. (2018a, 1–2)

While this is certainly true, and it is positive that there is more engagement around subjects such as the right to feed in public or the average weaning age – although arguably it is also worrying that there is even debate about whether people should breastfeed and where[2] – it is still the case that there are few works that explore breastfeeding in literary settings.

In terms of media generally, I have found some analyses of breastfeeding on TV, mostly focusing on programmes that adults watch (e.g. Foss 2018, which focuses on prime-time television, and Pollister 2012).[3] There have been some episodes of breastfeeding on children's television, such as *Sesame Street* and *Mister Rogers' Neighborhood*, but I have not found an academic exploration of this, although that does not necessarily mean that it does not exist. Pollister writes that

---

2. There has even been the claim that calling breastfeeding 'natural' could lead to people thinking that nature is always necessarily better than scientific advances and therefore rejecting medicine or vaccinations (e.g. Martucci and Barnhill 2016); it is, however, undeniable that humans are mammals and that we belong to this category because we produce milk for our young through our mammary glands. This is how nature works for mammals, so arguably the discussion should be about the promotion of, say, vaccinations rather than demonising what is biologically natural and normal. Despite this argument, in this book, I will not be discussing terms such as 'normal' or 'natural', nor will I discuss the history of discourse regarding breastfeeding, or the concept of how biological norms might be culturally constructed, or other such issues. These are interesting and important topics, but I want to focus on breastfeeding in fiction.
3. For example, Foss analyses TV shows and finds that they imply that breastfeeding leads to increased intelligence for the child, as in *The Big Bang Theory*, or to weight loss for the breastfeeding parent, as in *ER* and *Desperate Housewives* (2018, 96), and Prorokova explores films and TV shows, such as *A Clockwork Orange* and *A Game of Thrones*, which suggest that breastfeeding is deviant and perverse (2018, 138, 141).

bottle-feeding, rather than breastfeeding, is primarily seen in the media (2012, 222).[4] Greta Gaard, looking at American literature in particular, says that texts featuring breastfeeding are notable for 'their astonishing absence' (2013, 2). Ann Marie A. Short (2018b) analyses breastfeeding in one novel, which I will discuss in the chapter on adult literature (Chapter 3), but this is one of the rare examples.

Beyond fictional representations in the media, breastfeeding is appearing more frequently these days in advertising, and while this has been explored to a certain extent in popular sources, it has not been analysed from an academic perspective, to my knowledge. Charlotte Young emphasises how often bottle-feeding is seen in adverts, writing, 'Children play at feeding their dolls, popular TV shows, celebrities, adverts, magazines and news features all present imager that reinforces the bottle-feeding message. Gradually the concept of bottle feeding being linked with positive emotions has developed' (2016, 90). While this is still true, in the past couple of years, there has been a marked increase in companies showing breastfeeding women in their advertising. For example, in 2018, Gap showed a model breastfeeding her child, while wearing a Gap top (Bauknecht 2018), and in 2019, Adidas showed a woman breastfeeding, while, naturally, wearing Adidas clothing (Wordley 2019). And in 2021, Nike produced an emotional advertisement featuring pregnant women, breastfeeding women and women with their children, with the emphasis on the idea that all pregnant, feeding and/or parenting women are athletes, just by dint of doing what they do (Perry 2021). This can all be viewed positively, in that major companies are depicting breastfeeding in particular and mothering in general in their advertisements, and with a range of diverse skin colours as well (without an attendant range of body types, unfortunately), and some may find this empowering and exciting. But there is also a cynical reading: breastfeeding is being monetised. As in so many ways, women's bodies are being employed to sell things. It is interesting, and not really surprising, that these three prominent examples are all related to clothing; perhaps breastfeeding is being celebrated, or perhaps it is just a way of showcasing bodies that can purchase these clothes. As Sara Bauknecht notes, in reference to the Gap ad, 'It appears as though this ad has gotten people in the mood for spending', because some

---

4. Of course, it can be pointed out that the liquid in a bottle could be expressed milk and not formula milk, but I would guess that the general assumption would be that it is formula. And not only that, in one sense, it almost does not matter what is in the bottle; simply seeing a baby being bottle-fed gives the impression that breasts should not be on view and should not be used for feeding a baby. This could lead to people thinking that if they want to provide their child with breastmilk, this should be done with expressed milk through a bottle, rather than directly at the breast.

viewers were so pleased by the representation of breastfeeding that they decided to go shop at the Gap store afterwards (2018, n.p.). Money somehow makes breastfeeding acceptable, in some circumstances. Capitalism's reach does not yet seem to have encompassed literature yet.

But beyond these few academic and popular critiques of breastfeeding in the media, there has not yet been a sustained comparative analysis of breastfeeding in literature.

Methodology and Findings

I will explore methodology in more depth in the chapters on adult literature and children's literature (Chapters 2 and 3),[5] but I want to briefly mention it here as well. First, I have chosen to compare two different cultures, the United Kingdom and Sweden, in their depiction of breastfeeding in literature, because, as I discuss more later in this book, they have different rates of breastfeeding, different levels of support and encouragement for it and different views of women, all of which impact how they write about and depict women's lives and bodies. So this seemed interesting and instructive to me as an approach.

Besides reading widely and voraciously, I used keyword searches in library catalogues, although this more often turned up non-fiction works about the act of breastfeeding itself. I found it more useful to ask for recommendations from parents who currently were breastfeeding or who had breastfed and also from trained breastfeeding peer supporters and breastfeeding counsellors, both in the United Kingdom and in Sweden. These people – the majority of whom were women, with a very few who identified as non-binary – sent me suggestions. Most of the texts for adults that were recommended to me happened to refer to breastfeeding in one or two sentences, while only a very few featured breastfeeding in a sustained way. Even though the short references were sometimes instructive, I was more interested in the longer discussions of

---

5. I initially considered including plays and poetry, especially performance poetry (such as work by Hollie McNish (see Cook 2016)), but I found few examples of the former, and I felt the latter required a more in-depth analysis in its own project, so I have focused solely on picturebooks and novels here, with a few examples from graphic novels, short stories and young adult novels. I write 'picturebook' as one word rather than as 'picture book' in order to emphasise the interwoven nature of words and images in such a text. Natalie op de Beeck writes, 'The compound word *picturebook* presupposes interdependent nonverbal imagery and written language (a title at a minimum)' (2018, 20). I would suggest that sometimes the imagery and the words are more independent than interdependent, and that can be quite interesting, but that is not often the case in my corpus.

breastfeeding, which, as noted, were rarer to find, so I had to read many, many books for adults to find even a few mentions of breastfeeding.

This suggested to me that breastfeeding was seen more as a tiny and often unimportant part of life, even in the life of a small baby, rather than as a fascinating and vital topic in and of itself. And then there was the fact that so many of the depictions were negative, particularly in English-language works. They suggest that breastfeeding is hard, unsatisfying labour and that it may not be possible or worthwhile. I believe the chapter on literary fiction for adults (Chapter 3) shows, on the contrary, that for some Swedish authors, breastfeeding is seen as a worthy subject, and that parenting is considered important and not simply as 'women's fiction'.[6]

The situation was different for children's books; babies and breastfeeding were often the focus of books that included breastfeeding, rather than it being incidental to the story. This meant that in general, for children's books, I had to focus on works about new babies and/or about breastfeeding, and these books were not always of a high literary quality since they seemed intended to teach readers about getting a new sibling or to celebrate the breastfeeding relationship instead of being about a child's life in general. That is, they were often issue books, where the issue was breastfeeding or sibling rivalry. In addition, bottle-feeding was also much more common in English-language works than in Swedish ones.

As implied by the foregoing paragraphs, in regard to the methodology of analysis, I paid careful attention to my exploration of both words and images (with images relevant only to children's literature for the most part, with a few exceptions, such as graphic novels). I used a content analysis approach, thinking through the words and themes used in conjunction with breastfeeding. Dominic Strinati writes,

---

6. Through my use of quotation marks, I am not critiquing the concept of fiction by and/or about women, but rather the way in which it is viewed as its own genre, one that is less than other forms of fiction, presumably those by and/or about men. In an analysis of soap opera, Christine Gledhill and Vicky Ball note that culture is not gender-free, because women's spaces are named (such as women's pages in newspapers or women's programmes on the radio), while men's are not. So men's culture is seen as the norm and women's work as a 'deviation from the norm' ([1997] 2013, 341). Women's fiction (or 'chick lit') is likewise labelled in a way that tends not to be the case for 'men's fiction', because men are the norm ('lad lit' is a term used occasionally, but often in a joking manner). There is no space here to discuss the idea of genre and its limits, but it is important to note the problematic nature of terms and concepts such as women's fiction.

The capacity of the mass media to reflect the reality of women's lives in patriarchal, capitalist societies is something which is important to the liberal feminist viewpoint, and can clearly be examined using a content analysis methodology. Content analysis can be used to show how cultural representations of women, for example, in advertising, distort the reality of women's lives, portraying a fantasy world rather than the one women actually live in. ([1993] 2005, 177)

Additionally, patriarchy in part determines 'how women and men will be represented in popular culture, and how they will respond to those representations' ([1993] 2005, 180). In other words, it is useful to consider which words and concepts and tropes (and images, where applicable) are employed when representing or discussing breastfeeding, to understand how realistic or distorted these portrayals are, and also how readers may, as Strinati puts it, 'respond to those representations' (ibid.).

In regard to analysing representation, Stuart Hall, Jessica Evans and Sean Nixon differentiate between the semiotic approach, which 'is concerned with the *how* of representation, with how language produces meaning', and the discursive approach, which 'is more concerned with the *effects and consequences* of representation' ([1997] 2013, xxii; italics original). Here, I do not differentiate between approaches, nor do I find that particularly helpful. Rather, I want to understand both *how* breastfeeding is represented and what the messages, or *effects and consequences*, are in this representation. These two approaches seem obviously intertwined to me, and both are relevant.

I believe that literature does not exist in a vacuum; it is written, edited, translated and published in particular cultural and historical contexts by real people, who have power over the process. This relates to Hall, Evans and Nixon's 'how'. It is likewise purchased, borrowed and read in specific contexts by other people. Therefore, to me, it is essential to consider the impact that the words and images in books have on readers; this is the 'effects and consequences'. In a different research project, it would be worth exploring the responses to these texts experienced by real readers, and to do this through surveys and interviews; here, however, I have focused on analysing what messages the texts seem to be offering and how they might reflect or challenge societal beliefs.

As Philip Smith and Alexander Riley write, there are two main theories about or approaches to culture: '(1) those that see culture as something produced by society in various ways, and (2) those that see culture as an autonomous force steering society' ([2001] 2009, 3). Smith and Riley note that the second theory is more prevalent today (ibid.), but I suspect that, like nature and nurture, the two are deeply connected. In terms of breastfeeding, how a culture views women, mothers, breasts, and breastfeeding will influence whether women breastfeed and how breastfeeding is depicted in the media, including literary fiction. In turn, depictions in the media will continue to affect the way people understand gender, bodies, parenting and feeding babies, and this will impact choices individuals make about using their bodies, or not, to feed their children. Hall, Evans and Nixon talk about the circuit of culture, which shows the connections between representation, regulation, consumption, identity and production ([1997] 2013, xviii), and I feel the circuit is a useful concept here for understanding the way society both shapes and is shaped by how women use their bodies, and also the way that breastfeeding is depicted is both shaped by and in turn shapes how women are seen in society.

A final aspect of methodology to mention is that I have chosen to compare portrayals in two languages and cultures; I thought this would be revealing about the interplay between culture and literary production. The simple reason behind the choice of the two specific languages here is that they are the two I am most fluent in. In my analysis of the literary output in English and Swedish, I found significant differences, which to me implies a difference in the cultures, and I wanted to understand reasons why two cultures – both Western and with other commonalities[7] – might have such varying views about breastfeeding. I also wondered what we in the United Kingdom might learn from the Swedish example, in regard to normalising breastfeeding more and therefore portraying it more, which would lead to our society supporting it even more, and then depicting it more, and so on. That would be a circuit of culture, whether positive or negative.

In short, I believe that focusing in depth on the content of the words and images in books for adults and children in both English and Swedish is informative and edifying, and can help shape future societal change. If Sweden – while certainly no perfect country without any issues at all – can have higher breastfeeding rates and more positive portrayals of breastfeeding in literature, why is this not also possible in English-speaking countries?

Structure of the Book

This book has a simple structure, with a small number of rather long, detailed chapters. I start with a chapter of background discussion regarding breasts, breastfeeding and women's bodies. The chapter that follows analyses children's literature, and the one after that looks at literature for adults; due to the differing intended audiences and also the difference regarding the employment of images, it seemed simpler to separate the two types of literature in

---

7. Indeed, both are 'WEIRD' countries, i.e. Western, educated, industrialized, rich and democratic.

this way. Both chapters start with English-language literature and then move on to Swedish-language texts. I wanted to compare the two cultures within each chapter rather than separating them into different chapters. The chapter that follows these two explorations of literary texts focuses on analysing what might have caused such significant differences between the two cultures' literary outputs. Finally, the book closes with a conclusion, in which I emphasise how essential it is that we value women's work and also create a virtuous cycle or circuit of culture in relation to breastfeeding.

Terminology

I feel it is pressing to add a few words about terminology. I am aware that sex and gender are not the same thing, in that biological sex does not always determine gender, and I am further conscient of the ways in which gender can be considered a cultural and historical construct. I want to challenge some of the limitations that culture can place on people, simply by dint of their anatomy,[8] while also celebrating what that anatomy can do and how it can contribute to continued human development.

In general, in this book, I use the term 'breastfeeding'. As already mentioned, humans are mammals and we have evolved to feed our young through our mammary glands, which tend to be termed 'breasts'; we do not yet use the term 'mammary feeding'. However, I want to acknowledge that some people, especially in a US context, use the term 'nursing', while others, especially in queer circles, prefer 'chestfeeding', which removes the emphasis from the idea of breasts, as they tend to be linked to females, and of course, it is not always women who feed their children with their mammaries. Where relevant, I will use one of the other terms, but I hope that no one will take offense if I primarily use 'breastfeeding', especially because 'breasts' and 'breastfeeding' are employed in many of the works discussed here, and also because so much of what is shown in literature seems to reflect societal ideas about breasts and women in particular. Men's work is valued throughout the world, usually way beyond how women's contributions are valued. Women generally are the ones to carry babies and to feed them and care for them; although it perhaps goes without saying that women should also be free to choose not to have children, as there are many ways to embody womanhood, not all of which need to include parenthood. Hence, I have chosen to focus on the work women do.

---

8. Donna Haraway writes, 'Part of the reconstruction of gender is the remapping of biological sex. Biology is a historical discourse, not the body itself' (1989, 290). I am not a biologist or a scientist more generally, but I would say our culture does need to both recognise the body while also challenging cultural constructions about it.

But it is also important to acknowledge that in this era, many of us are more aware and accepting of the fact that gender goes beyond the binary, beyond the simple dichotomy of male versus female. So although in this book I mostly discuss the ways in which women's bodies are shaped, gendered, socialised, depicted and understood in Western society, I also acknowledge that some bodies with breasts are not female and that some breastfeeding or chestfeeding parents are not women or mothers.[9] However, since my emphasis is on the literal embodiment of gender and social roles in, on and within women, I will primarily focus on women and employ terms such as 'she', 'her', 'hers', 'female', 'mother' and 'woman'. I apologise in advance for any offense caused and wish you to know that my intentions were, I believe, good.

Elizabeth Johnstone, referring to Mary Wollstonecraft, writes that she 'sees breastfeeding as a means to power – an act by which they [i.e. women] may assert their worth outside the patriarchal sexual economy that oppressed and devalued them. Women, she argues, needed to reimagine their bodies not as entertaining "rattles" but as the locus of a domestic virtue that could reform the family and, by extension, civil society' (2018, 22). I am not sure I see breasts as 'the locus of domestic virtue', but I do see them – and women as a whole – as 'oppressed and devalued', and I agree that breasts and breastfeeding need to be reimagined, with their worth asserted. This, in turn, could change women's lives and the greater society. Considering how breastfeeding is depicted in literature and challenging negative portrayals is a step towards doing this. But this is just one of many topics to explore when it comes to the depiction in the media of the feeding of infants and of women and women's work more generally.

My Own Bias

Finally, I must acknowledge my own bias when it comes to this topic. As I write this, I have been a breastfeeding parent for more than seven years. When my wife and I had our first child, I had some struggles with breastfeeding initially.[10]

---

9. I must also note that some trans women breastfeed or chestfeed, but I found so little on this that I have not discussed it at all here. I found one personal essay about someone's experiences breastfeeding as a transwoman. One moving sentence reads, 'Lactating changed how I saw my body. Having breasts was great, but using them to feed another human being? That was magic. Specifically, it was mom magic. I might have been my daughter's sperm donor, but breastfeeding was how I knew I was going to be a mom. It validated my womanhood as much as any surgery ever could' (Fried 2017, n.p.).
10. On a physical level, I experienced vasospasms, blocked ducts and mastitis. Emotionally and practically, I dealt with a lack of knowledge or understanding from doctors, midwives, health visitors, friends and relatives. Accessing support was not a simple matter.

We were pressured to use formula (by midwives and health visitors), and I was also pressured by relatives and acquaintances not to breastfeed in public. Withstanding such pressure was not always easy, and I am not sure I would have been able to carry on without the steadfast support, belief and love my wife showered on me. This experience forced me to consider what people thought about my body, its appearance and its capabilities. This was by turns upsetting, frustrating and fascinating, and I ended up becoming a trained breastfeeding counsellor. Today, I am an IBCLC (an International Board Certified Lactation Consultant), I volunteer as a breastfeeding counsellor on the United Kingdom's National Breastfeeding Helpline, and I also provide breastfeeding support to clients in my role as a birth and postnatal doula.

Breastfeeding matters to me personally as well as politically. For me, it is feminist to breastfeed, because I am taking the time and space to do what I feel is right, emotionally and physically, for me and my children. Meeting my children's needs for sustenance in all its forms has helped me learn how to parent; it has taught me to slow down and to not buy into the idea that I must always be working for an employer, although I consider breastfeeding a form of work, so perhaps in that regard my children are my employers. What I mean is that I am prioritising my relationship with my children and their well-being rather than always focusing on paid work, and this is a challenge to capitalism and to ideas about what success is. Feminism, for me, does not mean trying to be like a man and to live and work as men supposedly and stereotypically do – working long hours, focusing on achievements and earning money, always contributing in a particular, accepted way to society – but rather about bringing my experience as a woman into my workplace and society as a whole. It also means changing how we think about what work is, perhaps by shifting how we calculate gross domestic product so it includes women's labour (e.g. Messac 2018) and redefining what a satisfying, healthy life might be.

So, my unapologetic perspective in this book is that breastfeeding matters and that depictions of breastfeeding matter, and although I am aware that some people do not agree with this, I do not feel a need to give voice to their views, which can in general be found easily on the internet or TV or in contemporary parenting books. Indeed, research has found that there is an 'association between use of infant parenting books that promote strict routines, and maternal depression, self-efficacy, and parenting confidence' (Harries and Brown 2017); in other words, books on parenting that are in support of bottle-feeding, feeding on a schedule, sleep training and other non-evolutionary-based approaches erode people's confidence in their parenting and can cause mental health difficulties. On the other hand, breastfeeding can calm both the breastfeeding parent and the baby and thereby help prevent depression, among many other things (e.g. Sunderland 2016, 265). My wish is that media would show this and help support breastfeeding in our culture. It has definitively been my experience that breastfeeding has increased my parenting skills and confidence and improved me as a person, and research suggests that I am far from alone in that.

Conclusion

Woman as mother, as object, as sexual being, as source of nurturing and nutrition, as well as pleasure and comfort. Woman as body. What gender-specific roles do we feel women need to fulfil and why, and how does our society encourage or pressure females into doing so? What do we think about breasts and breastfeeding in particular, and how do we reveal this thinking in literature? Does this differ from one country to another and, if so, why? These questions were the starting point for my investigations. Some of my findings have disappointed me, in regard to what they reveal, as I had started by hoping for the breast (apologies for the poor pun) and then, over the course of the years it took to carry out this research, learned to expect the worst. Still, I would like to think that this research will spur us on, both to conduct further studies into the topic and also to challenge and attempt to change some of the predominant messages in society today. Literary activism can help us ensure that society acknowledges these obvious facts: Women's work matters. Women's bodies matter. Women matter.

Chapter 1

BACKGROUND ON BREASTS AND BREASTFEEDING

Introduction

As Blakemore notes, 'It's one of the most culturally powerful symbols out there: the image of a mother nursing her baby' (2016, n.p.). Breastfeeding is much in the news these days, with researchers and reporters frequently contradicting and talking past one another. The articles and books approach the topic from many different angles, often not looking at the picture as a whole. Although the World Health Organization recommends that babies be exclusively breastfed for the first six months and then continue to be breastfed for two years or more along with receiving other food, the BBC reported that not even 35% of babies in the United Kingdom are breastfed at six months old, and only 0.5% are given their mother's milk at 12 months (Gallagher 2016, n.p.). It was unclear from this article why this is the case; it could be a lack of support, the belief that breastfeeding was wrong or unnecessary, the activism and marketing techniques of companies that produce formula milk or doctors who are sponsored by those companies, the lack of education regarding infant feeding and the risks of formula or many other reasons. Whatever the cause, the figures are almost astonishingly low.

Meanwhile, *Time* magazine referred to the 'breastfeeding wars' and argued that maternity leave was the problem (Luscombe 2016, n.p.), since women are not given enough time to be with their babies, including time to establish breastfeeding; indeed, the lack of a lengthy period of paid leave is an issue in many places. Other researchers suggest that since infant mortality has decreased in Western society, we need not worry about breastfeeding versus formula-feeding, and we should instead focus on what makes mothers happy, rather than what makes babies healthy and the mother–baby relationship strong (e.g. Lee 2014, 2–3; Burt et al. 2016, n.p.), although perhaps it is worth noting that breastfeeding is known to make mothers calmer and less depressed, even if some commentators think that the ability to leave their newborns and go out drinking would be a greater source of happiness (it might be for some women, but far from all). A short piece from the breastfeeding support organisation La Leche League discusses how many women perceive breastfeeding as a duty that they are pressured to undertake, rather than as something they are encouraged and supported to do (Burbidge 2015, n.p.), which suggests they find little pleasure in it, but it need not be this way.

Research published in the *Lancet* several years ago, which was then featured heavily in the popular press, discussed the amount of taxpayers' money that would be saved if more children were breastfed; it noted that 'breastmilk makes the world healthier, smarter, and more equal. [...] The deaths of 823 000 children and 20 000 mothers each year could be averted through universal breastfeeding, along with economic savings of US$300 billion. The Series confirms the benefits of breastfeeding in fewer infections, increased intelligence, probable protection against overweight and diabetes, and cancer prevention for mothers' (2016, n.p.).[1] I would point out that despite these amazing figures and facts, it did not calculate a monetary value for what women contribute to society with their bodies and their efforts. It is not just money that is at stake, of course; for example, despite the fact that infant mortality is lower than it was a couple of centuries ago, nonetheless, 'the United States has one of the lowest breastfeeding rates and one of the highest infant mortality rates – in the industrialized world' (Baumslag and Michels 1995, xxv). What is behind all this media attention seems to be a new realisation about the impact breastfeeding has on children's health and well-being, and indeed that of their mothers, too.

It has become obvious that many issues have intertwined here to make breastfeeding an emotive topic and not simply a practical one; if everyone agreed that it were important to breastfeed – as so much of the research suggests – then all that would be left to do would be to ensure that all new parents received support with it, but this is not the situation in society today.

Sexualised Breasts

A reason for this is that contemporary society seems to view women's bodies as being primarily sexual; breasts are revealed in advertising (e.g. Palmer [1988] 2009, 33; Gray 2012; Barker n.d.),[2] in newspapers (O'Carroll et al. 2015,

---

1. See http://www.thelancet.com/series/breastfeeding for a series of articles from the *Lancet* (n.d.) on breastfeeding and its health benefits or, rather, the risks of not doing it.
2. Breasts are used for persuasion, for selling all sorts of items unrelated to breasts (i.e. not bras), such as cars, beers, food and more. As shown in the introduction, breastfeeding itself is even being used in recent adverts, to make people believe that certain corporations are truly woman-friendly, regardless of whether their policies bear this out. But most often, it is breasts on view on their own, not with a baby attached.

n.p.), films[3] or TV shows, while women who breastfeed in public are asked to cover up (for just one of many examples, see Tran 2014). This is being combatted to a certain extent by more coffee shops, department stores and other public facilities claiming to be family friendly and breastfeeding friendly (e.g. Starbucks has said they want to accommodate families better (Alico 2016, n.p.)). But despite that, there is a clear confusion about what breasts are for and who they are for.

Women's bodies are viewed as public and always available, but only when it suits society, namely men. In her book, Caroline Criado Perez discusses how little research – medical and otherwise – is done on or about female bodies; instead, researchers use men as the 'norm' and then simply apply their findings or adapt them slightly for women, and often this is not accurate or appropriate. For instance, medicine types or dosages could be wrong because they do not take account of the differing hormones in women's bodies, and seatbelts are not the correct size for the average woman. In terms of why this is the case, Criado Perez writes:

> There is an irony in how the female body is apparently invisible when it comes to collecting data, because when it comes to the second trend that defines women's lives, the visibility of the female body is key. That trend is male sexual violence against women – how we don't measure it, don't design our world to account for it, and in so doing, allow it to limit women's liberty. Female biology is not the reason women are raped. It is not the reason women are intimidated and violated as they navigate public spaces. This happens not because of sex, but because of gender: the social meanings we have imposed on male and female bodies. In order for gender to work, it must be obvious which bodies elicit which treatment. (2019, 313)

We see women as sexual and their bodies as sexual and not functional, except for serving men. Women's bodies are visible, and this includes their breasts, when it comes to men's pleasure, but they should not be visible when not serving men.[4]

---

3. Actor Keira Knightley has recently announced that she will not perform in nude scenes directed by men, in part because of the male gaze (Anonymous 2021, n.p.).
4. Not all cultures view the breasts as sexual; in fact, most do not (Grayson 2016, 188–89). I return to this in the chapter on children's literature. But women's – and even girls' – bodies as a whole are seen as sexual and as available to men, which is in part why the #MeToo movement has gathered power: girls and women are fighting back against the objectifying and harassment that often define our lives.

Lisa Damour notes that in our society:

> girls develop their grown-up bodies while being inundated by images communicating the strong and distinct message that women are valued mainly for their sex appeal. Making matters worse still, widely seen marketing content often exploits young girls – think of adverts with a "naughty school girl" angle – or targets them as consumers, as in those now peddling thongs and push-up tops for seven- to ten-year-olds.' (2019, xix)

Similarly, Lucy-Anne Holmes writes in her memoir:

> We'd done something a bit weird with boobs, I reckoned. Because while it seemed as though boobs were everywhere, they were there purely for the titillation of men. And I guess I had just assumed that this is what my boobs were there for too. It felt a bit to me like we women didn't actually own our boobs anymore – the men did. And the weird thing is, I don't think men even wanted to own our boobs. The media and online porn industry had just given them our breasts. And us women hadn't even noticed. […] And what had gone on with our boobs? I don't even know where to start. Naked teenage breasts were in our daily family newspapers. Padded bras were being made for primary-school girls and sold in Tesco. Breast-augmentation surgery for purely cosmetic reasons was on the rise each year. […] [And yet] for one thing, breasts feed babies […] breasts are a woman's sexual hotspot. (2019, 46–47)

This short passage in some ways sums up the challenges to our society: breasts are 'owned' by men and are employed for their pleasure by the media, including newspapers, advertising and pornography (cf. Hausman 2003, 108, on how breasts should be for women's partners). Meanwhile, girls and women feel pressured to change the look and size of their breasts and do not feel ownership over their own bodies.

Angela Garbes insists:

> Breasts have only one functional purpose: to make food for our offspring. Amid the sexualised images of breasts that abound in our culture, it can be hard to remember this. But breasts exist for babies first – any adult enjoyment or appreciation is secondary. Breasts can only fulfill their true calling through pregnancy. If they've never produced milk, they simply haven't reached full biological maturity (though they can still play a part in a happy and fulfilling life).' (2018, 142)

While this is true from an evolutionary, practical, functional perspective, the pervasive sexualisation of breasts in our society makes it hard to remember that breasts have a non-sexual purpose. Charlotte Young notes that the 'irony of a culture that embraces scantily-clad females in almost every other context, from adverts to music videos, but recoils at a mum breastfeeding, is surely obvious. But why can't breasts be multifunctional, when so many other body parts are? Mouths can talk, eat, vomit, *and* kiss – why can't breasts be both sexual and functional?' (2016, 145; italics original).

In addition, since breasts are on the whole seen as sexual, women have begun to feel embarrassed about using and showing their breasts in non-sexual situations. Robert A. LeVine and Sarah LeVine write that 'shame about exposing the breast, stemming from its significance as a sex symbol, was the underlying reason for the avoidance of breast-feeding and [that] the mothers found it embarrassing to admit to feeling ashamed, hence their claims of physical inadequacy' (2016, 53). In other words, some women claim they cannot breastfeed in order to hide the fact that they do not want to, in part because they worry about showing their breasts to their baby or having their breasts exposed publicly, in a non-sexualised manner. We might pause over this: despite knowing the risks of not breastfeeding, despite potentially feeling sorrow or grief over not breastfeeding, women would rather pretend they cannot do it than have their breasts be seen as non-sexual. This, along with some of my other findings in this book, saddens me.

Perhaps it is worth remembering as well that breasts can be sensual for women and children, with no men involved, and this might be upsetting to the patriarchy and to ideas about who owns breasts (as discussed more later, challenging the male gaze is something breastfeeding can do). Kerstin Uvnäs Moberg (2019) explains the essential role of the hormone oxytocin in a variety of situations, including sex, birth and breastfeeding, and Sarah Blaffer Hrdy notes that oxytocin makes women want to be close to their children (1999, 139); breastfeeding is an intimate act between the mother and child, who intertwine to become a single dyad. Oxytocin makes lactation sensual – which is not the same as sexual, even if the hormone also appears in sexual situations – and this, too, may feel uncomfortable or inappropriate or frightening (cf. Lawrence 2020, regarding women who might even find breastfeeding to be a turn-on). Enjoying breastfeeding, particularly when most messages regarding it claim that it is usually painful (see Chapter 3 for more on this) and also when the overall impression given by our society is that breasts are for men and their pleasure, and not for women or babies, might add to the shame and confusion women feel about their bodies.

Also, part of the reason why breasts are not seen as multifunctional may be because, as Bernice L. Hausman writes, breastfeeding now 'seems dangerously close to other values that Americans specifically repudiate, such as a lack of defined boundaries between individuals, the uncertain regulation of the infant into cultural values, and an ambivalence about the mother's body as simultaneously a reliable source of nourishment for her baby and a site of sexual excitation' (2003, 94). In other words, breastfeeding is threatening not just because breasts are seen as sexual but also because breastfeeding itself is considered a challenge to Western or American values, such as independence (Hausman 2003, 15). When so many parenting guides encourage parents to leave their children to bottle-feed, to cry themselves to sleep, to sleep alone, to follow strict schedules, to sit untouched in pushchairs and to otherwise be 'independent', it is not surprising that parents who choose to do otherwise – to breastfeed, babywear, co-sleep, meet their children's needs on demand and so on – wonder if they are doing something wrong or unnatural (Harries and Brown 2017).

But is this the case? Is breastfeeding a challenge to independence or the way towards it? Indeed, what is breastfeeding?

Breastfeeding

Breastfeeding, quite simply, means providing an infant or toddler with breastmilk, usually directly from the breasts. Sarah Blaffer Hrdy explains the evolutionary importance of it:

> It is clear that the 'milky way' initiated the evolution of a charmed relationship between dependent immatures and their hostess [...] only among the followers of the milky way did that old opportunist Mother Nature get to try out different neuroendocrine combinations and select for the ones that promoted the *social relationships* most conducive to infant survival and to the mother's long-term reproductive success. Sex may not be destiny in the sense that it is necessarily a female that cares for offspring, but lactation requires a female to stay near her young. Prolonged association between mother and suckling young provided both the chance *and* necessity for 'social intelligence' to evolve.
>
> Lactation turns out to be a key player in the evolution of animals who were both social *and* intelligent. In this sense lactation was a shaper of destinies not just for mothers, but for all individuals who would evolve a capacity for compassion. (1999, 144–45; italics original)

Hrdy also notes that breastfeeding is a way of conditioning mothers to keep investing in their kids and to prioritise their children (1999, 538). Humans have evolved to feed babies in this way, because it promotes health, social skills, intelligence, a connection between mother and child, and more.[5]

Scientific analysis shows that breastmilk is healthier for children – or, to put it correctly, that it is the norm for children, while formula is risky (Young 2016, 162)[6] – and that those who are breastfed are better protected and have better outcomes later in life. Just as one example, Palmer states that 720 babies in the United States die each year between the ages of 1 month and 12 months because they do not get immunity via breastmilk ([1988] 2009, 48). Artificial milks 'lack all the enzymes, anti-infective properties and growth factors, they cannot really be compared with breastmilk' ([1988] 2009, 70). Breastfeeding also has benefits for the nursing mothers, such as a lower incidence of post-partum depression and a lower chance of getting certain cancers, and there are significant benefits to the mother–baby dyad beyond nutrition, such as comfort and bonding (see, e.g., Hrdy 1999, 141). In addition, responsive

---

5. When it comes to a strong attachment between the breastfeeding parent and the breastfed child, one would think that this would be an unqualified good. Taking a psychoanalytical approach, Mary Jacobus writes that:

   maternal milk not only gives the family its imaginary natural identity; it also provides the means by which social relations may be filtered of their impurities. In addition, maternal breast-feeding leads to permanent attachment to the mother, giving milk a single, unproblematic referent. [...] The mother comes to stand for conservation as well as for attachment, providing the grounds for signification itself. (1995, 214)

   While Jacobus may call this 'unproblematic', one could imagine that some people would differ, feeling that children should not have a 'single [...] referent' but multiple ones, attaching to fathers or other relatives as well as to mothers, and indeed, this is one reason why some people argue for babies to be bottle-fed (see Chapter 3 for more on the father–child relationship). Of course, breastfeeding does not stop others from connecting to the baby, but it does strengthen the bond between the feeding parent and the child, and there might be jealousy or anger around this. So this could be part of the reason why there is a preference for a woman's body to be sexualised, or even treated neutrally, rather than as a 'referent' and a source of attachment for a child.

6. An issue frequently discussed in breastfeeding support is the problem of saying breast is 'best', because that implies something else is 'second-best' or 'almost as good'. In fact, breast is the norm, and everything else is a risky alternative that may have to do in certain situations. As Charlotte Young explains:

   Once overwhelming research demonstrated that formula-fed babies were at greater risk of health problems, it became impossible to continue marketing formula as superior to breastmilk. Instead the formula companies adopted the technique described above, elevating breastmilk to 'best' – the equivalent of 'finest' or 'organic' – thus allowing formula to take the 'standard' tag. Elevating breastmilk to 'best' means it is associated with words including 'perfect' and 'optimum'. Marketers know that as a society we are drilled in the art of moderation. (Young 2016, 162 and cf. Palmer 1988/2009, xv)

parenting, including breastfeeding, fosters attachment between children and mothers, and leads to better parenting skills and more independent children (e.g. Landry et al. 2003; AskDrSears 2020). Given how we have evolved and the impact of breastfeeding, it has, until recently, been the biological and societal norm.[7]

There are multiple reasons why breastfeeding is now less common than formula-feeding in the United Kingdom, the United States and many other countries. Some have been mentioned above already, in terms of how women's breasts are perceived, but here, I want to briefly mention a couple of points that are relevant to the Western context and thus to the publication of the texts analysed in this book; for further detailed information on the topic, see Jennifer Grayson's book *Unlatched* (2016). One key point has been increased industrialisation and the pressure to earn money, where more women are required to work for longer hours, away from their babies (Grayson 2016, 73), which obviously makes it difficult to be with one's baby and to breastfeed on demand, while anyone caring for the baby can give a bottle of formula; increased paid maternity leave and an assurance that a woman's job will be waiting for her when she returns to work would help rectify this.

Also, the medicalisation of pregnancy, birth and childrearing could perhaps be said to have started this decline; from the eighteenth century, male professionals began to advise women on childbearing and childrearing, ignoring or even arguing against the information women had shared among themselves and the support they had given each other for centuries, and male doctors began to replace female midwives as the norm for healthcare during pregnancy, childbirth and the postpartum period (Hausman 2003, 10; also see van Esterik 1989, 111).

Medicalisation led to less knowledge about breastfeeding being shared, as men were inexperienced at breastfeeding and less knowledgeable about how it worked, while they also had much confidence in the artificial and supposedly scientific substitutes produced by male-run companies, because doctors and scientists were – and are – positioned as authorities who know more than the often less-educated women themselves. This in turn caused a loss of confidence around how to feed a child. Palmer writes, 'Confidence plays a huge part and if a woman has seen breastfeeding all her life and assumes it works, then she will have it. When you live in an artificial feeding culture, you miss the unconscious, lifelong lessons of how to hold your baby' ([1988] 2009, 28) The development of artificial milk was viewed as something scientific and correct,

---

7. There is no space here to discuss wet-nursing or the history of breastmilk substitutes; despite these two options, throughout history most babies have been breastfed or else they have simply not survived.

and women who were now uncertain about their breastfeeding skills or about the quality of their milk could instead rely on a product developed by these men of science; for some people, artificial milk is incorrectly 'considered to be an improvement on nature' (Maher [1992] 1995, 31) because it was developed by science and can be quantified; that it is missing many of breastmilk's qualities and ingredients is overlooked.

From about the 1960s, women in the West began to see breastfeeding as something that kept them tied to the home. Liberation discourse and the rise in feminism gave women the idea that feeding children artificial milk was freeing, because it was then a task that could be shared among a variety of people; in other words, feeding a baby was no longer solely women's work (Hausman 2003, 3). While this book is not the place to explore this liberation discourse in any depth, I would suggest that considering formula to be freeing for mothers is patently false. As van Esterik discusses, it does not seem that employing artificial milk helps other people take responsibility for infant feeding. And not only does bottle-feeding still rely on women to carry out the responsibility, but it also creates more work for them and places larger demands on them. Women have to learn how to correctly make up the formula, they need literacy skills, they have to get the water and ensure that it is clean, they buy the formula and bottles and teats, they spend more time preparing the formula, they wash the bottles, they may have to get fuel for boiling water and so on (1989, 183–90). So it probably is more of a burden in many ways than breastfeeding and requires more money, education, effort and time (see Brown 2016, 153, for more on this).

As Hrdy puts it, 'A mother (especially one without a breast pump) lives on a mammary leash' (1999, 537). However, that leash is perhaps preferable to another kind, one where they are objectified. Palmer writes that 'in the 20th century, women were presented with an illusion of liberation through the artificial feeding of babies, only to find their breasts appropriated by men and popular culture' ([1988] 2009, 3), and the pernicious influence of advertising and the media more generally has already been discussed above. That is to say, once breasts were 'freed' from their role as nurturers of children, they were then given a new role, which was to tantalise and serve men. For some women, it might be preferable to serve a man than a baby, but this should not simply be accepted as a given for all.

Greta Gaard notes that the idea of formula-feeding as liberation from women's roles is problematic. She writes that those scholarly works that 'denounce such ecological [i.e. attachment or evolutionary-based] motherhood using the rhetoric of feminist liberation, and at the same time function as backlash texts, since they devalue motherhood in that liberal feminist rhetoric' (2013, 15). That is, claiming to liberate women in this way ends up devaluing women and mothers generally, and breastfeeding in particular. Indeed, it can be women who devalue and oppress other women in this situation, contributing to divisions among women and among political movements that could be acting to improve rights and circumstances for all.

Besides industrialisation, medicalisation, the sexualisation of the female body and ideas about formula including liberation and scientific advances, Hausman refers to a number of other issues that changed how people viewed breastfeeding, such as a racial hierarchy where White people were seen as more rational, and thus, unlike 'irrational' minority others, they should feed babies formula according to a schedule and not breastfeed them on demand (2003, 12).[8] Ideas about race, superiority, place in the world, power and so forth have, of course, impacted more than breastfeeding.[9] All of these issues have combined to contribute to a steep decline in breastfeeding.

Formula is, of course, an important alternative for those women who cannot breastfeed or for those babies who are unable to have breastmilk (such as if they have certain variants of galactosemia) or who have sick, dead or absent mothers. However, it is well known that artificial milk does not have the same ingredients as breastmilk, does not offer the same nutrition or comfort and is not individualised for each child the way breastmilk is (see, e.g., Renfrew et al. 2004; Wiessinger et al. 2010, among many other such texts). 'Medically, nutritionally, immunologically, and emotionally, breastmilk and infant formula – breastfeeding and bottle-feeding – are entirely different and unrelated. [...] Infant formula is just food, but the living fluid, called breastmilk, is food and medicine uniquely engineered for human consumption' (Baumslag and Michels 1995, xxiii). In short, breastmilk is a living, changing substance perfectly adapted to each child's needs, unlike artificial milk.

In the West today, particularly as noted above, in countries such as the United States and the United Kingdom,[10] formula-feeding is more common than breastfeeding and subsequently more acceptable and more encouraged. This is a public health issue, as some of the quotes already cited here have made clear (e.g. the research in the *Lancet*). Palmer, whose 1988 book on the topic was

---

8. In other research on literature, I have found that perspectives on race and rationality have impacted how people write and translate (Epstein 2012, 12–17). I do not have the space here to explore how racist, colonialist, discriminatory views influence society, but given the continuing, urgent need for Black Lives Matter and similar movements, this is still a pressing issue.
9. As evidenced by continuing police brutality, a lack of support for refugees and asylum seekers, fewer supplies to fight Covid-19 in certain parts of the world and many other examples.
10. While formula-feeding is an issue in other cultures and locations too, since I am focusing here on literature published in English in the United Kingdom and the United States, my research has centred on breastfeeding in these nations.

reissued 13 years ago now, writes in her preface to the reprint, 'Twenty years ago when I was writing the first edition, more than three thousand babies were dying every day from infections triggered by lack of breastfeeding and by the use of bottles, artificial milks and other risky products. This is still happening' ([1988] 2009, xv). More than a decade on, this is still true. While in the United Kingdom at least, midwives and antenatal classes discuss and attempt to encourage breastfeeding, they do not seem to succeed in helping the majority of women breastfeed.[11] This is an urgent problem.

Besides the public health considerations (see, e.g., Palmer [1988] 2009, Brown 2016 or Grayson 2016), there are other reasons to support breastfeeding. As Hausman notes, and as implied here already, 'Breastfeeding as an act is no panacea for the subordination of women, but an examination of breastfeeding uncovers central feminist tensions around the meaning of women's bodies, the authority of science, and the social value of maternity in contemporary culture' (2012, ix). Van Esterik expands on this idea:

> Women's control over their own lives and bodies has much to do with the choices available to them for infant feeding. Their access to food, flexibility in scheduling and work load, and social support system influence their management of lactation or their decision to bottle feed. Ultimately, infant feeding choices relate to the position and condition of women, ideologically and economically, in different societies. (1989, 18)

In other words, supporting women to use their bodies in the way they have evolved to do, and as many women in fact want to do,[12] could enable women to take more control of their lives. It is without doubt a feminist issue (cf. Gaard 2013).

Women's work is not valued by Western society, and breastfeeding is seen as caring work, which is considered to be women's work. Francis et al. calculate the ways in which it is caring work (2002, 60–65) and argue that it is 'unwaged caring work', 'invisible and unvalued' (2002, 58). And if we did calculate all the work women do, including cleaning, childcare, cooking and, of course, breastfeeding (e.g. Gaard 2013, 3), gross domestic product (GDP) would look

---

11. In the United Kingdom, there is the National Breastfeeding Helpline, a phone and web chat service that provides free advice to parents about breastfeeding. As a trained volunteer breastfeeding counsellor there, I can attest to how many calls and chats the helpline receives, which is evidence for how parents want to breastfeed but are not receiving the support in person to do so. Specific statistics are offered in Chapter 4.
12. See Brown (2019, 8), where she discusses how 90% of women stop breastfeeding before they are ready, often due to a lack of support, and then grieve this decision.

significantly different (e.g. Messac 2018). I am not fully convinced about the importance of GDP as a way of evaluating people's time and efforts, because it puts too much emphasis on money as being of importance and value above all else, but since it is used as a metric, then it ought to incorporate all work, especially that which is usually invisible, underestimated and underappreciated. The Office of National Statistics (ONS) has an unpaid work calculator, which covers housework, childcare, laundry, cooking, transport, adult care and volunteering (Office of National Statistics, 2016). I decided to try to calculate the cost of breastfeeding. There is a wide range of normal infant feeding behaviour, but if it is thought that many babies feed 8 to 12 times a day, for between 10 and 40 minutes each time, I decided to go for an average of 10 times a day for 25 minutes each time. In a week, that is almost 30 hours. The ONS calculates that alone to be worth nearly £24,000 a year. That does not include the time people spend cuddling babies, changing their nappies and clothes, bathing them, reading to them, playing with them and so on. Nor does that include all the other tasks parents do – especially mothers, because research shows that even when they are the breadwinners, women in heterosexual relationships still do the majority of the labour (e.g. Hess et al. 2020; Rao 2019) – such as preparing meals or changing linens on the beds or hoovering, and so on. This also does not cover all the mental and emotional labour, such as helping children calm down from a tantrum, remembering to buy birthday presents, calling relatives to see how they are or booking appointments with the dentist. So £24,000 a year is an extremely conservative estimate of the value of a mother's unpaid labour in the home.

Also, as noted above, breastfeeding saves money, because people need not buy bottles, formula milk or other supplies, and breastfed babies do not suffer as many illnesses as those given artificial milk, so there is subsequently less pressure on health services (Francis et al. 2002, 78–81). So from a coldly financial outlook – and the emphasis on the bottom line in metrics such as GDP or the focus on finance by companies that seek to monetise breastfeeding is cold – it is sensible, never mind all the other risks involved in not doing it.

In addition, as Gaard points out, breastfeeding might contribute to 'self-worth for the nursing mother, whose milk seems to be the only material she can control' (2013, 1). While this might seem to link to the idea of the 'good' mother, which is explored in depth in Chapter 3, in fact this goes beyond that. It is about the woman's feelings about herself, about the way she values herself, rather than how others value her. It is, in short, a form of empowerment.

In sum, breastfeeding is better for children (and their mothers and the mother–child relationship), and the feeding of children is an issue for medical, cultural, financial and political reasons. And yet, it is currently subordinate to formula-feeding. This is, I believe, reflected in how literature for adults and children depicts the feeding of infants and toddlers, as I will show in the later chapters of this book.

The Body

Finally, to open up this discussion slightly, I want to discuss the female body a little more generally and consider the way the body in literature will be explored in the following chapters. Interestingly to me, one of the key texts on the study of the body, Bryan S. Turner's *The Body and Society* ([1984] 1996), does not once mention breasts. One would imagine that understanding the body in society – about things you do with the body, how the body is viewed, the way society shapes how you use it and feel about it, the way the body embodies values and opinions – would include exploring different functions of and stereotypes about the body and that, further, this would involve an analysis of gender and the body. Alas, it does not, in Turner's book. Still, Turner at least references women when writing:

> The body has become somewhat disembedded from many of the major institutions of contemporary society, particularly in terms of its relationship to the family, reproduction and property ownership. The body no longer functions within the crucial interplay of property, wealth and inheritance in the household economy; it is no longer so clearly a focus of marriage strategies, monarchical debates or inter-state violence as symbolized by the violent conflict of heroes. This social dislocation of the body means that the body has been more exposed to the playful manipulation of consumerist culture becoming a principal vehicle for what one might call consumerist desire. This separation of the body from its traditional sexual functions is associated with a women's movement which has questioned the relationship between sex and gender, and a gay movement which has problematized the nature of the masculine body. ([1984] 1996, 6–7)

I would suggest the queer[13] movement has also problematized the nature of the feminine body, but besides this, it is an important point that in some ways, women's bodies have become separated from 'traditional sexual functions', such as breastfeeding. This may be part of the reason for the apparent

---

13. Not everyone approves of the term 'queer', but here I use it as an umbrella term for lesbian, gay, bisexual, trans, questioning, asexual, intersex, kinky, queer and any other categories or labels that wish to be included.

discomfort we see in literature around breastfeeding; perhaps our society thinks women should have moved beyond such bodily functions.

Despite the lack of attention paid to breasts in particular, Turner's approaches can be quite useful. He explains how the body is a 'set of social practices', that is, 'that the human body has to be constantly and systematically produced, sustained and presented in everyday life and therefore the body is best regarded as a potentiality which is realized and actualized through a variety of socially regulated activities or practices' ([1984] 1996, 24) Turner also notes that '[a] second tradition in the sociology of the body conceptualizes the body as a system of signs, that is as the carrier or bearer of social meaning and symbolism' ([1984] 1996, 26) and that a 'third approach to the body interprets the human body as a system of signs which stand for and express relations of power' ([1984] 1996, 28). Some of this has already been raised in the foregoing paragraphs – such as the idea that a woman using her body how she chooses expresses power and may feel empowered – and all of it will be referred to in different ways in the chapters on literature.

Philip Smith and Alexander Riley also discuss the way the body is treated in society. They use Turner's ideas and note that the body has to be:

> regulate[d] and discipline[d] by social systems in the following ways: 1 Bodies must be reproduced to populate the society over time. 2 Bodies must be regulated in public space to prevent disorders such as crime. 3 Bodies must be trained to exercise internal restraint against unhealthy desires. 4 Bodies must be represented externally in such a way as to facilitate orderly interaction.' ([2001] 2009, 263)

All four points are interesting to consider, and all are relevant in various ways to breasts and breastfeeding, some of which have been referred to, at times perhaps obliquely, here: women's bodies (usually) are the ones to reproduce and nourish new bodies for society; women's bodies are sometimes the sites of crimes and violations and are seen as public property; potentially unhealthy desires – which can lead to said violations and also to the promotion of formula-feeding – caused by sexualising women's bodies seemed to be encouraged rather than restrained; and women are pressured to represent their bodies in a certain way, such as through sexual breasts instead of nurturing breasts. Women's bodies are 'regulated and disciplined' in other ways that are beyond the scope of this book, but clearly, breasts are treated in our society in such a way as to discourage breastfeeding and women's control of their own breasts. Breasts have almost become separated from women, or at least women have been made to feel that they do not have control over them.

Along these lines, Dominic Strinati writes:

[a] lot of the earlier work on women and popular culture concentrated upon what Tuchman has called the "symbolic annihilation of women." This refers to the way cultural production and media representations ignore, exclude, marginalise or trivialise women and their interests. Women are either absent, or represented (and we have to remember that popular culture's concern with women is often devoted entirely to their representation, how they look) by stereotypes based upon sexual attractiveness and the performance of domestic labour. ([1995] 2003, 162)

Again, then, women's depiction in society is very much about how breasts are sexually attractive; although the performance of domestic labour, including childcare, of which breastfeeding is one part, is important when it comes to women's representation, the sexual aspect seems to take precedence. Perhaps sex is viewed as a domestic labour that is more important than childcare; certainly women might be paid for sex in a way that they are never paid for breastfeeding.

Strinati goes on to say that in the media:

men are usually shown as being dominant, active, aggressive and authoritative, performing a variety of important and varied roles which often require professionalism, efficiency, rationality and strength to be carried out successfully. Women by contrast are usually shown as being subordinate, passive, submissive and marginal, performing a limited number of secondary and uninteresting tasks confined to their sexuality, their emotions and their domesticity. ([1995] 2003, 165–66)

My findings in this book confirm this view of women; while breastfeeding children could be seen as a domestic task, it is rarely seen in English-language literature, at least not in a positive way. Breastfeeding often creates an intimate bond between the breastfeeding parent and the breastfed child, and this bond would leave out men and perhaps thereby make them uncomfortable. A woman should be seen as serving men – whether sexually or by carrying out tasks in the home – or perhaps can be mocked because of stereotypes, but becoming close to a child might be considered to leave men out; it serves the woman and the child, and not the man in a direct sense, even though obviously a father would have something at stake in his genes living on.

So my argument here is that even though research into sociology and cultural theory pairs sexual attractiveness and domesticity when it comes to understanding the representation and embodied meaning of women's bodies, contemporary society – for a variety of reasons already discussed above – seems to have decided that breasts cannot be both sexual and domestic, and the sexual has won out. This limited idea of women's roles and women's bodies has infiltrated society to such an extent that it has impacted the depiction of breastfeeding, and even the actual act of breastfeeding itself.

Conclusion

In this overview, it has become clear that although mammals evolved to breastfeed and although there are medical, financial, emotional, mental, physical and other risks involved in not breastfeeding, contemporary Western society prefers to consider the breasts as sexual sites, primarily for men, rather than sites of comfort and nourishment, primarily for children and for the mother–child relationship. Breastfeeding, then, as an activity, a norm and a barometer of social beliefs, has been and continues to be much in flux over the years. The following chapters will take this further in order to explore in depth the messages literature for adults and children reveal about breasts, breastfeeding, mothering and women's bodies.

Chapter 2

LITERATURE FOR CHILDREN

Introduction

Breasts: as previously noted, among other things, they can feed a baby and they can titillate an adult, but it seems that in some societies, they can only do one or the other. This might especially be the case in picturebooks, where the readers and the read-to might be confronted with breasts and breastfeeding in both words and images. As Perry Nodelman discusses, in reference to nudity in picturebooks, 'boys can be naked without their clothes on, whereas traditionally, naked girls are nude' (1984, 28). In other words, an image of a woman breastfeeding her child in a picturebook may not be acceptable, because women (and girls) without clothes are always nude and sexualised, even if they are carrying out non-sexual tasks. Arguably, girls' and women's bodies are not behaving in a sexual manner in the great majority of picturebooks,[1] and

---

1. There are, of course, some exceptions. An obvious example would be books about reproduction, which often show presumably heterosexual people coupling and, therefore, may show naked adult bodies in sexual situations. However, it is possible to discuss how babies are made without sexualising or even gendering human bodies, as in Cory Silverberg's picturebook *What Makes a Baby* (2013). The illustrations by Fiona Smyth show bodies of different shapes and colours, and it is often hard to distinguish gender, which is part of the point, because the work leaves open for discussion different forms of conception, pregnancy, birth and families. Interestingly, however, feeding the baby is never referred to. Another exception to the idea that picturebooks are non-sexual is rarer than the 'how babies are made' text, and this is the new field of works about consent and/or pornography. See the Book Tastings from Svenska Barnboksinstitutet (the Swedish Institute for Children's Books) for recent works on this topic. An interesting example is the Norwegian picturebook *Sesam Sesam* (Sesame Sesame) by Gro Dahle (2017), with illustrations by Kaia Dahle Nyhus, which is about a young boy who sees pornography for the first time on the computer he shares with his brother. The illustrations clearly sexualise and objectify the female body, in part so the protagonist and his mother can discuss how porn is a fantasy and that sex in porn is not the same as sex in real life. I believe that there are more picturebooks about consent and pornography in Scandinavia than in English-speaking countries, but further research would be required to confirm this.

yet I would suggest that they are nonetheless viewed as nude, and thereby as sexual, which influences the depiction of breastfeeding.

In this chapter, I compare English-language picturebooks[2] to Swedish ones to explore how babies are fed and how this reflects or comments on the society in which the books are produced. As stated in the foregoing chapters, I take a feminist approach, arguing that breastfeeding is a feminist activity, and here that means that women's breasts can be bare and naked in public – including in literature – without being nude, even if the authors and illustrators do not necessarily agree with this viewpoint at this moment in time. It was interesting and somewhat surprising to me that even in some of the major recent texts on picturebooks (such as Kümmerling-Meibauer 2018), I found little mention of bodies, nudity/nakedness, breastfeeding, issue books or some of the other subjects and themes discussed here. Pregnancy, birth, infant feeding and the early years of childhood are very physical and embodied, so I had anticipated finding more representations of the body in picturebooks and more analysis of such representations, and yet there seems to be a shyness, or a shame, about depicting or discussing this.

My findings suggest a number of interesting points. First of all, in English, the breastfeeding of babies and toddlers is depicted mainly in books that are either about new babies or about breastfeeding in particular, and even when breastfeeding is seen in these works, the mother's breasts are often scarcely visible. The reasons that breastfeeding is not often depicted in children's books seem to be that society is uncomfortable with seeing breasts except as sexual objects and also that formula-feeding is more prevalent in many Western countries today. The Swedish case, however, is different, in that breastfeeding is the norm in these books, although there is still some ostensible discomfort with female nudity. As noted already, however, even if there is still some apparent anxiety around portraying breasts and breastfeeding in Swedish picturebooks, there are nonetheless more picturebooks in Scandinavia that show the female body, which perhaps implies that the problem is with breastfeeding itself rather than with breasts.

---

2. I decided not to explore middle-grade books here, because I wanted to limit my corpus and also because I wanted to focus on the connections between words and images. While some middle-grade works include images, not all do, and out of those images, they do not always depict many of the words. For instance, *Ramona's World* by Beverly Cleary includes the sentence, 'An almost empty bottle of formula stood on the lamp table' (1999, 56–57). No illustration goes with this, and although it is an obvious reference, I decided to exclude such works in a chapter on both words and images. It was disappointing to see formula so normalised in a popular classic work for children.

Methodology

One might imagine that books for children would generally feature any topic or issue that occurs in children's lives; in other words, any topic in the world because children live in that world. But as this does not actually appear to be the case, I want to discuss my methodology and process here because I believe it relates to the taboo regarding breasts and breastfeeding in children's literature.

To find books, I initially studied bookshelves and catalogues in libraries; for English-language books, I used my local library system, in the county of Norfolk, where the main Norwich library is considered the busiest public library in the United Kingdom (see Bury 2013); the collection is extensive. Despite the large collection, I was generally not able to find books on the shelves that featured breastfeeding simply as a matter of course. Instead, I had to get suggestions from parenting groups and breastfeeding groups, such as the Association of Breastfeeding Mothers, on Facebook, via email and in person, for books that they knew depicted breastfeeding, and I had to look for books produced by publishers that are pro-breastfeeding, such as Pinter and Martin in the United Kingdom. Since I regularly review books for the magazine of the Association of Breastfeeding Mothers, I sometimes was sent a work by a publisher that I had not found via my own means and contacts. Often, the books that did feature breastfeeding were not in my local library system and had to be requested from other libraries or purchased. The few books that the library already had that included breastfeeding were in a separate 'New Experiences' collection, as they tended to have storylines about a new baby joining a family (in other words, such books are thought to be only for young children who are getting a sibling and need to be prepared, rather than for children generally; see Epstein (2013) for an exploration of the problems surrounding issue books).

For Swedish-language books, I visited Svenska Barnboksinstitutet (the Swedish Institute for Children's Books) in Stockholm, which is a public research library dedicated to children's literature. The staff at Svenska Barnboksinstitutet kindly helped me as well, gathering books that they thought might be relevant. I did not focus specifically on literary or high-quality texts, but rather I read any book I could find that was about babies, especially new babies; my assumption was that such books would be more likely to show a baby being fed. This meant looking for picturebooks that seemed to aim at teaching young readers or those being read to about life with a new baby or else to emphasise the breastfeeding relationship. I also looked for books that were about families in general, especially diverse families, but I found few that showed breastfeeding. For both languages, I used a variety of search terms in the catalogues, such as breastfeeding, chestfeeding, *amning* (Swedish for breastfeeding), attachment parenting, baby-carrying, babywearing, sling, *bärsele* (Swedish for sling) and so on, to try to find additional books.

In short, my method was to be open to any books that might show feeding, no matter the publisher, style or quality, but the fact that breastfeeding was so difficult to find in English-language books is evidence of society's discomfort with it. It is a rare subject, and when it is featured, it is kept in a separate section: this points to it being a taboo. Further evidence of societal unease or embarrassment was found in the depiction of feeding in these works, as discussed later where I analyse the content of the words and illustrations.

I must acknowledge the obvious absence in this chapter of images from the books discussed. While I do discuss illustrations, I do not include samples from the texts for the reader to look at. Unfortunately, the simple reason for this is cost; most publishers made it prohibitive to reprint images from their works. I hope my descriptions will suffice, and I further hope interested readers will choose to purchase or borrow books so they can explore their words and images themselves.

The Prevalence of the Bottle: English-Language Books

I analysed 29 English-language picturebooks, of which 25 were English-language originals. The books were primarily 'new baby' works, which appear to be intended to help older siblings get used to the idea of a new baby joining the household; having milk is part of the baby's daily routine. Those that were not of the new baby style were works that were solely about breastfeeding. There were very few books that included breastfeeding as simply one aspect of the child character's life. Table 1 shows my findings in regard to the depiction of feeding babies and children in the images.

In short, only 12 out of 29 books (41%) depicted exclusive breastfeeding (with 4, or 33%, of those books being translations to English), 6 (21%) showed exclusive bottle-feeding and 5 (17%) had combination-feeding. Of the 29 books, 6 (21%) depicted no feeding of any type, although it is one of the main things babies do.

From one perspective, 41% is perhaps higher than one would expect, given breastfeeding rates in the United Kingdom (although not much higher than the 35% rate mentioned in Chapter 1), but I must point out that if I included only English-language originals in this table, then the figure would be 8 out of 25, or 32%. If I include only books that show some actual feeding (see Table 2), whether by bottle or breast, then the total is 19 for English-language originals, of which 8 show exclusive breastfeeding (42%) and 11 exclusive or combination bottle-feeding (58%).

Table 1 The results from English-language picturebooks that show feeding in the images

	Breastfeeding only	Bottle only	Breastfeeding and bottle	No feeding of milk depicted
Number of books	12 (41%)	6 (21%)	5 (17%)	6 (21%)
Comments	4 of these books are translations; 3 of those plus 1 more were published by Pinter and Martin.			Even if the words referred to the feeding of milk, if no breast or bottle was shown, I included it here.

Table 2 The results from English-language original picturebooks that show feeding in the images

	Breastfeeding only	Bottle only	Breastfeeding and bottle
Number of books	8 (out of 19) (42%)	6 (out of 19) (32%)	5 (out of 19) (26%)

Furthermore, an analysis of the words and images (following approaches and codes suggested in Moebius (2009) and Nodelman (1988), among other works) suggests that not all is positive here. To explore the words and images in more detail, I paid special attention to, among other aspects of the work, the language used to describe breastfeeding, the position of the baby at the breast and the position of the mother–baby dyad on the page, how much of the breast was visible, the presumed age of the nursling, the focus of the image and so forth. However, from the images alone, as discussed in Table 1, it is obvious that the bottle is prevalent.

Discretion: Not the Better Part of Valour

In the images in English-language books, it is often difficult to tell if a baby is being breastfed or is simply being cuddled close. Of course, as people are often at pains to point out, breastfeeding can be done discreetly, although as Wiessinger et al. note, using a cover or blanket over a baby while nursing often just attracts more attention (2010, 145), and babies regularly kick them off, because who would want to eat while under a blanket? The picturebooks that do feature breastfeeding bear – rather than bare – this out. For example, *Dogs Don't Eat Jam* by Sarah Tsiang is about an older sister who tells her newborn little brother what he needs to know for life. Her advice includes, 'You're learning to drink milk. You'll learn to hold your head up and how to look around' (2011, n.p.). The picture shows a baby nestled into his mother's chest, with her jumper artfully draped around his head; no skin is visible. The mother's lap is also fully covered up by a blanket; mother and baby are so wrapped up that only their faces can be seen.

Similarly, *My New Baby* (2009), which has an unnamed author, shows a baby breastfeeding in two pictures, and although there is a small line of skin visible between the baby's head and the mother's shirt, there is no areola, which one would expect to see if a baby is breastfeeding, and the skin could be taken to be part of the shirt or even part of the baby's head. In both of the breastfeeding pictures, there is someone sitting next to the mother, so she and her nursling are not even necessarily the focus of the images (see Moebius (2009, 316–18) on the size and focus of images). Indeed, this book focuses on the older child's feelings around the existence of this sibling. The older child, whose gender is unspecified, wonders why the baby 'always ha[s] milk' and how they can stop the baby from crying and when the baby will learn to walk, among other things (2009, n.p.). The book leaves space for explaining to an older child what it means when a baby joins the family and how the older sibling might feel. The baby is clearly breastfed, given the location at the mother's chest, but again, no breast is glimpsed.

Discretion is often key in both words and images, at least when it comes to books that feature breastfeeding but do not have it as their main topic. Some books that I read I ended up not including in the statistical analysis, such as the Caldecott Honor–winning book *All the World*, by Liz Garton Scanlon, with illustrations by Marla Frazee, due to how unsure I was about what an image was meant to portray. This book shows a variety of people experiencing life, generally in family and/or nature situations, and there was one page that showed a woman holding a baby to her chest while doing what looks like studying. This particular two-page spread depicts people alone or in pairs, holding each other, smelling food, rocking on a porch swing, patting a dog and so on, and the words read, 'Everything you hear, smell, see/All the world is everything/Everything is you and me' (2015, n.p.). The woman with the baby is wearing a long-sleeved top that is on as tops usually are and is pulled down to her waist, as one would expect, but a reader searching for images of breastfeeding might believe that the woman is wearing a breastfeeding top, and that there are flaps around the baby's face that are open for easy access to the breast, especially as the baby is basically in the cradle-hold position. But since the illustration is unclear and I doubted whether most people would read the image as being of breastfeeding, I ultimately discarded it.[3]

In fact, in many books, it is not certain that the baby is or has been breastfeeding, even if a reader might suppose that is the case based on the words. For instance, in *Hello, Baby!* by Jorge Uzon, there is the line 'You just ate for the very first time' (2010, n.p.). The picture shows a baby being held close to a chest, but it could be a breastfed or bottle-fed baby, depending on how the reader wants to interpret it, and the reader's interpretation will be based in part on their own experiences. What the adult reader says to the child read-to will also depend on what messages the adult wishes to impart.[4] In Uzon's work, there is a hand holding the baby next to or under a sweater, but there is no sign of a breast and the baby's mouth is relaxed rather than in a breastfeeding position.

Likewise, in *Cinnamon Baby* by Nicola Winstanley, illustrated by Janice Nadeau, the text reads, 'Miriam held the baby against her breast, but the crying continued. She jiggled it, sang to it, rocked it, walked it up and down and up and down the hallway. But still the baby cried' (2011, n.p.). In the image, Miriam is seen holding the baby against her clothed chest, but no

---

3. This book, as with many other contemporary picturebooks, appears to have diversity and inclusion as its aims, since the images show different ethnicities and possibly different types of relationships, even if the words never comment on this fact. Another picture in this specific two-page spread shows two women close together on a porch swing, with one holding her arm around the other, and a knowing reader might read this as a same-sex relationship. I would suggest that featuring diversity is enormously important and that it is better not to do so in a problematising way – that is, focusing on the problems someone of a certain ethnicity or sexuality might have or, in a breastfeeding-specific example, depicting discomfort with public breastfeeding, among other possible topics – but not mentioning the diversity at all in the words is also problematic in its way, as it creates invisibility and silence to a certain extent. In other words, adults reading this book with a child could easily make a comment that the two women were friends or sisters or that the baby was cuddling close, rather than acknowledging that they might be partners or that the baby might be feeding at the breast.
4. Not everyone agrees with this sort of analysis, in which we consider the messages in texts and how readers might receive them. Smiljana Narančić Kovač writes that 'Wolfgang Iser, who introduced the term [implied reader], defines the implied reader as a construct which should not be identified with any real reader' (2018, 416). Narančić Kovač goes on to discuss how the real reader 'often assumes the role(s) of the narratee(s) and blend[s] with the narratee(s)' (ibid.). While I recognise the distance many find or assume between the implied reader and the real reader, I feel that it is imperative to acknowledge the real readers or read-to of the texts. They read and/or receive texts, bringing their own experiences and backgrounds to the works. I do not think books can be divorced from the context in which they are written, the context in which they are received, the people who have produced them or the people who receive them.

actual breast is visible, and neither the text nor the picture is explicit about whether this is breastfeeding or only cuddling, though breastfeeding would be an obvious way of soothing an upset baby.

These examples can be interpreted as breastfeeding or not, and the words and images are imbued with so much discretion that ultimately they are unclear. One might argue that it is positive for readers and the read-to to be able to bring their own knowledge and experiences and opinions to a text and to be able to decide for themselves if a text is about breastfeeding, bottle-feeding or cuddling (this could be said to be a 'writerly' text, using Barthes's terminology, in that there is ambiguity that requires more work from the audience ([1970] 1991)), but I am slightly more pessimistic about it, or perhaps even prescriptive. Since English-speaking countries have such low breastfeeding rates despite breastfeeding being the biological norm for mammals, a category that includes humans, and since children's books provide an opportunity to educate children about a variety of ways of living, I maintain that picturebooks should explicitly discuss and show breastfeeding, with the dual aims of encouraging more adults to breastfeed any additional children they have and also of educating young readers about breastfeeding so that they too might consider doing it or supporting partners to do so in the future. This is to say that the discretion – potentially caused by embarrassment or shame about the female body – that many of these works show is misguided and can be interpreted as being negative about breastfeeding.

Intriguingly, one of the books that shows the most in terms of the breast being visible is also the book that is the most multicultural out of the entire corpus. Emery Bernhard and Durga Bernhard's *A Ride on Mother's Back* shows babies being carried around the world. In Guatemala, 'Newborn Rosha snuggles in the folds of the shawl tied around her mother. She rides safe and warm, close to her mother's body. Rosha nurses and sleeps, nurses and sleeps' (1996, n.p.). In the image, Rosha's mother makes food, cooking a sort of flat bread, while Rosha breastfeeds in the shawl. And in Papua New Guinea, Gogomo is carried in a net dangling from his mother's head; she wears only a small piece of cloth around her waist, so her two breasts hang clearly behind her son's body (1996, n.p.). While there is no areola visible, due to the positioning of the babies in their slings, it is nonetheless clear from both the words ('nurses') and the images (which show babies close to bare breasts) that these images are of breastfeeding. The mothers and their babies are at the centre of each image. But this book is not set in an English-speaking country and could be seen as a depiction of what foreign people do,[5] although obviously the Bernhards' work also normalises both baby-wearing and breastfeeding.

---

5. This relates back to the discussion in Chapter 1 about breastfeeding being for 'irrational' 'minorities' (cf. Hausman 2003, 12). Even today, some people argue that breastfeeding

Four of the five most explicit breastfeeding books are published by Pinter and Martin, a publishing company that regularly produces pro-breastfeeding texts. Interestingly, as noted earlier, three are translations, and this means that only one out of the four is an English-language original that emphasises breastfeeding. For instance, Mònica Calaf's *You, Me and the Breast* is a translation from Spanish (though no translator is named),[6] which perhaps suggests that some non-English-speaking cultures are more positive about breastfeeding. However, a study of Catalan-language children's books by Trias et al. found that breastfeeding was not often featured. As the English summary of their research notes, 'Forty-two percent of the 169 books selected showed images of breastfeeding; 12% of those referred to human breastfeeding, and the remaining referred to animal breastfeeding. Images showing formula feeding were present in 77.5% of the books' (2003, n.p.). That is to say, less than half of the books showed breastfeeding at all, and out of those that did, 88% depicted animals breastfeeding, not humans. Nonetheless, 42% of the books showed breastfeeding, some of them along with formula-feeding, which is not far off the figure of 32% listed earlier.

What is probably the most breastfeeding-positive work in my English-language corpus (even if it is not an English-language original) is Mònica Calaf's book *You, Me and the Breast*, which is illustrated by Mikel Fuentes. Each page features a breastfeeding image, and the whole point of the book seems to be to normalise breastfeeding; indeed, there is no plot, in terms of action, climax or resolution, as the words and pictures discuss and show a breastfeeding dyad only as they feed in different situations. For example, the text 'When you came out of my tummy [...] the first thing you looked for was my breast' is accompanied by an illustration of the umbilical cord being cut and the baby feeding (2011, n.p.). Other images show breastfeeding in a variety of situations, such as in the swimming pool, or while exercising, or in the garden. The texts are calm and affirmative, such as 'When you were breastfeeding, you were relaxed, happy and contented. We both loved these intimate and special moments' (ibid.). The images show the areola quite clearly, which is indeed what one would see if the baby's latch were correct, and they often show the nipple itself, in scenes where the baby has his mouth open and is about to latch

---

matters more in certain – usually less developed – countries than in others, although as research previously mentioned here shows, money would be saved and health would be improved if more people breastfed in the West.

6. As a translator who has, as of this writing, translated several children's books, which all feature my name, I find it problematic that translations are still produced that attempt to render the translator invisible. One would not attempt to erase the author or illustrator, and yet translators are regularly relegated to a line on the copyright page, if that. Breastfeeding should be visible and translators should be visible.

on. The areola and nipple are brown and prominent, while the rest of the mother's chest is white; there is no discretion here, no sweater pulled up, no cloth folded around the chest, no baby pressed tightly in to the breasts so no skin is seen. Breastfeeding does not take place under cover in this work. Still, although it is available in English, it is unfortunately not a good representative of English-language picturebooks.

Much the same can be said of Victoria de Boitiz's *The Mystery of the Breast* (2011), illustrated by Afra, and translated from Spanish (again, no translator is named); breastfeeding is the focus of the words and images, and breasts, nipples and areolae are all shown in the illustrations. In fact, there is one picture that shows clouds shaped like breasts, complete with areolae and nipples, and another where the breast is foregrounded, with a contented baby smiling behind it. Breastfeeding is the raison d'être of this work, and it is not carried out with discretion. This is positive in and of itself, but, as I will discuss more later, there is also something to be said for a story that features breastfeeding and has a plot about something else.

One of Pinter and Martin's few English-language originals for children is *Milky Moments*, which was written by Ellie Stoneley and illustrated by Jessica D'Alton Goode (2015). As in Calaf's book, Stoneley's work shows mother-and-baby or mother-and-child dyads breastfeeding in many locations: at the beach, on the sofa, on the bus, at play group, in a café, at the dinner table and so on. The scenes are usually one of two types: either the mother-and-child dyad are alone, breastfeeding and bonding, or else there is a larger group of people, usually women and children, socialising together, with breastfeeding happening at the same time. For instance, older children might be playing while their mothers sit and chat and breastfeed younger children. Whatever the scenario, breastfeeding is depicted as an activity that brings mums and babies together and that can take place anytime, anywhere. Breastfeeding is normalised in these images. Stoneley's work shows children of different ages breastfeeding, not just babies, and so implies natural-term weaning, and was one of the very few books I found overall that depicted anything but the breastfeeding of small babies.[7] There are a few men, presumably fathers, in the book, although there are also a couple of families that appear to have

---

7. Since writing this chapter, I have analysed six further breastfeeding-related picturebooks, all about weaning from the breast. Four were written in English, one was translated (poorly) from Spanish and one was available only in Swedish. All six featured a toddler whose mother was encouraging or insisting upon night-weaning or total weaning; the Spanish book included several children, the oldest of whom was 7 years old, and this was by far the oldest breastfeeding child I found in any of the books I read. I decided not to include these six books in this chapter because they are all 'issue books', aimed at

single mothers. I would suggest that given the attention to diversity here – families of different ethnicities are clearly depicted – it was a missed opportunity not to show a child with two mothers, or perhaps even two fathers feeding their child donated breastmilk, or a trans parent chestfeeding or employing a supplemental nursing system. It is interesting to consider how normative picturebooks featuring breastfeeding tend to be in general, with few of them featuring a variety of ethnicities or family types; I will return to this later.

I believe that it is important to show breastfeeding in picturebooks and for children and adults to see breastfeeding taking place throughout society, which is indeed what happens in the three books mentioned earlier (the books by Calaf, de Boitiz and Stoneley), since the stories focus on how breastfeeding can happen any time and anywhere. However, I also wonder who the likely target audience is for these works; my suspicion is that they are aimed at families where breastfeeding is already the norm, families that would enjoy seeing themselves reflected in a book.[8] That is to say, a book about breastfeeding is probably for those who have breastfed or continue to breastfeed. I imagine that it is doubtful that people who are against breastfeeding or who could not breastfeed or who are suffering with breastfeeding trauma or grief (Brown 2019) would choose to buy or borrow a book that celebrates breastfeeding.

Thus, it would be beneficial to see a book where there is a plot about something other than breastfeeding and breastfeeding just happens to be one part of what the nurser and nursling do together. Stoneley's images approach this, but the words do not. Indeed, an issue with books such as Calaf's and Stoneley's is that they have no plot per se. They appear to exist solely to depict

---

    supporting the breastfeeding dyad through the weaning process and would, I believe, be purchased only by a parent in that situation. Furthermore, nearly all were self-published, and there were concomitant issues with variable quality in both words and images because of the lack of editing. I have written a short article about these works, which will be published later in 2021 in the Association of Breastfeeding Mothers magazine.

8. I was in the children's section of my local library and actually saw a boy around 3 or 4 years old pick up Calaf's book and bring it over to his mother. She looked at the cover, snatched the book from the boy and said, 'We don't read books like that!' She then shoved it back into the large box of picturebooks. I was fascinated by this reaction. Why did she not want to read this book to her son? Had she not breastfed him? If not, was it because she had not wanted to and found breastfeeding unappealing, disgusting, unmodern, inconvenient or otherwise inappropriate? Or had she wanted to breastfeed but not been given enough support to do so? Was she scared she would be upset by the book? Was she worried about what her son might see in the images? Did she find the topic too 'sexual'? In short, why was a book about breastfeeding not something for her family? Who is the target audience for a book that depicts breastfeeding?

and promote breastfeeding, and while there is a need for that – just as there is a need for books that focus on race or sexuality or disability or death or divorce or a multitude of other topics – that is not the only sort of book that is needed when it comes to breastfeeding.[9] One of the very few books that does have a plot while also showing breastfeeding is *Katie Morag and the Dancing Class*, written and illustrated by Mairi Hedderwick. In the story, Katie Morag's mother is sitting nursing Katie's little sister in one image, with other adults standing near her, involved in tasks such as stirring food on the stove (2007, n.p.). The text on this particular page is about Katie Morag not wanting to take ballet classes, and no reference is made to breastfeeding. Indeed, a number of Hedderwick's *Katie Morag* books show breastfeeding in the background while other activities are foregrounded in both words and pictures. What could be problematic is that the colours of the mother and baby are quite pale – yellow, white, grey, with a hint of orange – so the two blend together and are muted (Nodelman 1988, 60), which makes it potentially difficult to distinguish the two bodies and the activity of breastfeeding. Nonetheless, breastfeeding is not problematised, nor is it focused on in a way that is to the detriment of every other aspect of the character's life; on the contrary, it is not discreet and it is normalised.

A final example is the board book *What Does Baby Want?*, which is a translation from Japanese (although, again, no translator is named) of a work by the husband-and-wife design team Tupera Tupera. The book is unusual for its shape, which is perfectly round. The pages show a close-up of a non-gendered baby, who clearly wants something and is not satisfied. The words suggest things that might cheer the baby up, such as a 'bouncy ball' or 'shiny tambourine' (2017, n.p.), but the baby rejects these items. The surprise twist – in reality not a surprise to breastfeeding parents – is that all the baby wants is the breast. The round shape is to reflect the roundness of the breasts. There is a two-page spread that shows the bare breasts, and this spread has no words on it. While I would not suggest that the breasts are sexualised, they are not attached to a particular body, and they are the definite focus of the page, with the nipples and areola in the centre. This is in contrast to a Swedish work that I will discuss later, where a wordless two-page spread focuses on the breastfeeding relationship rather than the breasts themselves. I think the

---

9. This is much the same as what I argued in my book on LGBTQ+ literature for children and young adults; instead of focusing on queerness as an issue, the better books feature LGBTQ+ characters who have other matters in their lives, although there is obviously also a need for coming-out stories and stories that show people who struggle because they are LGBTQ+ (Epstein 2013, 74–93). Instead of focusing on breastfeeding, it would be useful to have books that are about something else and happen to feature breastfeeding.

breasts are meant to make readers laugh and perhaps feel some shock, and then to reconsider and recognise that yes, babies do need their milk. I have read *What Does Baby Want?* aloud to groups of undergraduate students many times now, and every time I turn to that spread, there are audible gasps and embarrassed faces, and the students often say things such as, 'You can't show that in a book for children!' This, of course, is part of the point and leads to useful discussions, but I wonder if that attitude – that is, that breasts are not appropriate for children to see – would keep some adults from buying the work. After the breast spread, the next image shows the baby latching on and after that the baby is satisfied; the book ends with the baby going to sleep, with their hunger and thirst quenched, and their need for closeness fulfilled. *What Does Baby Want?* celebrates breastfeeding as a normal part of a baby's life and indeed shows breastfeeding as being the answer to a question that can puzzle parents: my baby is not speaking yet, so how can I figure out what my baby wants and needs right now? I do have a couple of other hesitations regarding the book, however. In considering diversity, I find it odd that a book produced in Japan shows a Caucasian-looking baby. In addition, the book comes with a sticker on the cover that says, 'A book about breastfeeding', which to me suggests that the book will be ignored by those who feel that breastfeeding is not relevant to their family's life.

In short, my findings suggest that English-language originals tend to be very discreet about breastfeeding, while translated works are more open about showing the breast and the baby attached to it. Also, breastfeeding-positive books are frequently focused on breastfeeding, instead of including it as one of many aspects to a baby's life.

Bottles, Bottles, Everywhere

As Table 1 shows, 6 of the 25 (24%) English-language originals showed only bottle-feeding and 5 (20%) showed combination-feeding, which means that 44% featured bottle-feeding. The figure increases to 58% if I calculate statistics only for English-language originals that depict any feeding in the images, regardless of what is stated in the words.

One example of combination-feeding is found in *Love That Baby* by Kathryn Laskey, which has pictures of babies being fed by breast and bottle on the same page. The main text says, 'Yum. Eating is what babies do best. Newborn babies feed all the time, but they only have one kind of food – MILK! They either breastfeed or take a bottle or do both', while around the pictures it has text that says, 'Newborn babies have to breastfeed – or drink from a bottle' (2004, n.p.). *Everywhere Babies* by Susan Meyers, with illustrations by Marla Frazee, likewise says, 'Every day, everywhere, babies are fed. –/by bottle, by breast, with cups, and with spoons,/with milk, and then cereal, carrots, and prunes' (2001, n.p.). Similarly, *The Baby's Catalogue* by Janet and Allen Ahlberg ([1982] 2012) depicts one baby being breastfed next to an image of a baby being bottle-fed; another image shows a bottle with what looks like pink juice in it. Books such as these three seem to treat all methods of feeding a baby equally and to thereby depict different foods, whether breastmilk, formula milk, cereal, juice or prunes, as equally good and acceptable for young humans.

A book featured in the Norfolk library's 'new experiences'[10] collection, *The New Baby* (Anonymous [1992] 2005), shows the mother, Mrs. Bunn, breastfeeding the new baby (presumably what was a 'bunn in the oven'), while on the same page, the baby's older brother plays and the older sister is feeding a doll from a bottle ([1992] 2005). This play bottle-feeding undermines breastfeeding positivity; surely the little girl could have pretended to breastfeed as well, as breastfed children are wont to do. And, of course, if bottle-feeding was going to be depicted, the boy could have just as well been doing it, since, as discussed elsewhere in this book, one of the arguments made for bottle-feeding is that anyone can participate in it, even if evidence suggests that this is not what actually happens.

One could argue that it is realistic to show combination-feeding or only bottles, given the high percentage of bottle-feeding of artificial milk in the United Kingdom and the United States. But one worrying oddity about bottles is that in some books, such as *Mr Super Poopy Pants* by Rebecca Elliot (2014) and *I'm Still Important!* (2000) by Jen Green, with illustrations by Mike Gordon, the infants are depicted holding the bottles by themselves or the bottles are nearly as big as or even bigger than the babies, which really emphasises them. Real bottles are never the same size as or larger than an actual baby, and it is dangerous to leave a baby propped up alone with a bottle; Brown (2018) discusses how it can be damaging to the parent–child relationship or even fatal to the child.

In addition, there is the question about what is in the bottle. Some readers might argue that these bottles contain expressed milk (Lowery (2019) writes that 85% of mothers pump milk some or all of the time, but it is unknown how many exclusively pump), but that is never stated in any of the texts.

---

10. It is, I would guess, considered a 'new experience'/special need/issue book because the thought is that families not expecting a new baby would not want to read it. While it is helpful for families who do want to read such works to know where to find them, surely it makes more sense for all books to be available to all readers, because even an only child or a child in a family that has finished reproducing might be interested in reading a story about a new baby.

A reader – especially a child being read to – is not likely to think too deeply about whether the liquid in the bottle is expressed breastmilk or formula milk or even water or juice or soda, and given the prevalence of artificial milk in English-speaking countries, I would guess that most readers would see the bottle and assume it was formula.

So a question is why so many books show combination-feeding or else bottle-feeding alone, and why the images seem to want to promote equality among feeding types. Besides the obvious fact that bottle-feeding is more common in the United Kingdom, there is also the question of appealing to the audience; showing breastfeeding might sadden or anger people who could not breastfeed or chose not to do so. Perhaps due to worries about non-breastfeeding families feeling defensive or offended or hurt by images of breastfeeding, some authors and illustrators appear to make a clear effort to treat all types of feeding as the same. As noted in Chapter 1, research provides evidence that feeding babies artificial milk is actually a risk (e.g. Young 2016, 60), so I question whether, instead of treading so carefully around this issue because of worrying about who might be upset to see breastfeeding, it might be more beneficial to promote breastfeeding in literature. This need not mean more books focused solely on breastfeeding, but rather more picturebooks that include breastfeeding as one of many activities in a baby's or child's life.

In addition, texts that feature breastfeeding would have the benefit of normalising the work women do when caring for their children. They would show that this is valuable and necessary work, and this could then bring about a shift in how society perceives what women do when on maternity leave or more generally when they parent.

To summarise my exploration of English-language books, most of the picturebooks that feature the feeding of infants are either books about families about to have new babies (which appear to be meant to teach and comfort older children who are soon to become big sisters or brothers) or they are books that are very explicitly pro-breastfeeding. The former books have a tendency to show breastfeeding and bottle-feeding in equal measure, and/ or they do not make it clear in the pictures that breastfeeding is taking place. The latter books tend to be plotless, focusing instead on normalising and celebrating breastfeeding in a positive manner, and I question the intended audience of these works, as I suspect non-breastfeeding families are not likely to want to read them. In all but the most breastfeeding-centric texts, breastfeeding is depicted discreetly, so much so that in many cases, it would be easy to miss or overlook the act. And in many books, it is also often shown as equal to formula-feeding, which I would imagine is so as to offend as few readers as possible and to thereby increase the audience; the bottom line matters for publishing companies, so they want books to reach as many readers as possible. Later in this chapter, I will discuss reasons for the overwhelming discretion when it comes to breastfeeding in picturebooks.

Here a Breast, There a Breast, Everywhere a Breast: A Comparison with Sweden

My findings suggest that in Swedish-language picturebooks, on the contrary, breastfeeding is depicted as a natural and common part of a baby's life, and there is no need for discretion. It is important to note that I found fewer books overall in Sweden to analyse, but Sweden has a population of 10 million people, whereas the United States has 382 million and the United Kingdom has 66 million, so combined they have 448 million (not to mention all the citizens of other English-speaking countries around the world). Given that those two nations together have 44 times the number of citizens, it makes sense that there would be fewer picturebooks in general and fewer specifically about new babies and/or breastfeeding. However, the English-language originals totalled 25, while the Swedish-language ones totalled 13, and that is not a 44-fold difference; even if I focused only on the United Kingdom, since the majority of my works were from there, there were not six times more English-language works than Swedish. In other words, though the raw figure for the Swedish corpus of texts is smaller, it is not as small as one might expect given the population differences. See Table 3 for my findings regarding images of breastfeeding.

Table 3 The results from Swedish-language picturebooks that show feeding in the images

	Breastfeeding only	**Bottle only**	**Breastfeeding and bottle**	**No feeding of milk depicted**
Number of books	9 (69%)	0	0	4 (31%)
Comments				Even if a book referred to the feeding of milk, if no breast or bottle was shown, I included it here.

I found that 9 out of 13 (nearly 70%) Swedish-language books show exclusive breastfeeding. While browsing books at bookstores in Stockholm, I found a book that did feature a baby and seemed to show containers of artificial milk, although they were not labelled, and since I was not absolutely sure and could not quite tell what the image showed, I have not included it. It is interesting to consider how often in this study I had to disregard a book because I could not tell what the image was meant to be; surely illustrations in picturebooks ought to be clearer than that, when it comes to books that are realistic in style.

While my Swedish sample is, as noted, smaller than my English one, it is nonetheless clear that more babies are breastfed in Swedish books. In Sweden, the breastfeeding rate at 6 months is around 63% (either exclusively breastfeeding or in combination with other food) (Anonymous 2018, n.p.),[11] which is clearly much higher than the figure of 35% in the United Kingdom mentioned previously. That suggests that breastfeeding is better promoted and/or more acceptable, which could be why it features much more often in children's books.

In many cases, as in the English-language books, the child being breastfed is a baby and the story shows the baby's life. In the English-language works, the baby's daily life, activities and routines are often the focus, as though to educate the older sibling about what to expect when the new baby arrives; on the other hand, in Swedish books, the older child's feelings are explored in more depth and the story is frequently about the older sibling's experiences with and feelings about having a new baby in the house. Breastfeeding can cause confusion or jealousy in the older child.

A typical example is *Emma och lillebror* (*Emma and Little Brother*) by Gunilla Wolde. Wolde writes that Little Brother 'tycker om att få mat ur mammas bröst. Men Emma tycker inte om när mamma matar Lillebror. Då vill hon ge bort honom till en annan tant. Då vill Emma bli bebis igen så hon får ha mamma för sig själv.' ([1975] 1998, n.p.) (likes to get food from Mum's breasts. But Emma doesn't like it when Mum feeds Little Brother. Then she wants to give him to some other lady. Then Emma wants to be a baby again so she can have Mum to herself).[12] When Little Brother is eating, Emma is jealous and wants that closeness with her mother, but when he is done, Emma decides she wants to be a big girl again, and she helps Mum change the baby's nappy. This acknowledges an older child's worries about being replaced and perhaps not as loved as the new baby. But it also shows how she enjoys some aspects of being a big sister, so for Emma, having a baby in her life brings about mixed emotions, and this is validated in the story.

---

11. According to the statistics, the breastfeeding rate at 6 months was 72% in 2004, so it would be interesting to know what had led to this drop and also if it has affected the writing of literature.
12. All translations from Swedish are my own, unless otherwise noted.

Similarly, *Nejlika och lilla lillasyster* (*Nejlika and Little, Little Sister*) by Hanna Zetterberg Struwe, with illustrations by Anna-Karin Garhamn, shows big sister Nejlika wanting to participate in childcare and perhaps to thereby be appreciated and needed by her parents. She gets upset when she cannot do the things she wants. When Nejlika wants to feed her new sister ice cream, she is told that the baby does not eat ice cream; instead, she is shown how she can sit with the baby and their mother while the baby breastfeeds, and she finds this to be 'mysigt' (cosy) (2008, n.p.). Through this exchange, she learns different ways of interacting with her sibling and her newly busy mother, and this helps her deal with the arrival of her sister and the change to their family.

A few books show breastfeeding but do not remark upon it, such as *Ninna och syskongrodden* (*Ninna and the Sibling Sprout*) by Matilda Ruta (2016) or *Rida ryggen* (*Ride on My Back*) by Ida Therén (2015), illustrated by Z. Keller, both of which depict a child breastfeeding in a sling. Breastfeeding and babywearing are normalised through the images; as noted earlier, in English, I found babywearing only in a book that featured people from other, non-Western countries. Incidentally, Therén's books are published by Nära Förlag, a Swedish-language publishing company that calls itself Attachment Publishing[13] in English and that is dedicated to attachment parenting. On Nära Förlag's Facebook page, they describe themselves in the following way:

> Känner ditt barn inte igen dig i alla småbarnsböcker om spjälsängar och barnvagnar? [...] Vi vill att fler barn ska mysa i en vuxens knä medan de tittar i en bok som beskriver en vardag som påminner om deras egen. Det finns få illustrerade småbarnsböcker som visar vardagen för ett barn som bärs i sjal, går på potta tidigt eller samsover med sina föräldrar. Vi bestämde oss för att göra boken vi själva ville läsa, ihop med våra barn! (Does your child not recognise themselves in all those picturebooks about cots and prams? [...] We want more children to have the chance to sit comfortably on an adult's lap while looking at a book that describes an everyday life that is like their own. There are few picturebooks that show everyday life for a child who is carried in a sling, uses the potty early or sleeps together with their parents. We decided to make the book we wanted to read, together with our children!). (Nära Förlag's Facebook page n.d., n.p.)

Writing specifically about *Rida ryggen* (*Ride on My Back*) and their desire for many children to see themselves in it, they note: 'Boken är därför könsneutral i största möjliga mån. Vi har därför valt att ha med partier som kan tolkas som amning, men som också bara kan uppfattas som närhet – för att både

---

13. 'Nära' means 'near' or 'close'.

ammande och icke ammande familjer ska känna igen sig!' (The book is [therefore] gender-neutral to the largest extent possible. We have therefore chosen to show scenes that can be interpreted as breastfeeding, but can also be seen as just closeness – so that both breastfeeding and non-breastfeeding families can recognise themselves!) (ibid.). Here, this can be viewed in contrast to some of the English-language works mentioned earlier, which either focused on breastfeeding or included it as one element of a baby's life, because Therén appears to want to reflect on and promote closeness in all parent–child relationships. In *Rida ryggen* (*Ride on My Back*) there is something of a plot, or perhaps more accurately a point, to the book, and breastfeeding can be seen in it, but the stated intention is to appeal to many different families, whether they breastfeed or not. This normalises breastfeeding even amongst non-breastfeeding families.

Ida Therén of Nära Förlag also produced a book solely about breastfeeding, and it has much in common with the Spanish books that have been translated to English that were discussed earlier. *Alltid tillsammans* (*Always Together*) (2016), which was illustrated by Nathalie Ruejas, depicts a breastfeeding dyad, and they breastfeed in a number of different situations. For example, the child likes breastfeeding 'mitt i naturen' (out in nature), when 'ledsen' (sad) or in the bathtub (Therén 2016, n.p.). There is no plot here, and the focus is clearly on breastfeeding positivity. There are several especially interesting points about this book. First of all, the child, whose gender is not clear (presumably in accordance with the gender-neutral approach the publisher mentioned earlier), and the breastfeeding parent look nothing like one another, in that the mother has red hair and is pale, whereas the child is dark-skinned and dark-haired; they do not look to be of the same race or even necessarily related. No other parent is seen in the work, which might make a knowing reader wonder if, for example, the child was adopted and if lactation was induced, or if the child was produced through a donated egg via fertility treatment; on the other hand, of course, not all parents and children look similar, and perhaps it sends a positive message about the closeness that breastfeeding can bring no matter what the biological connection. Perhaps adoptive or non-gestating or non-biologically-related parents would feel inspired to breastfeed.

Also, the book contains the only depiction of tandem breastfeeding I have found in children's literature thus far; indeed, it could actually be said to be tridem, as three children of different ages breastfeed. The book says that breastfeeding is 'kul att dela med syster och bror' (fun to share with sister and brother) (Therén 2016, n.p.), and the image portrays three children who look very different and have no obvious gender markers sitting with the breastfeeding parent; one, who is not the main protagonist, is feeding, but the implication from the words is that they will all get to feed.

Finally, *Alltid tillsammans* (*Always Together*) has a central pair of pages without words; the image is spread across the two pages and shows the dyad breastfeeding, only engaged with one another and not looking at the reader at all. This is a centrefold that works against the usual ideas of a centrefold, in that it is a child and a parent breastfeeding, having an intimate moment that does not include or invite the reader in. It is a potent and poignant example of the power of breastfeeding. This image in particular and the images of breastfeeding in general in this book do not reflect ideas of the male gaze (cf. Mulvey [1975] 2009; see more on this later in this chapter and elsewhere in this book); the concept of the male gaze means depicting females in a way that is aimed at heterosexual, cisgender men or considering men's needs and desires first when representing females. In our society, breasts are usually portrayed as sexual objects. But in Therén's book, bare breasts are not for the viewer's pleasure and especially not for a male adult's pleasure. They are there to feed, nurture, comfort and give pleasure to the breastfeeding dyad. Perhaps it can be said that the breasts reflect a baby's gaze, hungry, needy and loving. This is different from the centrefold/surprise pages in *What Does Baby Want?* because there the reader sees only the breasts, whereas in this work, it is about the dyad's relationship, of which breasts are one part. *Alltid tillsammans* (*Always Together*) was the only book in my Swedish corpus to be so purely focused on breastfeeding positivity, but there were many books that included breastfeeding as a normal part of life.

A couple of the Swedish-language books show both breastfeeding and what follows it, namely spitting up and excrement. It is interesting how detailed some of the descriptions are. For instance, in *Hej lillebror* (*Hi Little Brother*) by Elisabet Broomé and Cecilia Nordstrand Alin, first baby Arne spits up his milk and has to have new clothes, and then he excretes. The story notes that 'när Arne ätit kräks han nästan varje gång' (when Arne has eaten, he throws up almost every time) and also that 'bebisbajs är gult och luktar inte alls så där bajsigt. Vet du varför? Jo, för att bebisar bara äter mjölken från mammas bröst. Men när Arne börjar äta riktig mat kommer bajset att bli bajsbrunt och börja luka bajsilla' (baby poo is yellow and doesn't smell like poo. Do you know why? It's because babies only have milk from their mothers' breasts. But when Arne begins to eat real food, his poo will turn pooey brown and start smelling like stinky poo) (2005, n.p.). Despite the strange description of non-breastmilk items as being 'real food', as though breastmilk is not 'real' or 'food', this passage is informative and realistic. One could say that those adjectives generally describe Swedish picturebooks when it comes to breastfeeding and related matters. Babies breastfeed, spit up, poo and need to be changed and cleaned up. Older siblings get jealous or want to help, and do not always know how to handle this new, noisy presence. Breastfeeding is part of all this, but not the only focus.

As in English, there were a couple of examples of new baby-themed books that do not show any feeding at all, such as *Lillasyster är ett monster* (*Little Sister Is a Monster*) by Linda Pelenius (2012) or *Du ska få gröt och en lillasyster* (*You're Going to Get Porridge and a Little Sister*) by Solja Krapu-Kallio (2016), with illustrations by Anna Bengtsson, and they too focus on the older child's feelings, although one would think that this could therefore include images of the baby being fed. In *Lillasyster är ett monster* (*Little Sister Is a Monster*) by Linda Pelenius, Bob is so envious of the attention his new little sister gets that he attempts to throw her down a rubbish chute (2012, n.p.), acting out feelings that many parents and children can recognise, that is, that the older child wishes the younger one would go away forever. The lack of breastfeeding in these fictional works is sometimes strange, in that often the works show other things that the new baby does, but on the other hand, they do not show artificial feeding either, which is distinct from English-language works.

Perhaps the lack of feeding in these works is meant to either focus on the older child and/or to help encourage gender equality when it comes to the care of a baby. As Maria Andersson discusses, Frances Vestin's book *Mummel. En ny människa* (*Mummel: A New Person*) (1970) includes the lines, 'När barnet har kommit ut ur kvinnans mage, behövs inte kvinnan längre. Vem som helst kan ta hand om barnet och tycka om det' (When a baby has come out of the woman's stomach, the woman isn't needed anymore. Anyone can take care of the baby and like it) (cited in Andersson 2015, 13). This is perhaps meant to show that anyone can feed a baby, change the baby's nappy, dress the baby, rock the baby to sleep and so on, but it also has the effect of suggesting that breastfeeding does not matter, that the unique biological functions of a woman's body are unimportant and that women's work does not matter, or perhaps that women should do work other than childcare, which recalls the liberation ideology mentioned earlier in this book, with the idea being that women do not need to be tied to a baby.

Vestin's book was published in 1970 and may reflect feminist ideas from that time, but I do believe there is something of this belief influencing the production of children's picturebooks in English and Swedish still today. Many books or articles on parenting continue to advise that the non-feeding parent get involved in childcare by giving the baby a bottle; even the National Childbirth Trust includes it on their recent list of tips for 'What can I do to help support my partner with breastfeeding?' (National Childbirth Trust 2021). It is arguably bizarre to suggest that bottle-feeding a baby is a way to support breastfeeding, and indeed it undercuts the importance of establishing feeding at the breast while also implying that breastfeeding is not necessarily that valuable.

As a final note of comparison, most of the pictures of breastfeeding in Swedish-language books are both more accurate in terms of how they depict the way a baby is latched on and also more explicit, showing more of the breast and areola (e.g. Broomé and Alin's book or Therén's). In addition, sometimes they refer to the emotional effects of breastfeeding, such as describing in words or pictures the bond formed between the breastfeeding mother and the baby (also in Broomé and Alin, where baby Arne gazes at his mother, or in Therén, where breastfeeding is said to feel so 'skönt' (pleasant/lovely) (2016, n.p.)).

In sum, Swedish books discuss and portray breastfeeding much more often than English-language texts while also depicting bottles less often, suggesting that Swedes, including Swedish authors and publishers, are more comfortable with breastfeeding as a concept and with the depiction of breasts in illustrations in books for children. It is not very surprising that a country with a longer, more generous maternity leave package and a more breastfeeding-normative culture would be more likely to feature breastfeeding in picturebooks. Breastfeeding is the cultural norm, so it is depicted in books, which then encourages it to remain the norm, and so on. This will be explored more in Chapter 4.

Naked versus Nude: Breastfeeding as Taboo

Although breasts and breastfeeding are not listed as societal taboos in Holden's *Encyclopedia of Taboos* (2000), I suggest that in Western society today, breastfeeding is indeed a taboo, especially when in mother–child dyad public. Palmer writes that 'though any part of a woman's body can be a focus of eroticism, our era is the first in recorded history where the breast has become a public fetish for male sexual stimulation, while its primary function has diminished on a vast scale' ([1988] 2009, 2–3). And yet the West is apparently fairly alone in this view; as Grayson discusses, only 13 cultures out of 190 analysed 'commonly employ[ed] breast touching either before or during intercourse. And of the same 190, only thirteen indicated the size and shape of a woman's breasts as important to her sexual attractiveness. (Only three societies considered breasts erotic *and* integrated them into foreplay.)' (2016, 188–89; italics original). And as explored in Chapter 1, Palmer notes that in our society, since the breast is thought to be stimulating and useful as a marketing tool, we may have begun equating it to the genitals as a site of sexuality ([1988] 2009, 146–48). That may help explain the missing breasts in the English-language children's books; neither do we see bare genitals in most children's books, and especially not in adult books. Genitals are to be hidden away, and children are even taught in school that anything covered by underwear or a swimsuit is private and should not be seen or touched by anyone else (NSPCC n.d., n.p.); for girls and women, of course, swimsuits usually cover the nipples and breasts, and this would increase their belief that the chest is private and should be kept covered. Breasts are erotic, not practical, and definitely not both.

As noted earlier, when breastfeeding is depicted in the English-language original books, if any of the breast is visible, it is simply a thin line of skin. In general, one does not see much of the breast, and certainly not the areola or nipple. The babies' heads tend to hide the nipple. Nipples may be seen as too sexual for children's books. For example, Palmer describes how children's author and illustrator Jan Pienkowski's picture of Sleeping Beauty was edited so the nipples were removed in the US version 'even though in the illustration she had just given birth to her baby' ([1988] 2009, 3). But even if publishers wanted to avoid the nipple, they could show more of the breast or attempt to make it more obvious that babies are being breastfed in either the words or the pictures or both; that they do not suggests they see the entire breast as sexual rather than as the source of nourishment. In the translations to English, from Japanese and Spanish, and also in the Swedish books, the nipple and areola do not seem to be such challenging sites, and breastfeeding is normalised, which also means that the breast is normalised. There is no squeamishness or discretion in these non-English-language original texts.

Perry Nodelman's article about nakedness in children's books focuses on the depiction of naked children; however, it seems from my research that many of his points are still valid, and they hold true for the depiction of naked adults, particularly women's breasts, as well. Nodelman describes illustrations of naked children in literature as 'androgynous naked torsos' with a 'curiously sexless sensuality' (1984, 27). In his research, he finds that most naked babies in children's literature are male. His 'theory is that we are so used to thinking of naked females as nudes that the only way we can look at a naked body innocently, without overtones of sexual titillation, even a baby's body, is to make the body a male body' (1984, 28). Nodelman continues, 'That the naked young bodies in picturebooks are not without sexual significance is made clear by the almost total absence of female frontal nudity in the entire history of the genre' (ibid.). He calls our category for naked females the 'pinup' and reminds us, echoing John Berger, that 'boys can be naked without their clothes on, whereas traditionally, naked girls are nude' (ibid.).

I suggest, then, that we see few bare breasts in children's literature for the same reason; in English-language cultures, we sexualise women's bodies to the extent that the historically normal act of breastfeeding – an act that female mammals have evolved to do – is not accepted as a subject for discussion or illustration in books for children, because breasts are seen as sexual, even when feeding a baby. Even the books that have breastfeeding as their main topic often show breastfeeding taking place discreetly, with little of the breast, and none of the areola, visible (with Swedish books and books translated to English as the exceptions).

It is known that the literature made available for children was and is 'fastidiously controlled by institutions such as the school, the increasingly privatized family, and the church in order to ensure that the literary experience taught the child the value systems of the society into which it was to be integrated' (Miller 2014, 128). And children's books are the most challenged and banned, with the majority of the top 10 challenged books in the United States each year intended for the children's market (ALA 2021), because adults are concerned about what information children have access to. It is not a surprise, then, that in a society where women's breasts are considered to be sexual and for men's pleasure, those breasts would not often be depicted in the non-sexual act of breastfeeding in illustrations. The analysis in Chapter 3 likewise shows significant discomfort with non-sexual breasts, implying that using breasts for another purpose interferes with adult lives and relationships.

In my analysis of Swedish picturebooks, I found quite a few naked baby boys, with their penises depicted clearly (such as Stark (2007, 2016), and Broomé and Nordstrand Alin (2005)), but no naked girls. So even though the Swedish books showed more acceptance of the naked breast, to the point that a breastfeeding mother is a centrefold in one of the works (Therén 2016), female genitals seem one step too far.[14] While I am reluctant to speculate too widely about the depiction of genitals in children's books in the West as I have not carried out enough research into it, I think it is possible to suggest a real discomfort with the female body; females are nude and sexualised and passive,

---

14. I have noted that even in Swedish-language books, which can often seem more open and progressive than English-language ones, it is more common to see male genitals than female ones, including in works not explored here in my breastfeeding corpus. For example, in two board books that I happen to own and to read to my children, *Kanin-bad* (*Rabbit-Bath*) by Lena Anderson (2015) and *Leka tittut!* (*Play Peekaboo!*) by Maria Nilsson Thore and Annika Thore (2014), the stories both revolve around undressing. In the former, the protagonist is a boy who has come home and is undressing to get into the bath. In the latter, the protagonist is a girl who has just woken up and is taking off her pyjamas while playing peekaboo with the reader. The boy in *Kanin-bad* (*Rabbit-Bath*) undresses completely, and his penis hangs visibly before he gets into the bath. The girl in *Leka tittut!* (*Play Peekaboo!*) undresses down to her underwear. Her nipples are little dark dots, but her genitals are not glimpsed. One could argue that female genitals are somewhat more hidden, but even so, Vira in *Leka tittut!* could take off her underpants in order to then put on fresh clothes for the new day. These are two representative examples, from well-known and popular authors and illustrators, which provide further evidence for the idea that males are naked while females are nude.

while males are naked and active and free to move and to be in a way that females are not. Children's literature appears to reflect societal beliefs about gender and power, as discussed in Chapter 1.

An alternative reading of this absence of female breasts is possible, though. Nodelman argues that males are active in the illustrations of children's books, while females are passive and apparently exist to be gazed at (1984, 29; cf. Mulvey [1975] 2009 on the male gaze). I wondered, therefore, whether not showing breastfeeding would be a way of fighting back against the idea of women as being subservient and inactive. If the illustrators mostly show females, especially the mother characters, as busy, energetic and full of motion, then perhaps they are deliberately attempting to depict women in multiple roles. In other words, since breastfeeding requires that a woman slow her movements, sit or lie down, and focus mainly on her infant or toddler, images reflecting this may suggest that women serve their children and are 'creatures who must smile at those who have the right to look at them' (Nodelman 1984, 29). Unfortunately, this rather complex, challenging perspective does not seem borne out by the literature. Women in these books serve their children in other ways, including by giving them bottles of what is presumably artificial milk or spoon-feeding them other food, while men are rarely glimpsed feeding a baby. Women hold their babies, rock them, clothe them and otherwise put their children's needs first. The women seldom seem to be active in other ways and are frequently shown to be sitting down. All this suggests that we are comfortable with women fulfilling the traditional roles required by mothering and we believe she should be carrying out the work of childcare, but that we are not comfortable with seeing the women's breasts in the process of a breastfeed.

I claim, then, that breastfeeding is a taboo in English-language children's literature. Breasts are too sensual to be seen carrying out their primary evolutionary function. This taboo is not seen in quite the same way in non-English-language children's books, but there is a general taboo about what girls' and women's bodies can be seen doing and how much of them can be revealed, and there are different standards regarding females than males.

Diversity (or the Lack Thereof)

The subject of diversity has come up in a multitude of ways in this chapter already. Breastfeeding in reality is something that happens across races, classes, ethnicities, religions, genders, sexualities, ages, abilities and family types, but this is rarely seen in literature, whether for children or adults (see the next chapter for more on adult literature).

My corpus was heavily White, which is not a surprise given the findings that resulted from the study *Reflecting Realities – A Survey of Ethnic Representation within*

UK Children's Literature 2017 by the Centre for Literacy in Primary Education (CLPE). In this study, the CLPE found that characters who were Black or who belonged to an ethnic minority group appeared in only 291 out of the 9,114 (4%) children's books published in the United Kingdom in 2017 (CLPE 2018, n.p.). This is a shockingly low number, given that the most recent UK census I could find statistics from, in 2011, suggests that 20% of the UK population is non-White (Anonymous n.d.c, n.p.). One would expect, then, that at least 20% of characters in UK children's books would be non-White, to reflect the make-up of society. In her analysis of adult literature from the United States, Greta Gaard states, 'Narrative texts providing examples of free mothers, from diverse races, classes, and species, able to choose whether, where, and how long to breastfeed their own offspring, do not yet appear in U.S. literature, possibly because the conditions for such cultural and economic freedoms have yet to exist' (2013, 1). This seems to be the case for literature in English generally, for both adults and children, and perhaps reflects larger societal ideas about who breastfeeds and why.[15]

Furthermore, I found no families that were explicitly non-heterosexual, although of course some characters might be intended to be bisexual, even if this is never stated. However, because there is widespread biphobia (see Epstein 2014) and bisexuals are often invisible, I do not think many readers would consider the possibility that any of the women in these books were bisexual. Although there were some single mothers, whose sexuality was not made explicit, and there were a couple of images of women breastfeeding while accompanied with other women (such as in Stoneley's picturebook (2015), although her list of the cast of characters seems to imply that those other women were sisters or mothers rather than partners), I believe that readers would be likely to regard the breastfeeding parent as heterosexual, as that is the societal 'norm'.

Likewise, I saw no explicitly differently abled characters in the images and read no descriptions of someone working through any challenges to breastfeeding related to this topic. Breastfeeding is possible, and encouraged, in the majority of situations; to name a few, a parent can breastfeed if they have seizures, are in a wheelchair, have a stoma bag, are autistic, have learning difficulties or have most other physical, mental or learning differences or disabilities. The main considerations might be differences in positioning and attachment or thinking through medication and its transfer into breastmilk (see the Breastfeeding Network's advice on this, 2019). However, the fact that

---

15. There are known cultural barriers to certain groups breastfeeding and a lack of diversity in lactation support (see Durdin (2019) about why Black Breastfeeding Week is needed, for instance).

differences in ability are compatible with breastfeeding was not at all reflected in literature.

I also found no obvious portrayals of non-Christian families, even though breastfeeding is considered an important part of Muslim and Jewish parenting (e.g. Hawwas (1988) and Eidelman (2006), respectively; both religions encourage breastfeeding for two years or longer), among other missing religious and ethnic groups. Class also was not referred to in any of the works.

I also found no discussion of feeding to natural term, or until a child herself or himself decides to stop feeding, or of tandem-feeding, although I did find a couple of pictures of these things, with older children feeding in Stoneley's and Therén's books, and tandem-feeding in Therén's *Alltid tillsammans* (*Always Together*) (2016). As noted earlier in this chapter, I have subsequently studied a number of weaning-focused picturebooks but have not included them in this analysis. If I had, then older children would have come up more often in these works, as those books are intended to be read to older children whose mothers have decided to wean them.

In other words, there is an overarching lack of diversity in these books. Breastfeeding appears rarely in its unadulterated form, completely openly and accepted, but when it does feature, it tends to be an activity for White women and their babies.

Conclusion

Palmer comments that 'it is now known that even in a rich country, a millionaire's baby who is artificially fed is less healthy than the exclusively breastfed baby of the most disadvantaged mother' ([1988] 2009, xv). Clearly, then, the topic of how to feed babies is an important one. And yet, as mentioned earlier, the percentage of women in the United Kingdom who breastfeed is quite low. So from the perspective of bottle-feeding being a societal norm today, it is not strange that bottles are seen more often than breasts in picturebooks, on television, on cards congratulating new parents, on signs for baby-changing and baby-feeding areas and as accessories for dolls, among other places (see, e.g., Burbidge 2015; Baumslag and Michels 1995, xxvi).

While terms such as 'norm' and 'normal' are complex and problematic, in this case, I would state that they are accurate. Breastmilk is the biological norm for feeding babies, and it is the cultural norm in the majority of the world's countries. And yet, authors, illustrators and publishers do not seem to want to depict it in English-language books for children. The few children's books I have found that feature breastfeeding tend to be ones that are specifically about breastfeeding or about baby-wearing or attachment parenting more generally; in other words, someone would have to already be passionate about breastfeeding to seek out these texts. A parent is arguably not likely to pick up a work such as *You, Me and the Breast* or *Milky Moments* or *What Does Baby Want?* if their child was not breastfed; the books' covers and marketing materials focus on breastfeeding, which would be a reason for some children and parents to avoid them.

In Swedish books, however, the common method of feeding babies is by breast, and the plots of Swedish-language books tend to focus on issues other than the breastfeeding itself. Breastfeeding is thereby normalised. However, as discussed earlier, breastfeeding is normalised mainly for specific groups of people; the protagonists are overwhelmingly White and from apparently or nominally Christian, middle-class, heterosexual homes, and the breastfeeding children are babies, not toddlers or older children.

A large part of the reason that breastfeeding is less common in English may be due to discomfort with breasts; as Nodelman writes, 'I suspect that picturebook artists avoid depictions of female nakedness simply because it is so hard not to turn female nakedness into traditional nudity' (1984, 28). If society is uncomfortable with and unaccepting of the female body and sees it as sexual and nude, then it will not show a breast, even if the breast is feeding a baby. LeVine and LeVine note that many women choose not to breast-feed because of 'shame' (2016, 53) of the exposed breast. Breasts are seen as sexual, so women will not use them for feeding, and they will not be depicted in books about feeding babies, which increases the shame and the squeamishness around breasts in society.

An additional explanation is that as bottle-feeding has become more common and more accepted, it seems old-fashioned, and perhaps even anti-feminist, to feature breastfeeding. That is, some people might suggest that women might be stuck at home, feeding a child at the breast, instead of being able to go out and continue their life as before; obviously, breastfeeding can and does take places in public, and life with a child can be similar to life before a child, or drastically different, or anywhere in between. I contend that not only is it healthier to promote breastfeeding, but it is also a feminist issue. Van Esterik writes that 'feminist goals, however envisioned, require a variety of core activities: political mobilization, legal changes, consciousness raising, and popular education to deal with women's issues as they emerge' (1989, 69–79). Increased education leads to more breastfeeding (e.g. van Esterik 1989, 90), and 'the only foolproof means of protecting breastfeeding is to ensure that every family, community, health worker, and policymaker has full access to factual, scientific, and unabridged information – both about the benefits of breastfeeding and also about the risks involved in foregoing the practice' (Jolly 1995, xv). Children's literature can be seen as a form of education and a way of normalising a topic, for both adults and children. It is feminist to say that a woman can use her body to feed her child and that she can do this at home or in public. It is also feminist to say that we must recognise how vital and valuable the work of breastfeeding is to our society. We need to take control of our own bodies and how we use and view them, rather than allowing the male gaze and/or limited ideas about women to define us.

The statistics for how often breastfeeding is portrayed in children's books in English and Swedish match quite closely the statistics for breastfeeding in the respective cultures; these numbers can be increased, but based on my findings here, it seems that doing so would require societal change, including the minimising of the sexualisation of women's bodies. Ann Marie A. Short writes of the 'deeply held cultural anxieties about the female body and the underlying tension between maternal and sexualized interpretations of its function' (2018, 3), and these anxieties and tensions seem clearly depicted in English-language works for children. As the next chapter will show, this is the case in literature for adults too, but perhaps to an even greater extent.

Chapter 3

LITERATURE FOR ADULTS

Introduction

In contemporary English-language literature for adults and young adults, breastfeeding is primarily described as a negative, painful, disgusting act and as something only for a select group in society. Many of the examples that I explore later in this chapter, which are typical of the stories and books that I found, depict suffering, ashamed women, who breastfeed out of a sense of duty because they believe they are supposed to, but do not enjoy it and do not generally do it for more than some weeks or months. They may also find that breastfeeding interferes with their relationship with their male partner. The great majority of these women are White, able-bodied, Western, middle-class, heterosexual, educated and otherwise 'norm', and the breastfed babies are likewise from the same categories and also tend to be full-term, single-birth newborns.

In other words, the depictions of breastfeeding in English are quite limited and tend to focus on practical problems and negative emotions. The Swedish examples, on the contrary, may show practical issues and negative feelings, too, but they also portray people thinking through such things and working to overcome them. As with the children's books discussed in the previous chapter, there is a sense in Swedish that breastfeeding is simply one part of life with children, with both good and bad things about it.

One English-language short story, 'Orange World' by Karen Russell (2018), can serve as a representative for what is explored in depth in this chapter. In her story, Russell writes about a character, Rae, who 'in order to guarantee the health of the baby she's about to have, [...] agrees to breastfeed the devil' (Davidson 2018, n.p.). As Russell points out in an interview, becoming a mother is often imbued with fear and uncertainty, and society places much responsibility and blame on women when it comes to the health of the baby (ibid.). While it may be true that a typical mother worries a lot about her child and wants to protect the child, it is interesting and revealing that the deal Rae makes in this story specifically involves breastfeeding. The devil causes Rae great pain while feeding from her: 'the devil has dozens of irregular teeth, fanged and broken, in three rows; some lie flat against the gums, like bright arrowheads in green mud. Its lips make a cold collar around her nipple. She feels the tugging deep in her groin, a menstrual aching' (Russell 2018, n.p.). The devil also bites her. Furthermore, the devil has a better latch than Rae's own baby, getting more milk from her, which perhaps reflects worries about low supply, which is something often discussed in breastfeeding support (in fact, only 1–5% of women usually do have low supply, so this is a widespread myth (see Francis et al. (2002, 31) for statistics or Hookway (2016) for more on actual low supply versus the issue of perceived low supply)). Rae notes:

> Unlike her son, the devil has no problem latching on. The pain is bearable if she focusses on the nursery window, gleaming on the opposite side of the empty road. Then it starts to chew, and reflex gets the better of her. She shrieks, unthinking, and pulls its snout from her breast. No sooner is she free of the latch than the visions pour into her, a dark flood. (Russell 2018, n.p.)

While it is true that Rae feels some joy when feeding her own baby, and she recognises the role of hormones in breastfeeding (ibid.), she has had to make this Faustian pact with the devil in order to get to this point in her parenting relationship and to keep her baby alive. Other women in the story know about the devil and its deals and tell her she made a 'mistake', but Rae is so paralysed with fear for her child that she continues to feed the devil, who says to her, '*Tits out, bitch*' (ibid.; italics original). Rae says, about breastfeeding, in what sounds like quite a sarcastic remark, 'I feel lucky to know what it means to be food, before I am dead' (ibid.). That is to say, our bodies decompose in the earth and nourish other creatures, and Rae appears to feel that her body is being consumed now as well. Perhaps she might as well be dead, or maybe she feels that her pre-baby self is dead. Of course, Rae may be suffering from postnatal depression or even experiencing hallucinations, but given that other women in the story also see and feed this devil, the message appears to be that it exists and preys on new mothers. There is much that can be said about this particular short story and its context in a contemporary society where women are pressured to be 'good' mothers and perfect parents and spouses and to take most of the responsibility for their children, while also holding down jobs, managing the household, doing volunteer work and otherwise contributing to their homes and the greater world, but what is perhaps most relevant here is the overall idea that breastfeeding is for the devil. It is something women are forced to do or choose to do in order to protect their babies and their families and in order to be 'good'[1] mothers. It is a deal with the devil, and it only causes physical and emotional pain and suffering.

In this chapter, then, I first look at a number of examples of recent literature in English[2] to explore what messages it offers about breastfeeding to readers. In short, I argue that even if some authors are trying to be realistic about what breastfeeding might be like – it can at times be painful, especially if a breastfeeding parent is not offered the necessary support, and it is also true that some people can be critical about the act itself or those who perform it – the overall implication in English-language literature is that breastfeeding is wrong. This reflects the low rates of breastfeeding in many English-speaking countries.

There are moments of pleasure in breastfeeding in some of these works – even Rae in Russell's story talks about her love for her child, including nursing him – but in general, breastfeeding brings about the opposite of joy. Western culture may have once thought there was something natural and beautiful

---

1. After this, I will simply write 'good mother' without quotation marks around the first word. I think it is sufficiently clear that I question the idea of the good mother and do not subscribe to the ideas that women must be mothers at all and that mothers must be good, and thus I do not need to mark it each time.
2. In older literature in English, breastfeeding is depicted quite differently. For instance, as Tamara S. Wagner writes:

   In Victorian fiction, breastfeeding fulfills a range of different narrative functions, from comic relief to strategic device in social problem fiction. By mid-century, maternal breastfeeding was both medically recommended and socially sanctioned. It featured throughout popular culture as a common sight, a part of everyday life that was also sentimentalized as a central aspect of the mother-child bond. In fact, the Victorians generally codified the baby at the breast as a domestic icon. Comical scenes are evidence of – rather than undermine – the growing prevalence of this association of breastfeeding with middle-class domesticity. However, as a sentimentalized image of breastfeeding became appropriated for specific social agendas, the discourse surrounding breastmilk became newly problematized. Simultaneously, the second half of the century saw an increasing medicalization of breastfeeding. In stressing the nutritional qualities of breastmilk, scientists asserted medical control over this body fluid in a new clinical and often inconsistent terminology, and child-rearing manuals popularized the concept of baby care as expert knowledge. Fiction participated in topical debates on shifting, class-bound practices, weighing in on the changing role that breastmilk played in these debates. (2019, 18)

   An example I found that Wagner also discusses is Mrs Micawber in Charles Dickens's *David Copperfield*, who feeds her children from 'Nature's founts' ([1850] 2008, 250). The Victorian depiction, with its occasional comical scenes and the nutritional focus, is quite different from the modern one, which is one reason why in this book I look only at contemporary literature, as I am interested in what modern society has to say about breastfeeding and what modern society might learn.

about breastfeeding,[3] and this might have at times been accompanied by the arguably oppressive belief that women belonged at home, nurturing children, rather than also being out in public and experiencing and contributing to other aspects of society, but I would suggest that we have gone too far in the opposite direction now. It is as though women's bodies cannot be seen performing their biological functions and women cannot be depicted as enjoying those functions. Instead, women's bodies are meant to be sexy – as though breastfeeding and sexiness are incompatible – and women should not be 'food', as Russell put it (2018, n.p.), until dead. In what follows, I try to parse the messages in the literature and to understand what got us to this point.

After studying the literature in English, I move on to compare it to work in Swedish, where the overall messages are quite different, as already mentioned. Swedish-language literature suggests that women can breastfeed but can also do other things with their lives and can challenge societal ideas about gender-specific roles.

Methodology

Methodology was already mentioned in the introduction to this book, but I want to add a few more details here that are relevant to adult literature. To find literary works that feature breastfeeding, I used several different sources. One was to simply read as widely as I could from contemporary works in English and Swedish, which is something I do for pleasure and for work already. Another was to use keyword searches in libraries and on the internet, although, perhaps not surprisingly, this did not yield much when I focused on breastfeeding in and of itself, except when it came to non-fiction guides to breastfeeding. I had to broaden this search to look for novels or memoirs about mothers, especially new ones, but even then, I had no way of knowing whether breastfeeding was depicted until I read the book, and often it was not, as though mothering seldom includes breastfeeding.[4] As noted in the chapter on children's literature, I was surprised by how frequently books featuring new babies either skipped over the feeding of those babies entirely – even though it is one of their main activities – or only mentioned sticking a bottle in a baby's mouth.

I also asked other breastfeeding parents and breastfeeding counsellors for suggestions, but this did not help me add too much to my corpus in English, because people often said to me, in a puzzled tone, 'I cannot think of any depictions of breastfeeding in literature!' Nonetheless, I have a fairly large

---

3. Terms such as 'natural' are problematic, as noted in the introduction.
4. Although I read memoirs and other non-fiction about mothering and parenthood, I only discuss fiction here.

corpus of English-language texts, and many of the works discussed here were ones I found by chance, just through my own reading.

My original intention had been to travel to Sweden to carry out additional research into Swedish literature. I felt that a trip to Sweden, where I could read at Kungliga biblioteket (the National Library in Stockholm) and buy books at the bookstore would provide plenty of additional texts to analyse. However, the coronavirus pandemic changed my plans and forced me to cancel all trips. Instead, I asked for recommendations from people I already had contact with, such as other translators who are members of the Swedish-English Literary Translators' Association. Translator and writer Saskia Vogel told me that an author she translated, Karolina Ramqvist, depicted breastfeeding in at least two novels, so I was able to then get those works. I already knew from my own translation experience that one of my authors, Kristina Sandberg, wrote about breastfeeding as well.

I also made contact with Amningshjälpen (Breastfeeding Help), a Swedish national breastfeeding support organisation that has supported breastfeeding parents since the 1970s; I discuss them more in the next chapter, when I explore the voluntary support they offer. Their administrator, Yamina Hamidi, kindly sent out a message to all their peer supporters, asking for recommendations for books that included breastfeeding. I collated the suggestions I received from Amningshjälpen, translators, friends and others, and then tried to access as many as I could from my bookshelves and through e-books; unfortunately, not all were available online or for purchase.

Frankly, my Swedish corpus is much smaller than my English-language one, and I can only imagine that if I had been able to spend time researching in Sweden, I would have had a larger corpus. I would suggest, however, that the texts are nonetheless revealing in what they say about Swedish culture and breastfeeding. The quantity of the texts may be small, but how they represent breastfeeding is fascinating in how it diverges from the English-language works. I also feel that being forced to limit the corpus in some ways turned out to be a strength, because instead of trying to cover every possible text across a range of genres and time periods, I was able to choose to focus in depth on a smaller number of works and to consider them relatively representative of what has been published.

Breastfeeding as Painful or Difficult

I will start this chapter by analysing contemporary adult literature in English. In these works, breastfeeding is often shown as challenging, with problems ranging from low supply to struggles with latching, so the message implied is that it is physically challenging. While these problems do exist in reality, I found no examples in the corpus of struggling mothers being offered support. There were no breastfeeding counsellors or lactation consultants, or concerned midwives or doctors, or caring friends or relatives, or breastfeeding groups or cafés to attend in person, or groups on social media; instead, women in literature are left to suffer alone and to eventually quit breastfeeding.

Latching the baby on in the first place is hard in *The Forgotten Waltz* by Anne Enright. 'And weaning Evie off her medication was easy compared to weaning her off the breast, for example, which was a major production only slightly less fraught than the three-act opera of getting her on the tit in the first instance' (2011, 294–95). In other words, as phrased in Enright's slightly humorous way, latching the baby on is compared to a 'three-act opera', and both latching and weaning the baby from the breast are harder than weaning someone off prescription drugs; to make this even clearer, breastfeeding is considered more challenging than a drug addiction.

In television shows, Katherine A. Foss likewise finds that latching is depicted as difficult and painful. She comments, 'On television, obstacles are limited to initial problems with nursing and are focused on individual problems. In the hospital and shortly after, characters face latch issues with their babies, which are easily resolved with a little coaching from a nurse, partner, or lactation consultant. Characters also complain of sore nipples in the early days of breastfeeding' (2018, 97). Perhaps issues with latch are easier to depict on TV than in books, given that it is simpler to show a baby missing the breast or incorrectly attached in images than in words, as Foss seems to have found more examples of incorrect latch than I did, but the quote from Enright is revealing about how latching is considered a challenge in literature as well.

Even if someone can get a baby to latch on, they do not always have enough milk to feed them with. Low supply is a perennial issue in both literary fiction and in general societal belief now, as noted previously. Kathryn Pollister finds that some TV shows portray women whose babies die because of insufficient milk from their mothers (2012, 225), implying that it is dangerous to have low supply, as a child could die. There is no solution for this offered except for formula. Also, and not coincidentally, some TV programmes are even sponsored by formula companies (ibid.). Formula companies are known to have marketing strategies that reach across many areas of society, which aim to encourage as many people as possible to buy their products (e.g. Tanrikulu et al. 2020). Baby Milk Action (see their website), along with other organisations and individuals, work to reveal the ways in which the formula industry exploits cultural or political contexts – including issues as disparate as coronavirus or other crises and countries not signing up to the WHO code – in order to get consumers to buy their products, usually to the consumers' own detriment; this, in turn, has led to various boycotts of companies that make artificial milk, both on a large scale and by individuals, from the 1970s through to today. In researching the marketing strategies of formula companies, I did not find any literary fiction sponsored or published by them – although it is entirely possible that there are links between some publishing companies and some of the large multinational companies that produce formula. But it is clear that some of the concepts that formula companies wish people to believe, such as that formula is the solution for low supply or other issues, definitely do appear in my corpus.

For example, in *Unbecoming* by Jenny Downham, Mary has a baby out of wedlock 'but the milk doesn't ever come in. Not really. Not enough so the baby will ever stop rooting for more' (2015, 166); the baby does not get any 'satisfaction', and this means that the 'baby's mother is useless. Mary knows it. And now the child knows it too' (2015, 167). In other words, Mary is a failure as a mother because she has low supply; indeed, this failure goes so far that Mary ends up giving her child to her sister to raise, and this sister is able to give baby Caroline 'satisfaction' with a bottle of formula milk. More on being a good versus a failed mother is discussed later in this chapter, but what is interesting here is the idea that it is hard to satisfy a baby; formula is suggested as being more satisfactory, and indeed, it might even be better for someone other than the child's mother to feed the child.

Low supply and satisfaction come up again in *When Will There Be Good News?* by Kate Atkinson. 'Louise wasn't breastfeeding when she took drugs, her milk had never come in properly and ran out after a week. ('Stress,' the GP said indifferently.) Archie seemed to find a bottle more emotionally comforting than his mother's breast' (2010, 265). A lack of supply is blithely mentioned, and Louise, as with other characters in fiction who are said to have low supply, appears to receive no support for this apparent problem. No doctor checks to ensure she has not, for example, retained some of the placenta or does not have any endocrine problems or that the baby does not have any anatomical issues, such as tongue tie, among other possible reasons for low supply. The GP throws the word 'stress' out, but does not appear to discuss whether Louise was actually stressed and, if so, whether something could be done about this. Instead, formula in a bottle is an easy solution, and indeed Archie, as with Caroline in the previous example, receives satisfaction and comfort from his bottle.

The Gustav Sonata by Rose Tremain shows low supply too. Erich and Emilie have baby Gustav, but Emilie seems unable to satisfy Gustav at the breast. The scene is as follows:

Erich sits on the bed watching Emilie trying to feed his son. Even in her maternal state, her breasts, which had grown large during her first pregnancy, are meagre. It's clear to Erich that Gustav is slowly dying from lack of sustenance. He snatches him off Emilie's breasts, and carries him round to the pharmacy, where he lays him down on the counter and takes off his clothes.

'Look!' says Erich. 'Look how thin and weak he is! He needs milk. [...] My wife [...] she's trying to breastfeed him but I don't think there's anything *in her breasts*!' (2016, 187; italics original)

The pharmacist gives Erich powdered milk, and one of the other customers, a woman, says, 'You know he must have the breast as well. Or else your wife will get depressed' (2016, 188). This shows a rare understanding in contemporary literature of how hormones work and the importance of oxytocin for breastfeeding and for the baby and the mother's mental health. Still, 'when Erich gives Gustav the bottle, [Emilie] sees on the infant's face an expression of bliss, whereas, on the breast he's restless and agitated. And she knows she's clumsy with him. She can't seem to get him entirely comfortable in her arms. He kicks and screams. But when Erich picks him up, he goes quiet' (ibid.). In this book, Emilie never is able to show love or kindness to her son, Gustav, and her apparent inability to feed him is depicted as the starting point for her depression and lack of motherly feeling. Meanwhile, Gustav is happy and relaxed with his father; this is similar to the way Mary's sister appears better at feeding and caring for baby Caroline in Jenny Downham's *Unbecoming*. Low supply once again suggests a failure on the part of the mother.

The physical problems depicted in literature are mainly limited to latch and supply, and while I argue that it is problematic in some ways to focus on such things, as it suggests that breastfeeding is inevitably painful and hard, another way of looking at it would be to argue that such depictions could actually feature a wider range of issues. As Katherine A. Foss notes in regard to TV:

No storylines address breastfeeding a premature, jaundiced, or tongue-tied newborn, or address mastitis, thrush, clogged milk ducts, inverted nipples, or other issues that can impede success. And since these issues are not part of the storylines, remedies for these obstacles are also missing. Research has shown that women's concerns about lactation issues and the baby's nourishment are given as the most frequent reasons for weaning (Li et al.). These programs could help allay these fears – thus extending breastfeeding duration by counteracting myths about insufficient milk and offering solutions to typical problems. Furthermore, such depictions could reassure viewers these issues are normal and, therefore, not a reason to wean. Solutions could include dried breast milk for sore nipples, medication for mastitis and thrush, and pumping to boost supply. (2018, 98)

So, in what might seem to be a contradictory recommendation, I would suggest both that we move away from focusing on low supply, especially if no support is given in the works with this problem, and also that breastfeeding depictions in literature (and on TV or in films) could show a wider range of breastfeeding problems in order to normalise them and offer solutions. This sort of realism is desirable, because it would show that certain issues are easily solved, with the right support, and this could in turn lead to more people persevering with breastfeeding because they know that seeing a lactation consultant or talking to a peer supporter or calling a helpline would help them fix their engorged breasts or their baby's uncomfortable latch or get through their breastfeeding aversion or whatever the situation might be. In fact, in her analysis of breastfeeding on primetime television, Foss comes to a similar conclusion. She writes:

> Storylines about hospital practices hindering breastfeeding, breastfeeding policies and legislation, and lack of public support for breastfeeding could highlight problem areas and help to shape cultural attitudes. [...] More specifically, these messages help shift responsibility for breastfeeding success to the institutional level, highlighting the need for cultural change (and not simply an increase of individual women breastfeeding). Programs could also address strategies to help working women breastfeed – including onsite childcare, flexible working arrangements, sufficient pumping breaks, and extended maternity leave [as] such representations could alert potential employers to the need of working mothers and garner public support for policies to protect them. Improving working conditions for breastfeeding is especially important given that working fulltime has been shown to decrease breastfeeding. (2018, 99)

In other words, although Foss is not specifically referring to pain in breastfeeding, she is arguing that including stories about problems with breastfeeding could educate people and help shape policy. Besides that, however, I argue that also including scenarios where breastfeeding is working well and is problem-free or where workplaces have breastfeeding-friendly policies can encourage women and show that breastfeeding is not always a physical or political issue and can indeed work well and be beneficial to the breastfeeding parent-and-child dyad and to others as well. Breastfeeding is not solely about physical pain or low supply, and should not be depicted as such.[5]

---

5. In previous work I have carried out on LGBTQ+ literature, I have argued that while there is certainly a need for coming-out stories that show challenges related to coming out (such as rejection by family and friends), we also need more positive LGBTQ+ stories, ones that show that LGBTQ+ lives are not necessarily sad or hard (Epstein 2013). The same argument applies here: there is room for literature that features breastfeeding problems, and there is also room for literature that shows solutions to those problems, and there is also room for literature that shows no problems with breastfeeding at all.

Breastfeeding as an Emotional Impediment

Besides being a physical challenge, breastfeeding is shown to be an obstruction in multiple ways, including getting in the way of the woman living her life to the full, or interrupting marital relations, or becoming a blockage to the baby/child developing a relationship with their other parent.

While breastfeeding itself is not depicted as difficult in Meg Wolitzer's *The Wife*, it does interfere with the marital relationship because it makes Carol feel 'touched out', to use the phrase many employ today (e.g. Atkins-Boyce 2016). This phrase refers to when a breastfeeding parent feels overwhelmed by all the touching and closeness with the nursling, and then does not want any physical intimacy with their spouse, other children or friends. In Wolitzer's book, Joe wants to sleep with Carol, but she 'refused, telling him she wasn't ready to be touched, she already had enough human needs to deal with, what with nursing the baby every few hours. And when finally he insisted, she howled in pain as though he were stabbing her with a pitchfork, and he felt like a rapist, a murderer' (2003, 123). Indeed, due to the lack of sex and his desire for a new, more willing partner, Joe leaves Carol, and the daughter he has with her. He moves on to Joan and has children with her, but although Joan enjoys breastfeeding – 'I was a nursing mother, and that was all I had to be' – she feels pressured to stop, because Joe again wants control over his time with his wife and more sleep at night (2003, 124); that is to say, although Joe is not the one breastfeeding at night, he finds that it interferes with his sleep and his sex life, so his preference would be for his wife to stop.

Joe also feels anxious, because he wants to 'imprint' on the children and believes that Joan has more influence because she is breastfeeding (ibid.). Joe clearly thinks the breastfeeding has gone on too long because he snidely remarks, '"I hope you're not planning on doing this forever." Or, "I could be wrong, but I thought Dr. Spock said it's a good idea to stop nursing them before they start graduate school. It gets in the way of their classes." And so I did stop, sooner than I might have otherwise' (ibid.). Joan ends up spending her life supporting Joe and his career – in fact, the big twist in the book, which is not much of a surprise, is that Joan actually produces the literary work that Joe passes off as his own and gets credit for – and she feels that although some women might make other choices, perhaps supported by a 'husband who lactates' (2003, 184), the world will not recognise those choices. Here, then, Wolitzer's book depicts a woman who believes women have to be useful; one way of being useful is to breastfeed and nurture children, but an apparently better way, one that takes precedence, is to quit breastfeeding and to support a husband's needs, which might include sleep, sex or even their career. A woman can only have a life of her own if she has a wife of her own – the supposed 'husband who lactates' – and as this is usually not possible, Wolitzer's book shows the protagonist prioritising her husband over herself and her children.

In Diana Evans's novel *Ordinary People* – one of the very few books I found with Black or mixed-race characters – Michael and Melissa are in bed together. Although breastfeeding itself is not depicted, Michael tries to make love with Melissa, who has milk-filled breasts; indeed, he even tries to suck on them. This makes her uncomfortable and she does not want him to do it:

> She wrenched her neck away from him cat-like and he moved downwards to the vicinity of her milk-designated chest, which he couldn't really suck with any degree of self-respect but what the hell.
>
> 'I'd rather you didn't do that,' she said.
>
> She felt his hardness against her leg and resented the obligation that she should do something for it. She just didn't feel like it now. And it bothered her not just that he had proposed to lap at her shore of milk, but that he had started on the left. He always started on the left. (2018, 26)

Michael does not mind the milky breasts – perhaps, in fact, he finds her especially alluring because of them – but Melissa is 'bothered' by it, and she also 'resent[s] the obligation' to satisfy his sexual urges. So although Michael does not pressure Melissa in the way Joe did with Joan, both women seem to feel that the man's needs come first and are an 'obligation', and that breastfeeding, and the presence of milk in their breasts, is an inhibition and an obstruction.

As implied in the example of Joe and Joan, breastfeeding can also be depicted as interfering with a child's relationship with their other parent. As noted, Joe wants to imprint on the child and feels he cannot if the child is being breastfed. In Elske Rahill's collection of stories, *White Ink*, which are in the main about pregnancy, birth and parenting, breastfeeding is a way of keeping a child from the father. The unnamed protagonist in the title story – the title itself refers to breastmilk – separates from her partner and he gets visitations with the baby. A friend of the father's says to the protagonist, 'He said watching you feed the baby makes him wish he had breasts' (2017, 44). It is implied that it is not the feeding as such that the father envies but rather the time with and control over the baby. The mother, who is covered in 'milk stains' (2017, 45), and thus often is depicted as unclean and messy, provides breastmilk for the father to use while with the baby, and she pumps while separated from her child (2017, 53). However, when the baby is finally returned to her, it seems as if the father was starving the baby and did not give him the expressed milk, as a sort of punishment to the woman for breastfeeding and for the closeness she has with the child. The baby is 'wax-faced, blue-lipped, and your eyes are so big. You do not cry, but your big eyes grow bigger and you open your palms to me and before I can stop it my voice has betrayed us. "My baby," I say. "Oh my baby"' (2017, 53). The father calls the mother a 'bitch' and tells her, 'He doesn't want you [...] you know that, don't you? Just your tits' (ibid.). As a result of all this – the father being jealous of her breastfeeding, his refusal to give the baby breastmilk, his starving of the baby, his mockery of the mother–baby relationship and her worry that her complicated feelings towards her ex-partner somehow come through to the baby via her milk – the woman decides to stop breastfeeding. 'My breasts swell hot and sore at first, but I will not poison you again with all my braying rage. By the third day, your milk is gone' (2017, 59). In short, the woman's desire for a close relationship with her son in part through breastfeeding is depicted as affecting the father's ability, or even willingness, to engage with the child. It is worth pointing out, however, that the father does appear to be abusive and at one point frightens the main character by hiding the baby from her, but the overall message is that breastfeeding is part of the problem or that it is something that other people have control over, not just the breastfeeding parent. The mother in this story stops feeding both because she thinks her anger will infect the baby through her milk and also because she needs to distance herself from the baby in order to help him have a relationship with his father.

Similarly, in Rahill's most recent novel, *An Unravelling*, breastfeeding is again seen as difficult and an interference at times. *An Unravelling* is, in brief, about a family torn apart by money and art, and different generations of women in the story have different feelings about and experiences with breastfeeding. The matriarch, Molly, tries to feed her baby herself, but she is criticised by a midwife for missing her first, dead child, as if this is wrong, and so 'Molly's breasts grew shy and no milk came' (2019, 278), revealing how stress can affect supply (something hinted at but not explored in Atkinson's book, as mentioned earlier). Also, Molly feels that her husband's focus on his career and reliance on her make it hard for her to feed:

> It made Molly hate him so much that for the first days of Aoife's life, her nerves tingled, her breasts were aflame with milk that didn't come. She was sick with it. [...] She fed Aoife bottles with sugar and egg yolk in them. Molly is ashamed to think of it, how she allowed her failure and his to fester. (2019, 182)

As in Wolitzer's book, the man's career comes first, and that can negatively impact on breastfeeding. All these years later, Molly is still 'ashamed' by her 'failure' to breastfeed; she does not understand or have a good relationship with Aoife when her daughter is grown up, and it is implied in part that this is because of the lack of breastfeeding.

Meanwhile, Eileen/Lily, Molly's youngest child, has mental health problems. She tries to use having babies as a way of keeping her lover Liam, a married man who already has children with his wife, attached to her, but instead, this pushes him away. Eileen/Lily initially likes her older child, Cara, then begins to think of her as a devil because Liam transfers his affection from Eileen/Lily to the baby. 'How she loved that child – for the first six weeks she even fed her from her breasts. She should have known immediately [that the child was a 'gremlin'], of course she should have. She was expecting a boy to carry on Liam's gifts' (Rahill 2019, 229). So as long as she loves the baby, she feeds her, but then she begins to see the baby as a 'gremlin' because she interferes with Eileen/Lily's relationship with Liam. In some of the earlier examples, it was the father who considered breastfeeding to be an interference, but here, it is the mother, and in this case, she has mental health difficulties, which implies there is something wrong with her that makes her unable or unwilling to connect to her baby. There is no discussion of whether she might have postpartum depression or if she is receiving appropriate support.

Indeed, Eileen/Lily goes to the hair salon while her baby, who is still breastfed at that stage, is tiny, but instead of returning as planned, she walks away and stays out for hours. When she returns, the baby is 'sucking at a sugared rag, her little chest heaving in the aftermath of tears', and Molly is so angry at her daughter's treatment of her grandchild that she says she could hit Lily (Rahill 2019, 432–33). It is soon after this that Eileen/Lily quits breastfeeding, and she feels that there was no point to having these children, because not only do they take Liam's attention from her, but he ends up leaving her anyway. Later, Cara, the baby she left without milk for all those hours, grows up and has her own children. Cara gets repeatedly pregnant, and though she does breastfeed and show affection to her children, unlike her own mother, she is exhausted by motherhood and finds that it gets in the way of her artistry and her life generally. For instance, she, her husband and some guests smoke a joint after dinner. Cara says, 'This will be the one big perk of weaning Peig. No need to pump and dump' (2019, 221). Quitting breastfeeding, in other words, will simplify her life, including the ability to smoke marijuana and socialise with other adults.

Obviously, these examples may seem specific to Rahill's authorship and her own views on breastfeeding, whatever they may be. But the concept of breastfeeding interfering with other relationships and with the mother's life in general is not limited to Rahill's oeuvre, as was evidenced from Meg Wolitzer's book and some of the other examples. Another novel that suggests that breastfeeding, and maybe even being a mother in and of itself, holds a woman back is Kate Atkinson's *Emotionally Weird*. At first, breastfeeding appears to come easily and naturally for Kara and her baby Proteus. Kara is a student and she feeds Proteus in any situation (e.g. Atkinson 2000, 74, 174, 196), including during class, which makes another student 'blush [...] in horror' (2000, 74). Kara, unlike Rahill's Cara, who worries about pumping and dumping, even happily rolls and partakes of 'an enormous loose joint of home-grown grass' (2000, 197). Kara also expresses a desire, seen rarely in English-language literature, to breastfeed until natural term (i.e. until the child chooses to wean, which is usually between the ages of 2 and 8), though others mock this. 'They had embarked on a heated discussion about the age at which you should stop breastfeeding. Jill favoured two years while Kara thought you "should let them decide for themselves." A decision she might live to regret when Proteus was a thirty-year-old civil servant commuting daily from Tring' (2000, 197–98). Besides joking about natural-term breastfeeding, Atkinson also seems to make an ironic point about breastfeeding on demand for as long as the child desires when she has Bob, a lazy, sleepy druggie character, argue 'vehemently against feeding on demand because it would lead to a generation of layabouts and slackers' (2000, 202). However, despite her apparent comfort with and support of breastfeeding, Kara eventually abandons baby Proteus, leaving him with other students. Not knowing how to care for him, they give him a variety of non-breastmilk, adult foods, and he seems perfectly fine with them. A possible reading of Kara's breastfeeding relationship and behaviour, then, could be a mockery of long-term breastfeeding, and again we find the message that even though a woman may want to breastfeed, she will find that it can stop her from living her life and that, at any rate, a baby can thrive on other foods and does not need the breastmilk. Kara, unsupported in her intention to feed to natural term, leaves her baby, and it does not appear to harm him.

Besides interfering with life and relationships, on a more practical level, breastfeeding is also often shown as difficult and exhausting, getting in the way of a mother feeling rested or carrying out other tasks. In Kate Atkinson's novel *Behind the Scenes at the Museum*, Alice breastfeeds, but seems overwhelmed by both the act specifically and being a wife and mother more generally:

> [She] nursed the newly-christened Eleanor. Baby Nell had fallen asleep at the breast and Alice herself was dozing miserably, quite unable to face the unwashed clothes, unfed children and unsatisfied husband that comprised her lot in life. She was thinking, in a glumly metaphorical way, that she felt as if a great stone had been laid on her breastbone

and she was being slowly suffocated by it, like one of the martyrs of old. (1995, 435)

Alice is so 'suffocated' by breastfeeding and her other tasks that she even feels like a 'martyr'. Indeed, as discussed briefly in Chapter 1, one of the many arguments people make for feeding a baby with artificial milk is that then someone else can feed the baby and give the mother a break, even though much research suggests that it is still usually the mother who makes and gives the bottles and who does much of the work around the house and for the family (see Brown (2016, 153), which discusses studies that show that breastfeeding mothers spend more time feeding their babies, while formula-feeding mothers spend more time preparing and feeding formula, and also get less help with general care of their babies; she also discusses this on 274).[6] Alice, then, is unlikely to be less miserable or tired or to be able to do other things were she to stop breastfeeding, but it nonetheless sounds in the book as though breastfeeding were one of her main problems.

Similarly, in *This Must Be the Place* by Maggie O'Farrell, breastfeeding is depicted as exhausting and as something that wears on the mother. The protagonist has multiple children, a 'shocking, unjust number' and 'just seems to pop them out, one after another, her stomach permanently inflated, her breasts constantly being heaved out of her garments in the back garden for some infant or other to nourish itself' (2016, 210). Here, breasts are 'heaved', her stomach is 'inflated' and there is no indication of the specific bond between her and the breastfed child, as it is just stated that an unspecified 'some infant or other' is being fed.

Breastfeeding, in short, is represented in these books as keeping women from their real lives, whatever those lives might entail: daily tasks and chores, relationships with others, sex, education, careers, sleep, an identity of their own and more.

Breastfeeding as Disgusting or Wrong

Blushing 'in horror' at the sight of breastfeeding was mentioned earlier (Atkinson 2000, 74), but the concept of breastfeeding as being embarrassing, disgusting or wrong is quite common in the corpus. It is also suggested that breastfeeding should not take place in public.

In Kate Atkinson's *Life after Life*, breastfeeding seems to revolt or surprise some of the characters. For example, 'Mrs Glover couldn't suppress a slight

---

6. Indeed, as Carolyn Daniel finds, 'it is rare to find instances of males providing food in children's literature' (2006, 112); this would include via a bottle.

shudder at the sight of Sylvie's pale, blue-veined breasts surging forth from her foamy lace peignoir' (2013, 39). Here, breasts full of milk make another woman 'shudder'. There are also a couple of scenes in the book where a woman needs to find a place to breastfeed away from others, so she is not seen doing it. An example is where she finds a beach hut (2013, 45). Another is the scene where she searches for 'a discreet spot in order to feed Teddy. Girls brought up in nice houses in Mayfair did not generally duck behind hedges to suckle infants. Like Hibernian peasants, no doubt' (2013, 70). So middle-class and upper-class women in general, it seems, should not breastfeed like 'peasants' and certainly should not do so in public. This may in part reflect cultural and class-based norms from the early twentieth century, which is when these scenes are set, but they also show a discomfort with breastfeeding more generally.[7] Although focused on recent TV programmes, Foss finds that 'when women nurse in public onscreen, their actions are heavily criticized and conveyed as inappropriate' (2018, 100). This sense of inappropriateness prevails in the corpus.[8] Cindy A. Stearns writes, 'Breastfeeding raises many possibilities for public performance. The average newborn nurses about every two hours. Unless a woman stays at home for several months and is able to only breastfeed at home, and in private, most women must think about how they will go about breastfeeding in front of others' (1999, 311). This may be true in reality, but in literature, women are encouraged to stay at home and out of view.

Given that breastfeeding in public is often a subject that is up for debate in modern times (Stearns 1999, 312, among other sources, plus all the examples of women being asked to cover up, as already discussed in this book), I was actually surprised not to find more examples from literature where a woman is breastfeeding in public and this upsets or angers other people or even drives them to act inappropriately in return, such as by photographing a breastfeeding woman's bare breast (Blackall 2021).

---

7. As this is common throughout Atkinson's oeuvre, it is likely that this discomfort with breastfeeding reflects her own views, and she in turn was shaped by being raised in the United Kingdom in the twentieth century.
8. Although here I am focusing on English-language novels, I want to reference Clémentine Beauvais's novel *Piglettes*. Beauvais wrote and published this book in French in 2014, but as she lives in the United Kingdom and translated it herself to English in 2017, I feel it can perhaps be included. In the novel, Mireille is told her mother, a teacher, is expecting a baby. Mireille is disgusted and asks, 'Will you go to school and teach with the baby hanging from your boob? Some mothers do that sometimes. It's atrocious. I refuse to condone such behaviour.' Her mother replies, 'I won't be teaching, since I'll be on maternity leave. And I don't know if I'll breastfeed. Is that all? Any other questions?' (2014, 75). Mireille does not want her mother to breastfeed in public, especially at work, and finds the idea of a 'baby hanging from [a] boob' 'atrocious'.

Several of the examples from this section show how some find breastfeeding to be 'distasteful' or want to look away from it, but I did not find any scenes where someone was told to stop breastfeeding or to go breastfeed in a toilet or a separate room. When analysing television, Foss discusses a scene in *Married ... with Children*, which she says

> frames public breastfeeding as absurd and obscene, even in a show that aims to be obscene. Furthermore, Al's disgust is contrasted to his attraction to women's breasts, as he comments to his (male) associate: 'What is happening to this country when a woman of the opposite sex can just waddle into your place of business, your holy sanctuary, and bare her breasts. It's disgusting.' The other employee replies, 'It's repulsive.' They reach down and pick up magazines with the titles Big 'Uns and Black Big 'Uns. (2018, 102)

That particular TV show is known for its apparently humorous misogyny and is an influential, long-running programme; many people have seen it and imbibed its critique of women and their bodies, and perhaps been influenced by it. Foss further notes, 'When mothers breastfeed their new babies covered up in their homes, it is presented as beautiful and natural' (2018, 103), whereas breastfeeding in public is not, but that is not what my literary corpus suggests; rather, the 'beautiful and natural' is mostly absent throughout the fictional works and instead the idea of 'disgusting' or 'disturbing' is the main message.

In another Atkinson work, *Behind the Scenes at the Museum*, breastfeeding is described as 'distasteful' (1995, 56). This may be said half in jest, as this part of the story is narrated by the newborn infant Ruby and also because the scene does reflect ideas about feeding on a schedule and not spoiling a child, while also gently mocking them, but it nonetheless may encourage readers to share those values. There are still hospitals in English-speaking countries that use nurseries and encourage schedules and keep babies separated from their mothers, which of course interferes with breastfeeding on demand. The depiction in the novel is as follows:

> Bunty's settled in well in the maternity ward. The mothers all lie beached on their beds complaining all the time, mostly about their babies. We're nearly all being bottle-fed, there's an unspoken feeling that there's something distasteful about breast-feeding. We're fed on the dot, every four hours, nothing in between, no matter how much noise you make. In fact the more noise you make the more likely you are to be relegated to some cupboard somewhere. There are probably forgotten babies all over the place.

> We're fed by the clock so that we don't become spoilt and demanding. The general feeling amongst the mothers is that the babies are in a conspiracy against them (if only we were). We can scream until we're exhausted, it won't make any difference to the ceremonial feeding ritual, the time when all the little baby parcels are fed, winded, changed, laid down again and ignored. (1995, 56)

Here, babies are called 'parcels' and are ignored so they do not become 'spoilt'; there is obviously a sense of humour in this description of the nursery at the hospital, possibly poking fun at such beliefs, as it is actually known that babies cannot be spoiled. But it is worth pointing out that even though much research from anthropology and medicine shows that there are many different methods of childcare around the world (e.g. Lancy 2008, among other books), many baby books and much of popular culture in English-speaking countries still subscribe to these approaches, that is, to the concept of strict schedules, lack of physical contact and the feeding of artificial milk. So what might appear funny or even pointed to some readers is likely to be considered accurate and acceptable to others, including the concept that breastfeeding is 'distasteful'.

Later in the book, we again see this mixed, slightly ambiguous view of breastfeeding. Ruby's father and uncles catch sight of their neighbour, Mrs Roper, breastfeeding her child, and this 'elicits cries all round of "Bloody Hell!" said half in admiration and half in disgust' (Atkinson 1995, 299). Ruby notes:

> You expect her [Mrs Roper] to rummage around in her extremely untidy house and produce a lacrosse stick or a riding crop rather than the unprepossessing baby-David – or his accessory, a swollen breast, pumping with blue veins like a 3-D delta map. I am both repelled and fascinated by this sight. I have never seen anyone breastfeeding before Mrs Roper (we aren't that kind of family). It also makes an unfortunate contrast to Auntie Babs' chest, now entirely shorn. (1995, 301)

There is much to unpick in this short scene. Mrs Roper's breast is described as her baby's 'accessory', as though there is something wrong with him feeding from it frequently and as though it belongs to him, and her breast itself is portrayed in unattractive terms as 'swollen […], pumping with blue veins like a 3-D delta map' (ibid.). Ruby's thoughts reveal this now-familiar blended feeling of disgust and interest, and she feels that breastfeeding is not something for her 'kind of family', that is, nice and tidy and polite people. Meanwhile, she also thinks of these 'swollen' breasts in contrast to her aunt's chest, and her aunt had breast cancer and required a mastectomy; it is not clear whether it is Babs's or Mrs Roper's chest that is considered more repellent here.[9]

'White Ink', the main story in Elske Rahill's collection, which was discussed earlier in relation to breastfeeding interfering with the father's relationship with the baby, is another example of a work where breastfeeding appears wrong and gross. The protagonist links 'giving you suck, giving him head, cleaning the toilet' (2017, 47). In other words, breastfeeding is the same sort of work as giving a man oral sex and scrubbing a toilet; perhaps this is true to some degree, in that these are all undervalued tasks that some women carry out without much respect or appreciation. The baby is also portrayed almost as a monster in his need for milk, which is similar to the idea of the devil breastfeeding from the mother in Karen Russell's short story (2018), which was analysed at the start of this chapter. In Rahill's work, the baby breastfeeding is described as follows:

> You wake too early – a ravenous mouth; a need; a wild, snorting, pulling thing, ferociously rooting for survival. Sleepily we lump you from his hands to my arms to milk, and there you mew and smack and, frantic for it, you miss and miss and catch and miss and latch. The lock and pull of you sends a rush through the other breast and three white arcs cross the bedroom – elegant, confident shapes, and shocking for their reach – leaving a sprinkling of tiny blots on the mirror of our wardrobe […] you keep the nipple within suckle-clamp, two palms suckered to the swell-and-wobble globe that is now your touchstone. Your mouth is a stretch of red-sharp gum, a serrated streak of tooth cutting through […]

---

9. Unfortunately, there is no space here to analyse the depiction of breasts more generally in literature, given how much material I have on breastfeeding alone, nor is there the scope for discussing the portrayal of breast cancer. However, I can mention that I found another link between breastfeeding and breast cancer in Rupert Thomson's novel *Never Anyone but You*. Thomson's work, which is based on the true story of the lovers Claude Cahun and Marcel Moore, has a scene where Marcel dreams that a king has a wet nurse breastfeed his children, but he cuts off one of the wet nurse's breasts so that the child does not fondle it while feeding, as breastfeeding children are wont to do (2018, 122–23). Later, Marcel has breast cancer, and there is some discussion about whether the breastfeeding dream was a prediction, or whether it shows that Marcel subconsciously knew what was happening to her body, or whether it is in fact a comment on Marcel and Claude's passionate, co-dependent relationship and the way they need and use one another (2018, 128–29). Interestingly, this novel is one of the few that refer to breastfeeding that is by a male author. For more on breast cancer in literature, see 'Baring the Breast: Mastectomy and the Surgical Analogy' by Mary Jacobus (1995, 231–68).

satisfied little puke and I promise your daddy again about the sheets. (2017, 30–31)

The baby is 'frantic', 'ferocious', 'a wild, snorting, pulling thing'. He has a 'red-sharp gum' and a 'serrated' tooth that cuts, which suggests a knife, something that hurts and maybe even kills. The baby 'pukes' – a rather violent, slangy choice of term, though a more common word might be 'spits up' or 'possets' – and makes a mess, and of course it is up to the woman to clean the vomit (she makes a 'promise' 'about the sheets'). All told, the baby's behaviour appears beastly and revolting. At least this behaviour is carried out at home, however, without disturbing people in public.

In Russell's short story and in Elske Rahill's novel, *An Unravelling*, breastfeeding was at times linked to the idea of a devil. Mothers may have to make pacts with the devil, including breastfeeding the devil, to keep their children alive, or perhaps the breastfeeding children themselves are devils, interfering with the woman's life, her relationships with other people or the child's relationship with others. Breastfeeding as evil and devil-like is also a theme in Philip Pullman's *The Book of Dust*, one of the few male-authored books I have found that includes breastfeeding. In this novel, the 'bad' fairy Diania breastfeeds Lyra as a way of trying to steal her away (2017, 249–57). Diania's milk puts Lyra to sleep, but this is described as being evil rather than natural and common, though breastmilk does indeed help babies and children sleep (e.g. Sánchez et al. 2009); in Pullman's work, getting Lyra to sleep is a way of gaining control over her. Diania also wants to feed Lyra in order to help Lyra attach to her, which again is described as a bad thing, rather than as a positive bond. She is not the baby's mother, and through her behaviour, Pullman implies that there is something wrong with breastfeeding/wet-nursing. The novel suggests that Lyra is safer in the care of people who bottle-feed her. The scenes with Diania are quite long but nonetheless useful to quote in length because they reveal the clear message that breastfeeding is negative and wrong, and even an evil act:

> The little glade was clearly illuminated, and right in the middle of it sat Diania, bare-shouldered, bare-breasted, with Lyra sucking vigorously at her right nipple. The woman looked up, and gave them a smile so strange she might have been inhuman.
>
> 'What are you doing?' said Malcolm.
>
> 'Why, feeding the child of course! Giving her good milk. Look at her suck!'

She looked down proudly. The nipple slipped out of Lyra's mouth, and the woman lifted her up to her shoulder and patted her back. Lyra obligingly belched, and the woman promptly brought her down on the other side, and the child's little mouth began to work open and shut even before she found the nipple. Then she closed her eyes and went on sucking vigorously.

Malcolm thought that she never sucked the bottle like that. Asta whispered, 'This woman is trying to steal her.' [...]

'She's doing that to make her belong to her,' said Alice. 'She en't normal, Mal. She en't proper human. [...] She's doing some magic or summing, I swear. You know the fairies, in stories? Well, they take human children. [...] They steal kids and they're never seen again. It's true,' she said [...]

'She won't have had milk like that before,' said the woman.

'No, and thank you for feeding her,' said Malcolm, 'but we're going to go now [...] And we'll take Ellie [what they call Lyra to trick others] now.'

'No you won't. She's mine. [...] She's mine. She's drunk my milk. Look at how happy she is in my arms! She's going to stay with me! [...] Because I want to, and I have the power. If she could speak she'd say she wanted to stay here too.'

'What are you going to do with her?'

'Bring her up to be one of my people, of course.'

'But she isn't one of your people.'

'She is now she's drunk my milk. You can't alter that.' (2017, 450–53)

Lyra seems happier and more comfortable when breastfeeding, and it is noted that she 'never sucked the bottle like that' (ibid.), but this is clearly depicted as a problem. Breastfeeding may be comfortable, but in this case, it is wrong; this is the opposite of some of the earlier examples, in which breastfeeding was less satisfying and comfortable than bottle-feeding. When Malcom and Alice finally get Lyra away from the evil Diania, she howls, and says Lyra is her own baby. When they tell her that she is not her baby, she screams, 'I waited a thousand years to hold a baby to my breast! But she's drunk my milk! She's mine!' (2017, 456).

While Pullman's novel is obviously not about the 'real' world, given the magical, fantastical elements, it can still be argued that fiction comments on life. Another writer of fantasy fiction, Ursula K. LeGuin, included breastfeeding as an expected habit for her fantastical beings but later noted that she regretted what a short breastfeeding stage she depicted in her writing

(6–8 months). She acknowledged that she was influenced by the societal views of breastfeeding at the time she wrote, which emphasised that breastfeeding was 'lower-class', and if a woman was to do it, she must supplement her child with formula and breastfeed only for a short period of time (Mishan 2009, n.p.). In the case of this fantasy work, LeGuin was affected by the views around her and then reflected them in her writing, which in turn may have impacted her readers.

Pullman does not call breastfeeding 'lower-class', but in the scene in his book, breastfeeding is evidently bad, and it is a tool used by someone who is morally corrupt and mentally disturbed. Diania uses her breastmilk to try to control Lyra; rather than the milk nourishing Lyra and making her feel close to Diania, it is employed to try to 'steal' Lyra and make her 'one of [Diania's] people'. Lyra, it appears, would be better off being bottle-fed artificial milk. It is true that given other elements of their characters and the plot, Lyra would not be safe with Diania, but it is nevertheless rather telling that Pullman chose to employ breastfeeding as the evidence that shows just how malevolent Diania is.

As these examples reveal, breastfeeding tends to be portrayed not as a positive way to nourish and nurture children but rather as something that others find off-putting and wrong. In Chapter 2, I found that the naked woman or girl is viewed as nude and that there seems to be a taboo about seeing women's breasts in literature. Given how common it was to find breastfeeding described as disgusting in literary texts, I wondered whether breastmilk was seen as a taboo, because it comes from a bodily orifice, and whether this would then impact these ideas of wrong/dirty/disgusting. Turner writes that 'metaphors of risk and danger are characteristically associated with the orifices of the human body' ([1984] 1996, 7), and this links back to anthropological work on dirt and taboo, such as by Mary Douglas ([1966] 1994). Since some people say breastfeeding should be done in private or covered up, the way one would urinate or excrete in private, I had expected to find more references in literature to the supposed 'dirtiness' of breastmilk and to be able to argue that it was more of a taboo in English-speaking cultures. Shame and disgust are certainly linked to the ideas of dirty/clean and impurity/purity, but this was not the overarching negative idea about breastfeeding found in my corpus. Furthermore, in information about taboos around the world, I found taboos on dairy milk but not regarding breastmilk (e.g. Holden 2000). So while breastfeeding in public seems verging on taboo in this corpus and in some swathes of society and while breastfeeding anywhere – whether in public or at home – appears to upset and disturb people, I cannot quite claim that it is a taboo, although it seems undeniable that breastfeeding generally is viewed as wrong and obscene.

Sexual Attractiveness versus Breastfeeding

Our society, I would suggest, seems to believe that women should be sexual and attractive at all costs and that this should take priority over the biological usage of our bodies. In other words, we may be mammals who have mammary glands in order to feed children, but this is not as important as being attractive to other adult humans, primarily men (see Flood (2017) for a discussion of a book on puberty that says breasts are meant to make women look 'attractive' or Stearns (1999, 309) for a discussion of breasts as women's 'crown jewels'). Some of the previous examples, where women are pressured to quit breastfeeding in order to be attractive to men and to sexually satisfy their men, reveal what is given priority in society.

An image that sums up this issue is from a short story by Kate Atkinson, in her collection *Not the End of the World*. 'Romney had managed to adopt a pose similar to the models in the pornographic magazines – her huge, milk-swollen breasts offered to the camera like gifts' (2002, 170–71). Here, a breastfeeding woman takes on a sexualised pose, as though in pornography. A woman must always look sexual, even when focused on her child. This reference in Atkinson could be argued to be similar to the English-language translation of the Japanese children's book *What Does Baby Want?*, where there is a two-page spread of just breasts, or the Swedish children's book *Alltid tillsammans* (Always Together), where we see the breastfeeding dyad. However, in the images in the children's books, breasts and breastfeeding are the clear focus (see Chapter 2 for more on this), while in Atkinson's work, the text suggests that the woman is sexualising her own breasts, offering them to the viewer. Therefore, I would argue that rather than taking her breasts back from the purely sexual realm and insisting on their biological use, as is the case in the two children's books, Romney in Atkinson's story is attempting to show that though she is being a mammal and feeding her child, she is nonetheless still sexual and attractive. Thus, although this may initially appear to be a positive depiction, I believe in the end, it emphasises the apparent dichotomy between breastfeeding and attractiveness, and the pressure on women to focus on the latter.

There have already been a number of examples discussed earlier that show how breastfeeding and breasts filled with milk can interfere with a woman's relationship with her male partner, especially in regard to sex, and this too gives the message that a woman must make a choice between feeding her child and satisfying her man. In *The Gustav Sonata* by Rose Tremain, which was mentioned previously, it is even suggested that a woman might have to choose between being sexually attractive and available to men and having a child. Lottie says to her lover Erich, 'I don't want my breasts to be sex objects any more. I want to suckle my babies' (2016, 181). Erich does not seem to want to accept this. He thinks:

> Her breasts. Why did she have to mention them? He used to lie on her and suck like a child, loving the way the nipples hardened as she became aroused, even imagining that some beautiful dewy substance came out of these pert nipples, to nourish him and bind him to her – bind her for ever, because he knew he would always need her. (ibid.)

Erich, then, wants to be the one who sucks on her breasts 'like a child', and he wants to be fed by them; not, it would seem, fed milk, but rather a 'dewy substance'. It is interesting that the word 'pert' is employed, as one concern about breastfeeding is that it makes breasts droop, although this is actually something that happens in pregnancy. Lottie never does have children of her own, so her breasts are used to 'nourish' and 'bind' men to her – or to be bound to them – rather than connect to and nurture babies; this harkens back to Pullman's novel, where the unstable Diania tries to bind a baby who is not hers to her through her breasts.

In her review of television programmes, Foss finds that 'many of the breastfeeding representations sexualize breasts, especially in programs geared toward men' (2018, 101). So here, women must be sexually attractive, even when breastfeeding, or else, it might be argued, they are seen as not fulfilling their natural role as sex objects for men. Foss continues, 'Showing breastfeeding in episodes that also sexualize breasts may do little to change perceptions that breastfeeding differs from public nudity or indecent exposure. Although it may be difficult for actors to mimic breastfeeding, doing so would be a significant step toward normalizing breastfeeding, especially since mainstream media as a whole rarely include images of real breastfeeding' (2018, 102–3). And Tatiana Prorokova, who analyses television and films in her work, notes that breastfeeding is often seen as 'perverse', because it requires that breasts be non-sexual. She sums up this concept as follows:

> Although a naked breast is an overt symbol of female sexuality that draws attention of heterosexual men, its usage as a 'living bottle of milk' provokes men's hesitation and eventual repulsion. The paradox of the sexualized breast with its biological and nonsexual function has been artificially created by patriarchy, which vehemently diminished the role of a woman to a biological and sexual object only. It is, however, pivotal, that though imposing both functions on the woman, patriarchy draws an explicit line between the two, as the two can manifest each other only separately and never simultaneously. Moreover, the agents that

participate in the act of using female breasts can never meet: breasts as a sexual object are meant for men, whereas breasts as food containers are only for infants. Breaking these rules leads to social and cultural confusion, and is, evidently, exploited by the genre of comedy to make the viewer laugh (or, by the horror genre, to make the viewer uncomfortable). (2018, 137)

Although I did not find breastfeeding employed in a humorous way in my corpus of texts and also did not find horror in the sense of the genre rather than the general sense of people being horrified by breastfeeding or considering it horrible or horrific, I agree with Prorokova's conclusion: breastfeeding is depicted as problematic in some texts because it gets in the way of men's access to breasts and disgusts or horrifies men, who want to see breasts as solely sexual.[10] Breastfeeding challenges the patriarchy and suggests that there are different ways of viewing women, their bodies and the functions of their bodies, but many of the literary texts emphasise the dichotomy between sexual and maternal, rather than trying to break it down. There is a hard border between the two, without an acceptable liminal space.

The books discussed here use terms such as 'distasteful' or show people 'shuddering' at the sight of breastfeeding women and their breasts, stressing the idea that this is not what breasts are for. Stearns notes that the 'good maternal body is not commonly believed to be simultaneously sexual, despite the obvious facts of human reproduction' (1999, 309), and it seems that in our society the sexual is prioritised over the maternal. Interestingly, in her research with breastfeeding parents, Stearns finds that 'breastfeeding women fear that the exposure of their breasts will be misread as a sexual invitation to male strangers and they fear potential consequences of that misreading' (1999, 316), suggesting that avoiding breastfeeding, especially in public, is one way of not blending the maternal with the sexual.

Neutral Breastfeeding

In a very few cases, breastfeeding is, if not exactly negative, not positive either. It is simply a fact in the book, treated neutrally. For instance, in *The Familiars*

---

10. One article I found discussed breastmilk as an addition to sexual activity for the novelty factor (Bartlett 2010, 179–88), and a cursory internet search reveals plenty of pornographic videos that feature lactating women, so it is clear that some men find breastfeeding and/or breastmilk erotic, but the predominant message in literature and other forms of media seems to be that breastfeeding breasts are not sexual and that breasts should be sexual.

by Stacey Halls, 'At that moment the baby began crying from his bed in front of the fireplace [...] my breasts were full and threatening to spill, so I got up' (2018, 407–8). This shows no pain or disgust in relation to breastfeeding, possibly because it is a book set many centuries ago, when breastfeeding was the cultural norm, but nor does it mention any joy in feeding or connection between the breastfeeding mother and the baby. Given how overwhelmingly adverse most portrayals are, I would be glad to see more neutral ones, if our society is not yet ready for additional positive ones.

Positive Breastfeeding

Although the representations of breastfeeding in her work are mostly negative, as discussed earlier, Elske Rahill does show some positivity towards breastfeeding in *An Unravelling*. Breastfeeding might be frequently portrayed as difficult and wrong, but it is in places also shown both as a way to create a close relationship between mother and child and as evidence for who experiences real motherly love. The matriarch, Molly, says of mothering, 'Of course, it took something out of you, but, oh, it was marvellous too. She wouldn't have chosen anything else. She wouldn't swap anything for that night with her first baby suckling at her breast' (2019, 49). More on good mothering is discussed later.

Interestingly, a couple of the books that feature more positive descriptions of breastfeeding are actually contemporary young adult (YA) novels. I refer to them in this chapter rather than the one on children's literature, since in that one I focus on picturebooks. It could, of course, be chance that YA novels are less negative about breastfeeding. Or perhaps authors for younger readers are deliberately making the choice to show breastfeeding as something that works and is pleasant because they want to fight against prevailing cultural views and to influence the next generation to consider breastfeeding or supporting a partner to breastfeed. It may also be that the writers of these texts are themselves a bit younger and have had better experiences with breastfeeding. Without contact with the authors and further research,[11] it is difficult to say for sure what has made their depictions of breastfeeding less negative than literary texts in English in general.

As an example, in Sally Nicholls's novel *Close Your Pretty Eyes*, Grace is described as 'a big black girl with a baby sucking on her boob. She was the other foster kid' (2013, 4). Unlike Kara with baby Proteus in Kate Atkinson's

---

11. I did in fact write to some authors to ask if I could talk to them about their depictions of breastfeeding, but none replied. I do not know if they found this an odd inquiry or if they were simply too busy.

Emotionally Weird, the fact that Grace is a young mother who breastfeeds baby Maisy does not hold her back. On the contrary, Grace studies hard and by the end of the story gets accepted to the London School of Economics, and manages to get a flat there and childcare for the baby. So Grace can both breastfeed and also be successful in other spheres, and she does not have to abandon her baby to fulfil her dreams. She is also one of the very few examples of a non-White character that I found.

In another work by Sally Nicholls, *All Fall Down*, Isabel's stepmother, Alice, breastfeeds baby Edward, and this is depicted as something that satisfies both people in the feeding dyad and also is lovely to watch. Granted, *All Fall Down* takes place in the fourteenth century, and not breastfeeding a baby would have likely led to her or his death, if a wet nurse could not be found, but even so, the descriptions of breastfeeding are unusually positive for the corpus of texts analysed here. The book begins, 'It's dark still, the pale grey light before dawn, and below the floor of the solar my baby brother Edward is crying [...] [Alice] lowers herself on to a stool and opens her slip, revealing her heavy, mottled breast. Edward's screams are quietened as he suckles. Alice looks up and smiles as she sees me watching' ([2012] 2013, 5). Later in the novel, there is another breastfeeding scene that paints nursing in religious tones:

> I prop myself up on my elbows and lift the blanket-curtain aside, so as to see into the room below. Alice comes through from her chamber. She's holding the candle in one hand and Edward in the crook of her other arm. Her hair is wild and dishevelled under her nightcap and her woollen slip is open at the breast. She settles herself at her stool, and lets Edward find her breast and start suckling. I watch from the solar, expecting Edward to finish and Alice to go back into bed with Father, but she stays there in the dark chamber, murmuring to Edward or perhaps to herself. In the yellow candlelight, there's something beautiful about the two of them – a little like the painting of the Virgin Mary in the church, but more earth, more solid.
>
> From the safety of my hiding place, I watch the two of them. After Edward has finished suckling he falls back quickly to sleep, but Alice stays awake for as long time, sitting at the stool by her loom, her rough head bent over her sleeping son. ([2012] 2013, 96)

Breastfeeding here is special, 'beautiful', both spiritual and earthy. There is a bond between Alice and Edward, and while it is between the two of them and technically does not include Isabel, it is something that she can observe, admire, learn from and be inspired by. The reference to the Virgin Mary is especially interesting, as she is depicted in Christianity as the archetypal good mother. Like Mary, Alice is a good mother in the way she feeds and cares for her baby.

Another YA novel in my corpus is Becky Albertalli's *Simon vs. the Homo Sapiens Agenda*, which is about a teenager named Simon coming out as gay. When he talks to his parents about it and is assured of their continuing love for him, the following scene takes place, with Simon's mother speaking first:

> 'I actually remember holding you for the first time. Your little mouth. You latched right onto my breast—'
>
> '*Mom.*'
>
> 'Oh, it was the most incredible moment […]'
>
> […]
>
> 'Actually, we have something for you.'
>
> 'Is it another awkward anecdote about me breast-feeding?'
>
> 'Oh my God, you were all about the boob,' my dad says. 'I can't believe you turned out to be gay.'
>
> 'Hilarious, Dad.' (2015, 249–50; italics original)

Breastfeeding is 'incredible' but also the source of gentle humour, as Simon's father jokes that his gay son has lost his apparent breast obsession. Discussing breastfeeding is 'awkward' and yet also allows parents and child to talk and connect, and to lighten the mood during what could be a stressful time for them.

Although in this book I do not have the space to discuss the depiction of breasts in society in general, there are a couple of examples that are worth looking at, and of course the portrayal of breastfeeding reflects on the societal view of breasts. In *Patience and Sarah* by Isabel Miller, Patience and Sarah are two women who develop a relationship. Intriguingly, but perhaps not surprisingly given the lesbian love story, the portrayal of breasts is much more positive and tender than it is in many literary works, and there is a definite link between admiration of the breasts and a desire to feed from them.

> Monday when I woke I thought first thing of Sarah. Instantly my bosom filled, as though with milk, and tingled. I lay there thinking how fine it was to be a woman and have a part that could please me the way my bosom did from just a thought, and imagining Sarah, waking now too, thinking of me and glad to be a woman. ([1969] 2005, 54)

Here, Patience is sexually aroused, thinking of Sarah, and she feels as though her breasts are filled with milk. Instead of Patience being aroused by the thought of Sarah's milk-filled breasts, as sometimes happens in literature to men in heterosexual relationships with breastfeeding women, it is the aroused woman herself who links her arousal to the feeling of milk-fullness. This is not the male gaze, and nor is it a queer female gaze exactly; it is more a sense of gratitude for the life-giving force of breasts, a sense of the uniqueness of a woman's body and an awareness of the potentially arousing nature of a woman's body. Later, Patience also describes appreciating Sarah's mother, in part because, 'I like her strong body for making you and her big bosom for feeding you and her hands for petting and dressing you' ([1969] 2005, 119). Breastfeeding has nurtured Patience's beloved, Sarah, and so she is grateful for it.

It is quite telling that it is a lesbian story that is more positive about breasts and breastfeeding, and it is also very intriguing that YA novels seem to normalise it and use breastfeeding itself, or seeing it or discussing it, as a form of connection. Further research would need to be done into YA novels to see if this is true more generally, because although I read very widely in the field, I admittedly did not find huge numbers of books that featured breastfeeding at all.[12]

Breastfeeding and Good Mothering

The idea of the good mother has already been referred to multiple times in this chapter. There is much societal pressure on women to be good in many ways, including in terms of mothering. Carolyn Daniel mentions the link between 'the good mother and food/love/comfort and between the bad mother and lack of food/love/comfort' (2006, 95), but there is no suggestion in any of the books analysed here that because the mother is not feeding breastmilk, she is a bad mother. Indeed, artificial milk has been blithely accepted as a replacement for breastmilk in many English-language books. Nonetheless, anxieties around breastfeeding, or not, certainly are connected to the concept of the good mother.[13] Stearns, in her sociological study of breastfeeding mothers, notes, 'To transgress the precarious boundaries of the good maternal body is to risk being labeled a bad mother and/or sexually inappropriate or deviant' (1999, 322). So a question is whether, in literary texts, a good mother breastfeeds or bottle-feeds her child. Some women suggest they feel pressured

---

12. I must also acknowledge the Beauvais YA novel that was discussed earlier, as it was not positive in its depiction of breastfeeding.
13. As others have noted, formula-feeding is so prevalent in our society that newspapers and other publications report on breastfeeding 'with the comment "Here's another

to breastfeed, but then again, there is no real sense of guilt or sadness when they do not, although they might feel some other consequences, such as a lacking relationship with their child.

A number of the examples already discussed offer implications about whether the mother is good or not (see Weiss (2014), among other texts, on the good mother). Rose Tremain's *The Gustav Sonata* is one instance of this, where the mother never forms a bond with her child, and this lack of relationship starts with the lack of breastfeeding. There is a slight irony in this sort of negative view in literature, because it suggests an impossible choice for women. If breastfeeding is actually always painful, difficult, disgusting, wrong or an impediment to relationships, then one would expect that not breastfeeding would be depicted as the better choice, one that would not cause guilt or potentially break the mother–baby bond. In a bottle-feeding scenario, as depicted in many of these books, more people could potentially engage with the baby, including feeding the baby; the mother can do drugs, attend classes or otherwise carry on with her life as it was pre-baby; the mother can still be sexually available to men; and no one need be revolted by the sight of breasts lactating and a baby sucking on them. However, it does also make sense that not breastfeeding comes with criticism, in that to a large extent, Western society still believes that a woman's highest and most important role is to be a mother.[14] And if she does not put her baby above everyone else, including herself, then something is wrong with her and she is not a good mother. To use a cliché, a woman with a baby in literature is damned if she breastfeeds and also damned if she does not.

A typical example is C. J. Sansom's *Tombland*. Two women are contrasted, one who is not an engaged parent and one who is, but who dies. The former is described this way: 'Edith Boleyn, God rest her soul, was no good mother to the boys. As soon as they were born she handed them over to a wet-nurse and wanted nothing more to do with them' (2018, 74). The latter mother, the good one, is the protagonist Shardlake's old friend Josephine. When Josephine is

---

study to make women feel like failures." Surely it's society that is contributing to why women feel like failures, not the scientific research?' (Young 2016, 160). Formula-feeding has become the norm, but breastfeeding or not has become a hugely emotional and also lucrative subject, with companies making money off of women's desire to do their best for the children.

14. This connects to the cult around Mary, the virgin who became a mother without having been sexual; arguably, Christianity has had a strong influence on societal ideals regarding women's roles (cf. Turner ([1984] 1996, 12), on how 'Mary was untouched by the corporeal features of birthing and motherhood, because her embodiment could not threaten the spirituality of Jesus', and cf. as well the Nicholls novel mentioned earlier, where the breastfeeding mother is compared to the Virgin Mary ([2012] 2013)).

murdered, Shardlake takes the baby, named Mousy, and finds a wet nurse, Liz. Liz is described as a good person whose own child died and who 'just keep[s] producing milk' (2018, 762). Her care and feeding of Mousy help her survive, and a doctor friend of Shardlake's pronounces: 'This is a fine, healthy child, and I give the credit to your wet-nurse. Perhaps she should be promoted to full nurse' (2018, 788). There is, then, a very clear dichotomy between Edith and Josephine/Liz. Edith is 'no good mother' and does not breastfeed or engage with her children, while Mousy had a good, breastfeeding mother and then has a good wet nurse, and this keeps her healthy.[15]

Good mothering, whatever that actually means, is also related to the idea of a woman not being a 'failure'. Giving formula, like using a wet nurse in works set in times past, is sometimes seen to be a choice or a last option for women who fail at breastfeeding and thus at mothering. This theme comes up in multiple works, including in the graphic novel *Blame it on the Boogie* by Rina Ayuyang (2018), which is about growing up and becoming a mother. And yet, as already noted, being a good wife/partner often takes priority over being a good mother; a woman can quit breastfeeding in order to 'succeed' at satisfying her male partner. Stearns finds that 'women actively create the good maternal body before an audience that is more familiar and comfortable with the sexualized breast than the nurturing breast' (1999, 321), but this does not seem to be the case in literature in English; rather, women must forgo a 'good maternal body' and focus on the 'sexualized breast' and not the 'nurturing' one in order to be 'good' women.

Not breastfeeding – whether because of low supply or other reasons – can signal failure, as in Elske Rahill's collection of stories, *White Ink*, the title of which refers to mother's milk. In one story, 'Valerie knows she is not what people call a "natural mother." She is not "made for it", the way some women are, with slings and breast pumps and all that. But she does her best' (2017, 13). In the story, Valerie, the supposedly unnatural mother, does not appear very well liked by her family. It is interesting that giving breastmilk – presumably through expressed milk gotten by a mechanical breast pump – makes someone a good, 'natural' mother, but it is not said that breastfeeding at the breast is more natural.

Sadly, there is little acknowledgement in any of these books that if a woman does not breastfeed, this may not reflect on her personally but rather on society

---

15. As a side note, Sansom's book is the only one in the entire adult corpus to comment on the smell of a breastfed baby's excrement:

> Liz was changing the absorbent rag for her [Mousy's] bottom. I was surprised at the lack of smell. Liz smiled. 'Breast milk doesn't stink, sir.'
>
> I smiled. 'I did not know that; but I know little of children.' (2018, 768)

as a whole. She has not failed; the system has failed her. The literary texts explored here reflect and reveal failures of education, health care, support, policies and more in our society, and also emphasise widespread institutional and societal racism, classism, homophobia/biphobia/transphobia, ableism and other forms of prejudice. Women who do not meet their breastfeeding goals may blame themselves and feel like failures and may feel guilty and ashamed about this (Brown 2019, 37–39), but they are not, of course, individually to blame at all. It is the formula companies, the ill-educated doctors or midwives or other authorities, the publishing companies and other aspects of society that ought to feel ashamed.

Palmer writes:

> Many women have denied themselves the experience of reproduction because they know it handicaps their economic and career advancement. Others have children but do not breastfeed for the same reason, or because it went wrong in the hopelessly unsupportive medical and social system. When we see a suckling pair it does not summon up associations of tenderness and pleasure, but of rejection, failure and pain both in our relationships with our own mothers and with our babies if we have them. ([1988] 2009, 148)

Being a good mother, whatever exactly that means, is an unfeasible goal when faced with, and combined with, 'career advancement', an 'unsupportive medical and social system', various social pressures and mixed messages about womanhood, relationships with partners and complex feelings about how we ourselves were parented, among other issues. Literature rarely shows women getting support with any of these things or managing to overcome them and to breastfeed as part of their mothering role.

Clearly, too, the range of ideas around being good shows how this is an impossible standard to meet for women. Also referencing the 'natural', in Kate Atkinson's *Life after Life*, Sylvie 'took Ursula back into bed with her and the baby rooted around for her nipple. Sylvie believed in wet-nursing her own children. The idea of glass bottles and rubber teats seemed unnatural somehow but that didn't mean she didn't feel like a cow being milked. The baby was slow and floundering, confounded by the new' (2013, 132). Here, Sylvie suggests that using a bottle is 'unnatural', but she still feels like a cow, as though there should be a separation and a difference between humans and other types of mammals. She also distances herself from the act, calling it 'wet-nursing' instead of simply 'nursing' or 'breastfeeding' or 'feeding'.

Few representations show any benefits to breastfeeding other than this supposed proof that the person breastfeeding their baby is 'good'. Foss finds that there was little discussion within televised depictions about larger meanings or purposes behind breastfeeding. She writes:

> Most representations offer little information as to why mothers should breastfeed. From these depictions, the correlation between intelligence and breastfeeding is conveyed through several exceptional characters. Viewers learn that top forensic anthropologist Dr. Temperance Brennan in Bones as well as the genius characters in The Big Bang Theory were all supposedly breastfed. Additional benefits conveyed in television include weight loss for the breastfeeding mother (ER and Desperate Housewives) and increased breast size (The Secret Life of the American Teenager). (2018, 96)

In other words, being breastfed is said in some TV shows to increase someone's IQ (in actuality, it is that formula-feeding seems to decrease IQ (e.g. Isaacs et al. 2010)) and to supposedly increase the size of the woman's breasts, which apparently is a positive thing because bigger bReasts are more attractive to men (Flood 2017),[16] and as we have already seen earlier, no one wants breastfeeding to get in the way of sexually satisfying their man. There is, then, little exploration of breastfeeding as the biological norm or the fact that it promotes health and bonding for both the breastfeeding parent and the baby/child (Moberg 2019, 84–106). Although I found no mention of the 'benefits' of breastfeeding, such as the few that Foss found, perhaps more importantly, I found no reference in my corpus to the risks of formula-feeding.

Carolyn Daniel argues that food choices in literature add to 'implicit judgments about a woman. [...] There is a surprisingly narrow range of what constitutes good feeding and thus good mothering' (2006, 108). Many literary works show anxiety about mothering and being a good mother, which is understandable given the vast range of ideas and obligations our society seems to have for women; one dichotomy seems to be that women should both take care of children but also act as if they do not have children, and another can be said to be to both nourish children while also being sexually available to men.

---

16. Major children's publisher Usborne published a book on puberty aimed at boys that claimed that the reason why girls/women have breasts is 'to make milk for babies' and 'to make the girl look grown-up and attractive'; this rightfully, in my opinion, attracted criticism from parents, teachers and others, who found it overly sexualising of girls'/women's bodies (e.g. Flood 2017). It is not all societies that find breasts sexual, and that is not the reason why mammals have breasts.

In short, instead of focusing on breastfeeding as an act in and of itself, the focus seems to have shifted to the person with the breasts doing the feeding; breastfeeding, or not, has become a way of judging the 'goodness' of a mother, but many of the examples here continue to emphasise this idea rather than pushing against it. As Mary Jacobus acknowledges, 'To place maternal nurture – that is, breast-feeding – unequivocally in the personal domain is to forget that, for the eighteenth century at least, wet-nursing was both a social institution and a state-regulated industry' (1995, 207). This is to say that although we link breastfeeding to being a good mother now, this was not always the case in all historical periods or all places. As mentioned before, Mary, the mother of Jesus, is viewed as the perfect specimen of motherhood – a virgin, a parent who does not defile her son's spirituality with her physical body, a breastfeeding mother – and this has surely impacted Western views of motherhood and goodness, but it has not always been the sole perspective on the topic, and as some of the non-English-language examples discussed later show, the concept of the good mother can be fought against. Indeed, rigid gender roles must be fought against.

Lack of Diversity in Breastfeeding

One thing that is very clear from the examples analysed in this chapter is that diversity is sadly lacking. By diversity, I mean in terms of both the people who are breastfeeding a child and the babies or children who are breastfed themselves, but also in regard to the types of breastfeeding experiences depicted. Breastfeeding is generally something that White, middle-class, heterosexual, able-bodied, average-sized, married women do in these texts, which suggests that it is perhaps only for the privileged and not an activity or a choice that other people can or do make. And it is also usually shown as something painful or disruptive that takes place for a short period in a full-term baby's life, which implies that one does not breastfeed premature babies, multiples, older babies or children and also that breastfeeding cannot be easy, pleasurable or a source of a bond for both the feeding dyad and others. The lack of diversity in terms of family types and sexuality also meant there were no mentions of co-feeding, where two parents share the feeding. Despite the apparent preference for artificial milk, I did not see combination-feeding depicted, nor were there many references to women expressing milk or giving milk through another device, such as a cup or syringe or an at-the-breast supplementer. In sum, there is a very narrow range of breastfeeding experiences in literary fiction in English.

For example, in *Unbecoming* by Jenny Downham, the family is White, English and red-haired (the red hair, in fact, is of significance in the story and is often emphasised). The breastfeeding mothers in Rahill, O'Farrell and Atkinson are also heterosexual, White, British or Irish, and able-bodied. While colour, sexuality, class, size and able-bodiedness are not always mentioned in these stories or novels, the fact that it is not referred to could lead many readers to simply assume that these characters are part of the dominant cultural norms.[17] Although some books mentioned in Chapter 2 imply that breastfeeding is for 'primitive' people – often those who are non-White or are non-European – interestingly, one might also think that given negative stereotypes about non-norm, non-WEIRD groups of people,[18] breastfeeding would be shown as the more civilised choice.

Similarly, in her exploration of breastfeeding in contemporary television programmes, Kathryn Pollister finds that it is only 'white, attractive, thin, and middle-class' women who breastfeed (2012, 232). Foss likewise notes:

> The limited diversity in breastfeeding women and experience is highly problematic, as it suggests that only one type of women breastfeeds, ignoring women of colour, adolescent mothers, and other women. More mothers of colour need to be shown; the absence of other representations could discourage other women from nursing by failing to present them as normal women who nurse. Many opportunities to promote breastfeeding for different women and with different experiences are missed. (2018, 95)

As mentioned earlier, I found only two mentions of non-White characters breastfeeding, one in a novel for adults and one in a YA novel. As for other aspects of diversity, their absence was depressing but unsurprising.

Pollister refers to other research findings that show that breastfeeding on TV is only shown to take place in 'middle-class or celebrity families', whereas bottle-feeding is for 'ordinary' people (2012, 225). Perhaps the undertone here as well as the main message is that even if breastfeeding is difficult or disgusting, it is still only privileged women from majority or 'norm' groups who choose to suffer this pain on behalf of their children (which is rather contradictory in and of itself, given that some texts suggest that it is savage or lower-class to breastfeed). It is, to return to the Karen Russell short story that opened this chapter, the 'diabolical' choice (Davidson, 2018, n.p.), but perhaps there is the implication that it is a choice that 'better' women make, the good mothers.

---

17. This is not how it should be, and I would not suggest that someone's ethnicity, religion, sexuality and so on always has to be mentioned or has to be the focus of the story, but if it is not referred to, then it seems likely that many readers will assume the characters are in the dominant cultural groups.
18. Western, educated, industrialized, rich and democratic.

The children being breastfed in all these books are infants and very young babies; I could not find an example of breastfeeding multiples or tandem-feeding; Foss, too, notes this lack when it comes to television (2018, 103).[19] Nor could I find an older baby, toddler or young child breastfeeding, though research suggests that the natural weaning age is between 2 and 8 years of age (see Hinde (2015, n.p.), where she also points out that weaning is a process and not something that happens 'at' a specific age). Again, looking at television, Foss writes, 'extended breastfeeding involves much older children and is presented as strange, inappropriate, and distracting [...] as deviant – an alarming finding considering that the health benefits for mother and child dramatically increase with duration' (2018, 104–5). As Ann Marie A. Short discusses in her analysis of Emma Donoghue's *Room*,[20] Donoghue's novel is one of a very few that show 'extended' or natural-term breastfeeding, that is, breastfeeding until the child decides to stop (see Dettwyler 1999). Short writes, referring to the child character Jack, who is five years old:

> Jack mentions breastfeeding, which he refers to as 'having some,' thirty-two times throughout the novel, and almost always describes it matter-of-factly. [...] Suckling throughout the day (and night) is presented as just another facet of Jack's daily routine in *Room*, alongside brushing his teeth, exercise, reading, and bath; in this context, his breastfeeding seems unremarkable. Yet the fact that I distinguish Ma's choice to nurse Jack as 'extended' in the title of this chapter reflects current and prevailing cultural attitudes about breastfeeding: despite the capacity of most biologically sexed female bodies to lactate for years after the birth of a child, nursing past infancy is considered atypical in most Western societies. Indeed, in most industrialized cultures, nursing a child longer than twelve months is considered 'extended' breastfeeding, even though

---

19. I also found only one example of a premature baby, and this was in a short story. In fact, although the mother in the story initially attempts to pump, the baby is in intensive care and is solely fed formula by her father. At home, he continues to feed her formula and to generally manage all her care; there is an implication that the mother had a troubled childhood and is now unstable and not able or willing to take care of her baby, including through providing breastmilk (Klam 2020). This links back to the discussion of the 'good' mother; she is not an involved mother and does not get too involved in childcare. Although breastmilk would be the better choice for a premature baby, this is not discussed at all in the story ('The milk of a woman who delivers a preterm infant is different from that of a woman who delivers at term, probably to meet the special needs of the low-birth-weight neonate' (Wambach and Riordan 2016, 137)).
20. I have not included this book in my own corpus in large part because Short's article so thoroughly covers it.

the World Health Organization (WHO) recommends 'up to two years of age or beyond'. (2018, 150–1)

Donoghue's story is about a woman captured in the titular room with her son, and while breastfeeding is natural and, as Short puts it, 'matter-of-fact' in this context, it is seen as something odd outside the room and in society at large. Short continues:

> However, as soon as she and Jack escape, literally within hours of being free, Ma encounters shock and disgust over the fact that she still breastfeeds Jack. Initially, she defends that choice, snapping at the police officer who stares at her she breastfeeds, 'I'm nursing my son, is that OK with you, lady?' (180), and informing her incredulous mother, 'You don't know the first thing about it' (241). Yet by the end of the novel, a few months after their escape, Ma ends up weaning Jack in a manner that feels not just profoundly meaningful for her relationship with Jack, but also necessary for her reintegration into society. (2018, 152)

This is to say, in this novel, natural-term breastfeeding is so 'shock[ing] and disgust[ing]' that a breastfeeding dyad cannot carry it out beyond a room where they have been imprisoned. In Short's article, she explores reviews of Donoghue's book, specifically ones that mention the breastfeeding relationship, and finds that in general, the comments about breastfeeding are either negative or neutral leaning towards negative. Some readers complain about the supposed 'sexual undertone' (2018, 154) to the breastfeeding or feel it is inappropriate and offensive to discuss 'bodily functions', a category in which they include breastfeeding (ibid.).[21] Short adds, 'Readers also mention and take issue with the fact that when Jack actively requests to nurse, or "have some," he is articulating a desire for both breastmilk and the comfort he receives from nursing' (2018, 155); in other words, they are disturbed that a mother is offering her child comfort through her breast.

In order to fit into society and to return from 'exile', 'Ma denies Jack's requests to breastfeed, particularly when there are other people around, and he reacts with sadness, frustration, and confusion' (2018, 158). Jack must be abruptly weaned from his source of nutrition and comfort so that he and his mother can become part of the larger society, and so they do not upset or disgust other people, although clearly even getting to this outcome bothers some

---

21. See the earlier comment about bodily functions and orifices and taboo (cf. Turner [1984] 1996, 7).

readers, who do not understand the apparent 'obsession' with breastfeeding in the novel (2018, 153).

This particular novel, with its unique depiction of natural-term breastfeeding, albeit with sudden, mother-led weaning, offers readers the message that perhaps breastfeeding an older child in an extreme situation is acceptable although strange, but that it is certainly not something to be done in civilised society; even such a message clearly annoyed many readers and reviewers, as Short shows in her article. Short refers to societal dichotomies and contradictions – 'home and work, public and private, childcare and leisure' (2018, 157) – and I would suggest that breastfeeding, both in Donoghue's book and in others discussed in this chapter, indubitably is shown as belonging to some of those spheres and not others. It should be done in private in the home, as part of necessary, but unpleasant, childcare. But it is not something to do in public, and it should not be pleasurable or comforting or leisurely, and of course, it should mainly be for babies, not children, especially those who can talk and can request it.

Again, comparing this to Foss's research into breastfeeding on television, her conclusion is as follows:

> Representations consistently convey that for a certain group of women in a private place and for a newborn, breastfeeding is natural, beautiful, and easy. However, outside this narrow definition of 'normal', breastfeeding is presented as absurd, unnecessary, socially unacceptable, or deviant. [...] Television has continued to perpetuate many of these stereotypes of the breastfeeding experience – as a private activity, primarily for infants. One positive change has been the expansion of who breastfeeds. In the last few years, more women of colour have been shown breastfeeding in fictional television. (2018, 106–7)

The main difference between her findings and mine in this regard is that I have not seen more women of colour breastfeeding in contemporary literature, but this may be partially a failing on the part of my corpus, or it could also reflect the low levels of non-White characters seen in literature in general. Perhaps there will be a positive change in this regard in the coming years, and breastfeeding depictions in literature will become more inclusive and diverse.

The Internalised Gaze

While the next chapter analyses differences between English and Swedish literature and attempts to understand why English-language literature depicts breastfeeding so negatively, I want to briefly discuss here the concept of patriarchy and the internalised gaze. As referenced a number of times already,

Laura Mulvey's important work on the male gaze ([1975] 2009) raised the concept of how women are depicted in the media based on what heterosexual men see and want to see, and how this in turn shapes the way that women see themselves. I would suggest that we could, perhaps, call this an internalised gaze; women are so used to misogynist and/or limited ideas about what a woman can be, do or look like that they struggle to view themselves in any other way. This, then, would influence how women write books about women's breasts and about breastfeeding (and, of course, the male gaze would shape how men write about such things, although, as my corpus shows, men are much less likely to depict breastfeeding).

Turner claims:

> Women still experience sexism in everyday life, but this is a defunct patriarchalism, an interpersonal strategy on the part of men who find their traditional sources of power increasingly open to doubt. Their sexist patriarchalism is a defensive response of a crisis of identities in a society where machismo values are brought into question by permissive state legislation on homosexuality, children's rights and women's liberation. ([1984] 1996, 156)

I disagree strongly that this is 'defunct', because it still affects women on a daily basis. On the contrary, I am suggesting that women have internalised this sexism and the concomitant male gaze. Women are oppressed by patriarchal society, but due to so many years of this, some women have to a certain extent bought into the prejudice and misogyny espoused by society and have started to constrict and oppress themselves and each other too.

Prorokova writes that the examples she explores from television and film 'shrewdly examine a potentially dangerous side of breastfeeding, which results from the social pressure and cultural anxieties surrounding breastfeeding and women's breasts' (2018, 147). Many of the examples I have discussed earlier not only reveal this 'potentially dangerous side' but also in fact reinforce it, rather than try to challenge it. This is not the same as in my Swedish-language corpus.

The Swedish Corpus

As noted, I could not get to Sweden and had to make do with what I could access online, what was already on my own bookshelves or what I could order from Swedish bookstores. This means that my Swedish corpus is not as large or comprehensive as my English-language one. Still, I discovered some interesting points.

First, a number of the works that were recommended to me by others were not, in fact, that recent. They were often early or mid-twentieth century rather than from the 1990s and later; this was in contrast to my English-language recommendations. Perhaps the people I got recommendations from were less likely to read modern literature, or maybe modern literature does not feature breastfeeding as often, although my two major case studies, as discussed later, suggest otherwise. It could also be that breastfeeding was so normalised in Swedish literature that it has featured throughout several generations' worth of books, whereas in English-speaking cultures, artificial milk has been so pervasive that books from the early twentieth century would not be likely to show breastfeeding. As I wanted a comparative sample, I primarily disregarded the older texts, except to read them for my own interest, and instead focused on contemporary literature.

Also, the books recommended to me were frequently by and about working-class people, a finding that must be analysed in more depth elsewhere but that perhaps suggests that formula-feeding was, for a time, a mark of wealth and class; again, I have no strong proof of this but raise it merely as a point of interest and in hope that someone else researches this subject in the future. This is in contrast to the English books, which nearly always were strongly middle class. Breastfeeding in these working-class Swedish works, such as by Moa Martinson, is simply a natural part of life. In these texts, there is often a line or two about a character breastfeeding, but it is never, at least in this corpus, the focus of the story. For instance, Moa Martinson's *Kvinnor och Äppleträd* (Women and Apple Trees),[22] from 1933, is about two women, sisters, who go against societal expectations by bathing every week. One of them, Sofi, who is often called Mor Sofi (or Mother Sofi), has had 15 children. Sofi's oldest daughter joins Sofi and her sister Fredrika one week and looks at her mother's 'magra kroppen' (thin body) ([1933] 2019, 14) and sees her breasts. The paragraph includes the description 'brösten hängde som två små påsar efter att ha blivit diade av femton girgia små munnar' (her breasts hung there like two small bags after having nursed 15 greedy little mouths) (ibid.). The scene also goes on to describe Sofi's body in more detail, with all its stretchmarks. Sofi's daughter, who has a young firm body, wonders what her father thinks and is told he does not see Sofi's body, perhaps suggesting that he would not find it sexually appealing. The daughter has much to ponder here, but she seems to accept the look of her mother's body while also turning away

---

22. All translations from Swedish are my own, unless otherwise noted.

from it, and there is a tension between a youthful, fresh body and an experienced, aged body. But breastfeeding is accepted and normalised, and Sofi has no shame or disappointment in regard to her appearance. It is the weekly bathing that people wonder at, not the number of her children, the fact that she breastfed them all, or the change to her skin and looks caused by bearing so many young.

On the other hand, the more contemporary works often are explicitly about motherhood, which includes breastfeeding, sometimes to a great degree. The depictions of breastfeeding are not idyllic, in that they do not imply that breastfeeding always is easy and goes smoothly, but rather they are realistic, with both positive and negative aspects. Sometimes they portray confusion about breastfeeding, such as showing conflict between medical advice (for instance, the old-fashioned idea that it is important to schedule and space out breastfeeds) and a mother's own intuition (to breastfeed on demand, when the baby wants and needs it). These works, which in English-speaking countries might be considered 'women's fiction', in that they are by and about women and focus on women's lives, are widely read in Sweden. Indeed, the two authors whose oeuvres I will discuss more later have been translated to other languages and have won major literary prizes in Sweden. This suggests that to a certain extent, women's stories are seen as human stories in Sweden, in a way they are not necessarily in English-speaking countries.

The two contemporary authors whose works contain the most breastfeeding depictions that I have found so far are Kristina Sandberg and Karolina Ramqvist. They write in realistic, open and nuanced ways about motherhood, which includes breastfeeding, and the tropes mentioned earlier in relation to English-speaking works – such as breastfeeding interfering with a mother's relationship with her male partner, or breasts not being both sexual and nurturing, or breastfeeding being challenging and nearly impossible, or formula-feeding being more satisfying for the baby – are generally absent. There may be the sense that breastfeeding is something that good and 'dutiful' mothers do, although often it is woven into the protagonist's feelings about what being a mother is, and some of the story may be about her unpacking, analysing and coming to terms with her role as a parent. Breastfeeding is not depicted as disgusting, solely painful or wrong, and breasts are not only for titillating men; breastfeeding is one facet of how women parent. These portrayals reflect a general sense that breastfeeding is the biological and cultural norm in Sweden, and the depictions are, in some ways, unremarkable in the Swedish context, though clearly they are in stark contrast to the English-language books discussed earlier.

Fighting against 'the Good Mother'

I will first look at what is known as the Maj trilogy by Kristina Sandberg.[23] Sandberg wrote these novels about a character named Maj, a young working-class woman in the 1930s who becomes pregnant out of wedlock and has to marry the older, wealthier man she barely knows who is father to her baby. The trilogy explores the shift in her class journey while also tracing her development as a mother and, later, as a grandmother, and this is all depicted against Swedish culture and history across the twentieth century. Although it features a working-class character in the early twentieth century, somewhat like the Martinson example mentioned earlier, the trilogy is significantly different, especially in regard to its exploration of societal and internalised voices, which shape and oppress women. Sandberg is also careful to depict the sense of shame that women often feel but do not express; Maj is a character who is constantly worried about getting things wrong, about how she appears or smells, about whether she is acceptable, about whether her feelings and experiences are valid, and so forth. Sandberg validates Maj, and women's lives more generally, through the trilogy. In 2014, Sandberg won the August Prize, which is the most important literary award for Swedish-language literature (she has also received many other awards, including the Moa Martinson Prize and the Selma Lagerlöf Prize).

The first book in the trilogy, *Att föda ett barn* (literally, To Birth a Child, though I call it Labour, which reflects both the actual physical labour in birthing a child and the labour of hard-working housewife Maj) (Sandberg 2010), depicts Maj as she gets impregnated by Tomas, a man she scarcely knows. She marries him, moves up several notches on the class ladder and gives birth to their first child, Anita. Once Anita is born, breastfeeding is frequently referred to and sometimes thought about to some depth (I may have missed some, but examples include pages 314–15, 318, 32–24, 326-27, 330–33, 334–35, 337, 338, 340-43, 347, 348, 350-54, 362–67, 371, 386–87, 391–92, 398–400, 407, 430–31, 435–36, 442, 453, 454 and 472). In the second book, *Sörja för de sina* (literally, Grieving for Their Own, though I think Sorrow works as a short title here) (2012), Maj gives birth to her second child, Lasse, and again breastfeeding is shown as part of their life together (e.g. 49, 83–84, 87, 137, 139, 142, 143, 145, 153, 159 and 177). The children are both older

---

23. I must confess to some bias regarding Kristina Sandberg. I have translated work to English by both her and her husband, the writer Mats Kempe, and I have known them since around 2007. I have tried to be objective when rereading and analysing her works, but this of course is not fully possible, as I have a personal investment in her writing and affection for her as a person.

by the third book in the trilogy, *Liv till varje pris* (Life at Any Cost) (2014), so breastfeeding does not appear in this work, although the final novel does continue the exploration of women's conditions and women's lives.

Maj could be described as an anxious person, who worries about everything from body odour to cooking the right meal for her in-laws, and obviously this also includes her mothering abilities. Formula milk is available and is mentioned as an option, but it is not something Maj chooses, perhaps because it seems clear that breastfeeding is the norm in her cultural and historical context. Although Maj accidentally got pregnant the first time and had not been yearning to be pregnant or to marry Tomas, she still seems to feel that breastfeeding is what she wants to do and what she ought to do. This is likely connected to assumptions about being a good mother and housewife, as in English-language works, and yet the approach to such pressures and desires is different.

When Maj gives birth to Anita and the nurse offers her instructions and advice, Maj thinks '*hon ser att jag inte är någon bra mor* [...] *men lär mig då, säg hur jag ska göra!*' (she can see that I'm not a good mother [...] so teach me then, tell me what to do!) (Sandberg 2010, 315; italics original).[24] This theme is carried through the books, as Maj yearns to be a good mother and sometimes struggles to connect to her children in the way she feels a good mother naturally should and could. She worries others can see that she is not secure in her role (e.g. 2010, 318). She constantly hears the voices of other people, telling her how to behave and how to parent (such as on pages 350 and 371, among other places), and Sandberg uses italics throughout the trilogies as a way of contrasting Maj's ideas with other people's. The voices can be contradictory – is breastfeeding for a long time advantageous and does it create '*ovanligt nöjda, sociala och nyfikna barn*' (unusually happy, social and curious children), or is it '*abnormt*', '*hämmande, osjälvständiga krävande barn*' (abnormal, making children 'repressed, dependent, demanding')? (2010, 350; italics original). Maj finds it hard to know what to believe, and she is not yet confident enough to trust her own intuition.

This idea of the good mother, of course, also occurs in English-language literature, as discussed earlier, and it comes up in society in general (e.g. Burbidge 2015, n.p.). So I would suggest that based on the Swedish- and English-language examples, we could surmise that breastfeeding has been seen as a duty in the West for some time, which perhaps therefore makes it

---

24. While it might seem negative that Maj is asking a nurse to 'teach' her how to mother, and while it is true that Maj is very anxious, this trilogy does at least suggest that nurses/midwives and others can provide some information and support, which is not seen at all in the English-language corpus.

understandable that from a feminist perspective, some women chafe against the sense of duty and view breastfeeding as shackles they want to break free from. They may want an easy solution to the concept of being tied to their children, as is evidenced in some of the English-language texts. But in the trilogy, Maj does not want to turn to formula; rather, she wants to understand what a good mother is, and to become one. This certainly places a lot of pressure on her as a person, and the reader is privy to her inner thoughts and concerns, which she usually cannot express to other people, but Sandberg's books never suggest that breastfeeding itself is to blame for the stress or that formula is the answer, nor does the work suggest that there is one right way to mother. Instead, Sandberg implies that it is society that pressures people, and that it can take time to relax into the role of a parent or to feel confident in it, and that perhaps some people never do, but that this does not necessarily speak badly about them. It is not the individual's issue or fault, but rather society's. The narrator of the trilogy – an authorial voice, potentially the grandchild of Maj – notes at one point, 'Jag vill inte skriva om en mamma som inte kan älska sitt nyfödda barn. Men jag vill skriva om kravet som läggs på alla mödrar, kravet på godhet, kärlek, intuition, omvårdnad, lyhördhet, fasthet, ja allt som ska till hos en mamma för att barnet ska få *en trygg anknyning*' (I don't want to write about a mother who cannot love her newborn child. But I want to write about the demands placed on all mothers, the demands for goodness, love, intuition, care, sensitivity, consistency, yes, everything that we expect of a mother so the child will have *a secure attachment*) (2010, 321; italics original). While Sandberg's books follow Maj's story, they also use it as example of what life was like for women in that time and place; the individual character, the setting, and the historical and cultural background all matter. The trilogy explores different ways to parent and the oppression women can suffer in different time periods.

While Maj herself continues to struggle with her confidence and does not always feel comfortable following her own intuition, she does learn to question what others say. In the second book, Maj is pregnant with her second child and is continuing to breastfeed Anita. Her doctor, however, insists that she stop breastfeeding, claiming that children '*måste också lära sig tampas med motgånger*' (need to learn to handle adversity) (Sandberg 2012, 87; italics original). In her own head, if not aloud, Maj thinks about how the doctor has surely not had to deal with an upset or sad child 'bara jag får amma blir världen hel igen' (who feels that if they just get to breastfeed, the world will be right again) (ibid.) Whatever Maj's own personal experiences, over the course of the trilogy, what the reader gets to consider is how many restrictions and expectations are placed on women and how many suggestions or instructions women are offered, especially when it comes to the idea of being a good mother. Women are not always given the space to think, feel and decide for themselves.

Sandberg shows that it is not breastfeeding itself that is a problem – which is a different message from some of the English-language texts explored earlier – but rather society as a whole that needs to be challenged. Women, like Maj of the trilogy, hear all these conflicting ideas and voices, and need to learn to dismiss them and rely on their own intuition and, more than that, society needs to get rid of the myth of the good or ideal mother. As Weiss notes in an analysis of this cultural myth:

> This depiction of motherhood isn't merely annoying. It offers cultural cover for attitudes that do real damage to women, men, and families, reinforcing baseless perceptions of women as less reliable in the workplace, low expectations for fathers at home. (If these are skills specific to moms, dads are necessarily secondary parents; despite some progress, fathers, on average, still spend less time on housework and child care, and more time at leisure, than mothers.) (2014, n.p.)

While Maj spends much more time on housework and childcare than her husband, in part because of the time and place her story is set in as well as her own expectations of herself, Sandberg insists on the importance of this work. Maj's labour is portrayed much more than her husband's is and seems much more vital in terms of their life together as a couple and as a family.

In short, in this Swedish trilogy, the myth of the good mother is portrayed in terms of how it affects one specific woman and family, and it is challenged at a larger, societal level, perhaps replacing it with Winnicott's concept of the 'good-enough mother' (1973). Maj is not perfect, of course, because no human is, but through her very being, she challenges prevailing notions and encourages readers to do so as well. She demands that readers pay attention to women and to women's lives.

Normalising Breastfeeding

In another contemporary Swedish author's oeuvre, breastfeeding is also normalised, although Karolina Ramqvist's work focuses more on the practicalities and realities of breastfeeding, instead of using it as one part of a greater analysis of cultural conceptions of motherhood. In addition, the author, like Sandberg, insists on motherhood as being an important and necessary topic to write about, and this includes breastfeeding. Ramqvist, too, is a prize-winning author (of the Stina Aronson Prize, the P.O. Enquist Prize and more), although of course it may go without saying that winning literary prizes does not necessarily attest to the quality of the work.[25]

In *Björnkvinnan* (The Bear Woman), as in Sandberg's work, the authorial voice interrupts and adds to the story. There is a comment: 'Jag hade betraktat moderskapet som en kliché om kvinnlighet som jag ville avlägsna mig från, men på samma gång var det en erfarenhet som inte gick att förbigå och som inte liknade något annat' (I'd considered motherhood to be a cliché about womanhood that I wanted to distance myself from, but at the same time, it was an experience that couldn't be ignored and that wasn't like anything else) (Ramqvist 2019, 215). So the author, while writing another story, also writes about writing, about breastfeeding and mothering while being engaged in her creative work. This links the creative with the re-creative, the productive with the re-productive, clearly showing how urgent it is to create – to create both literature and children – and to explore this creation. It also reveals how she had thought writing about motherhood was a cliché, but she realised there was much of importance and value to say about it.

Within the narrative itself – and not just the meta-narrative – breastfeeding appears, and it is described in detail, as here: 'Han börjar suga och hon tittar bara ner på honom då, hans böjda arm och handens fingrar som rör sig, spretar i takt med tungans tryckande rörelser mot hennes bröstvårta. Det lugnar henne att lyssna på ljuden han åstadkommer, att höra att han äter' (He begins to suck and she just looks down at him then, at his bent arm and his moving fingers, at how they move with the rhythm of his tongue's pressing movements against her nipple. It calms her to listen to the noise he makes, to hear him eating) (2019, 302). Although in the story she is armed, at this specific moment, the world is only about her and her nursling, and the peace she feels as she feeds him. Breastfeeding is normalised and is portrayed positively, reflecting the bond between the mother and her child.

The idea of breastfeeding as comforting and peaceful also appears in Ramqvist's earlier novel *Den vita staden* (The White City)[26] (2015). Karin finds breastfeeding to be soothing for both herself and her baby and also a connection between them (e.g. 2015, 25–27, 116 and 126). She watches her baby feed, and after the baby falls asleep, so does Karin (2015, 27); this is realistic as breastfeeding releases hormones that induce calmness and sleepiness for both the feeding parent and the child.

---

25. In the case of these two authors, my opinion is that they are deserving of their awards; I simply mean that for me to point out that a particular author has won a literary prize does not necessarily say much about their authorship.
26. This book has been translated to English by Saskia Vogel, who brought my attention to it, but I have not read the English translation, so any translations here are my own rather than the official ones.

And in this book, too, breastfeeding is described frankly, as is the mother's postpartum body. Karin's stomach hangs and her breasts sometimes are heavy and veiny (e.g. 2015, 6 or even 30, where she describes them as 'groteska' (grotesque)) or leaking (e.g. 2015, 43, 51, 100 or 172). Ramqvist also refers to issues such as feeling the uterus contract while feeding (2015, 23–24), keeping the milk moving to avoid mastitis (2015, 35), engorgement (2015, 88) and the muscle ache some breastfeeding parents might feel in certain positions (2015, 144); I found few other fictional works that showed such knowledge and honesty about breastfeeding as a whole. And while at times this may be seen as off-putting (such as leaking, grotesque breasts), it is realistic that women may have mixed feelings about their bodies.

Ramqvist shows both the mess of parenting, especially breastfeeding – the milk stains on clothes, for example – and the intimate intensity of it. Her work does not directly challenge the myth of the good mother, but like Sandberg's, it does insist upon motherhood, including breastfeeding, as an appropriate and essential topic for literary fiction. And Ramqvist shows both positive and negative aspects of it, which makes her work realistic and relatable. Such writing thereby normalises breastfeeding as one important aspect of a mother's life.

Swedish Summary

Admittedly, my Swedish corpus of texts is smaller than my English-language one, and the fact that I primarily explored the contemporary ones here and not the older texts I also read makes it even smaller. Nonetheless, it is clear from these examples that the overwhelming negativity towards breastfeeding that I found in English-language literature appears absent from Swedish-language writing. Rather than blaming breastfeeding, rather than depicting it as painful, disgusting, wrong and problematic, as is the case in many of the English texts explored here, the Swedish authors instead show that it is society that is the issue. It is possible to have heavy, leaking breasts and to also enjoy breastfeeding and to have pride in what one's body is capable of. It is possible to have a job and to breastfeed, to produce creative work and to breastfeed, and even to produce creative work about breastfeeding. It is also possible to challenge the voices and messages that society offers about women, motherhood and breastfeeding, by questioning those messages and by writing about women's lives.

Despite the commonalities of the good mother theme seen in both sets of texts, I would argue that Swedish literature does not seem to show the same liberation discourse in regard to preferring formula-feeding over breastfeeding. Swedish literary texts do not seem to depict breastfeeding as threatening, disturbing, intrusive or otherwise as negative, as English-language works do, which perhaps means that even though characters in Swedish literature do feel some pressure to breastfeed, they do not appear to see formula-feeding as a saviour. Breastfeeding is not an activity that interferes with or disturbs women in Swedish texts as much as it seems to in English-language works; reasons for this difference will be discussed in the next chapter.

Finally, I want to acknowledge that there was no real diversity in the Swedish corpus either. The characters were Swedish in ethnicity, and although working-class characters did appear in older texts and in Sandberg's trilogy, there was little diversity of experience or background beyond this. In Sandberg's second book, Maj breastfeeds while pregnant, which is a scenario that was otherwise not written about in my corpus. On the whole, however, breastfeeding depictions throughout both languages were not hugely varied.

Conclusion

As is seen in many of these examples, breastfeeding is treated extremely negatively indeed in literature in English, and yet there is also a strong sense, implied in some cases and overt in others, that women should be judged, criticised and found wanting if they do not breastfeed. Rather than critique these mixed messages and directly challenge and attempt to change the society that has given rise to them, English-language literature simply replicates them, agreeing that breastfeeding is a problem. Coming to a slightly different conclusion, Greta Gaard says, in reference solely to US-based literature, that 'these texts confirm that breastfeeding and nursing milk have been "backgrounded" in U.S. literature and culture, denying our animal dependence on the relational nurturance we first receive from our mammal mothers, and the eco-political contexts that shape possibilities for mothering and nursing children' (2013, 3). The eco-political contexts matter hugely, but few of the books in my corpus explore them or encourage the reader to challenge them.

On the contrary, in Swedish-language literature, breastfeeding is normalised and referred to honestly – not ignoring the pain or challenges that can sometimes accompany nursing a child – and it also asserts the primacy of women's stories and the need to reshape society's views of and pressures upon women. Women's work – the labour of childbirth, feeding and parenting, as well as creative work – is valued in Swedish literature in a way that I have not seen in English-language texts. In the next chapter, I will try to understand why there is such a stark difference between the two sets of literary works and thereby between the two cultures.

Chapter 4

ANALYSIS OF DIFFERENCES

Introduction

The chapters on adult literature and children's literature already began to tease out some of the differences between the cultures analysed in this book, such as the internalised male gaze or the fact that practical issues sometimes seem to be of more interest in English, while emotions are explored more often in Swedish. However, it is worth discussing these differences in more depth. Why are depictions of breastfeeding so different in English-language versus Swedish-language works? It is, I would suggest, quite a clear difference – and almost a shocking one – in that Swedish literature is so much more positive and open towards breastfeeding, while the English-language texts are in general negative about breastfeeding in words and more liable to depict bottle-feeding in images.

In this chapter, I will explore a few possible factors, such as demographics or views on women, although I must admit from the start that I do not come to any clear-cut answers. As with many issues, it is likely that a combination of factors has led to the situation we see in society and literature.

In what follows, I explore culture, politics, feminism, reading habits and more, and I focus on Sweden and the United Kingdom. While Swedish is also spoken in Finland, none of my example texts were Finland-Swedish ones, so I have chosen to just look at Sweden. The English-language situation is more complicated. Most of my English-language texts were from the United Kingdom, and some were from the United States; none were from Canada, Australia, New Zealand, India, South Africa or other English-speaking countries, although I believe some of the works analysed in this book are available in some of those nations.[1] So, in the following sections, I mainly look at the United Kingdom, mentioning the United States only when relevant, and I compare the United Kingdom to Sweden: two European nations that are

---

1. I hope in the future that more people will research breastfeeding in literature from countries other than those discussed in this book.

not far apart geographically, but that do seem very disparate indeed in regard to breastfeeding.

Breastfeeding Statistics

In an earlier chapter, it was noted that in the United Kingdom, the breastfeeding rate at 6 months is around 35%, which is considered the 'world's worst' (Gallagher 2016), while in Sweden, it is around 63% (Anonymous 2018, n.p.).[2] Literature seems to follow culture, in that there are more depictions of breastfeeding in Swedish literature than in English-language literature. To deepen these statistics, I was interested to know how many women reach out for support with breastfeeding in the two cultures. That is to say, if women struggle with breastfeeding, do they look to get help so they can carry on? Or does it seem simpler to quit breastfeeding and turn to artificial milk?

Both Sweden and the United Kingdom have breastfeeding support services run by trained lay volunteers. In the United Kingdom, this is the National Breastfeeding Helpline, which is staffed by breastfeeding counsellors trained by the Association of Breastfeeding Mothers or by the Breastfeeding Network.[3] In Sweden, Amningshjälpen (Breastfeeding Help) is staffed by 'hjälpmammor' (help mums), their term for peer supporters. In both cases, the counsellors/peer supporters have to pass exams and are expected to have read widely about breastfeeding, which includes anatomy, physiology, the contents of breastmilk, expressing milk, patterns of feeding, positions, illnesses, drugs in breastmilk, the WHO code and other relevant subjects. They also are expected to learn about counselling and support, which includes the idea of providing information and encouragement but not advice or instruction, and to agree to follow certain ethical guidelines, including not promoting artificial feeding. In most cases, the counsellors/supporters have themselves breastfed children.

Felicity Lambert, the administrator of the National Breastfeeding Helpline, told me that volunteers on the helpline answered 9,257 calls during 2019;

---

2. Rates for the initiation of breastfeeding after birth are higher, but people who face challenges when breastfeeding do not necessarily receive the help they need in order to continue. Also, the US Centers for Disease Control and Prevention state that around 57% of babies in the United States are breastfed at 6 months, although the number decreases to 25% when it comes to exclusive breastfeeding, which means that many of the babies are receiving formula and/or food as well as breastmilk (Anonymous 2020a). Also, the United States is a heavily pumping culture, in part because women have very short maternity leaves, which means that many babies may be receiving breastmilk, but it is from a bottle or other tool, and not always at the breast.
3. I am a trained counsellor through the Association of Breastfeeding Mothers and I volunteer on the helpline.

she noted that in that year, the helpline received the most calls it ever had up until then[4] (personal communication, 2020). The helpline also has a web chat function, and volunteers there communicated with families in 249 chats. Finally, volunteers provided one-to-one support through social media in 2,096 threads. Many volunteers on the helpline also work at in-person breastfeeding groups or cafés or give lectures or provide breastfeeding information or support in other formats, such as articles, but these things are not recorded in the statistics.

At Amningshjälpen, administrator Yamina Hamidi told me that in 2019, volunteers answered 1,872 calls; provided support over the internet, mainly on Facebook, 2,488 times; gave support via text 1,120 times; and answered 862 emails (personal communication, 2020). They also offered a significant number of video chats, lectures, courses, home visits and more. The type of support offered and the kind of statistics kept obviously vary between the two countries, but I think it is possible to compare them to a certain extent.

The UK population is around 66 million, while Sweden's is around 10 million. Based on what Lambert and Hamidi told me, it appears that a larger percentage of families in Sweden than in the United Kingdom requested breastfeeding support. Looking at phone calls and web chats, 9,506 out of approximately 66 million people means that 0.014% people in the United Kingdom requested support. In Sweden, 1,872 calls plus 1,120 texts (which I am equating to the web chats) is 2,992 phone contacts, and out of 10 million people, this equates to 0.03%. This means that twice the number of people in Sweden appear to look for phone-based support versus in the United Kingdom, and perhaps coincidentally, Sweden's breastfeeding rate at 6 months is twice that of the United Kingdom's.

I do not want to push this statistical analysis too far, because there are too many factors that are not included here, such as attendance at an antenatal breastfeeding class or the ability to get to an in-person breastfeeding support group.[5] However, the fact that more people seem to contact Amningshjälpen than the National Breastfeeding Helpline may imply that there is a higher degree of motivation to breastfeed in Sweden and perhaps a greater awareness that getting support can mean the difference between breastfeeding or not.

---

4. As I write this, the coronavirus situation in 2020 has changed this, because many families are not getting in-person support and so are turning to the helpline. But I do not have statistics from 2020 for the United Kingdom or Sweden.
5. This would be a fascinating area for future research: Who reaches out for support and why? How does it impact on their breastfeeding journeys? How does this change depending on circumstances? Brown and Shenker (2020) explore this in connection to the Covid-19 crisis, but there is room for even more analysis.

In Chapter 3, many books in English suggested breastfeeding was painful or showed problems with it, such as low supply, but these depictions did not include the protagonist receiving support from a breastfeeding counsellor or midwife or friend or attending a breastfeeding group. So there was an awareness of problems in English, but no suggestion of possible solutions. Meanwhile, Swedish books seem less likely to show problems, or if they do, the problems are overcome, so the fact that more Swedish parents seek out support through Amningshjälpen suggests that they realise there is indeed help to get.

I also feel it is important to acknowledge that the reliance on volunteer support is in itself problematic. Volunteer breastfeeding peer supporters or counsellors are nearly always women, and as these positions are unpaid, this is yet another example of invisible and undervalued women's work. If breastfeeding were recognised as being as essential to women and children's mental and physical well-being as the research shows it is, and if women's work were included in financial calculations, the situation would be different. For example, doctors, midwives, health visitors, daycare providers, teachers and others who come into contact with parents and children would receive thorough training in regard to what breastfeeding is and how best to support it. Furthermore, those who work on helplines or who provide in-person support would be paid and would not be expected to give their time and energy for free. So while these statistics around support are useful to compare, they are also linked to the overall issue that is a theme in this book, that is, that women's contributions to society are persistently overlooked, ignored and disregarded.

Demographics

I naturally wondered, given the different statistics on breastfeeding, what was behind this difference. One possibility, I thought, might be demographics, such as ethnicity, class or religion. Certain groups of people in a particular country might be more or less likely to breastfeed.

Ethnic Differences

I pondered the idea that the ethnicities in the two cultures were different and that various groups are known to breastfeed more or less, depending on circumstances. I had assumed that the United Kingdom would be more diverse and that perhaps varying cultural perspectives on breastfeeding or attitudes towards it, such as breastfeeding in public, might account for some of the differences. However, I found that nearly 20% of the Swedish population was born outside the country, with 25% of the total population having a foreign background (Anonymous 2020e, n.p), while in the United Kingdom, it is about 14% (Vargas-Silva and Rienzo 2020, n.p.). Forty per cent of these immigrants to the United Kingdom were born in the European Union (ibid.). I could not find out how many of the foreign-born immigrants to Sweden were born in the European Union, but 11% are from other Nordic countries, while the other largest groups seem to be from Poland, the former Yugoslavia, Germany, Syria and Iraq (Anonymous 2020e, n.p.). So it is difficult to make a direct comparison, but I would not suggest that the ethnic make-up has influenced attitudes towards breastfeeding. Still, it is worth highlighting that while some people assume a homogenous population in Scandinavia, the statistics show otherwise.

It is useful to consider, however, the fact that certain groups are less likely to breastfeed and more likely to face barriers and prejudice that prevent them from getting support. Part of the goal behind the United Kingdom's Black Breastfeeding Week, for instance, is precisely to support and encourage Black families. But a lower breastfeeding rate among Black people is doubtful to be the cause of the small amounts of breastfeeding seen in English-language books because, even if 20% of the UK population is non-White (although another set of statistics lists this as closer to 13% (Anonymous 2020g, n.p.)), this is not in evidence in literature. Even contemporary literature is overwhelmingly White; for example, Flood (2020) notes that only 5% of characters in children's books are Black, Asian or minority ethnic. If Black families featured often in books and were described in words or portrayed in pictures as bottle-feeding their babies, I might argue for there to be a cultural influence on the depiction of breastfeeding in books, but unfortunately they are not often included in books. Only one of the adult books in my corpus specifically mentioned a character being Black (Evans 2018), and one young adult novel did likewise (Nicholls 2013). So I do not think that the ethnic make-up of the respective countries has had an impact on breastfeeding's portrayal in literature.

Religious Differences

If not ethnicity, my next thought was that then perhaps religion plays a role. The UK Index Mundi lists the population as 60% Christian (Anonymous 2020g, n.p.), and this was confirmed by the most recent census. How many people actually go to church and consider themselves religious versus culturally Christian is not clear, and it is true that labels do not always reflect people's real beliefs or ideas of themselves. In Sweden, 60% of the citizens are said to be Lutheran, with additional percentages of other forms of Christian, such as Catholic or Baptist (ibid.), but this is not the whole story. 'A Gallup Poll in 2016 found that 18% of Swedes self report as atheist and 55% as non-religious' (Anonymous 2016a, n.p.), and 'just five percent of Swedes are regular church goers' (Anonymous 2015, n.p.). Nominally, then, the percentages of people who identify as Christian are similar, but given how many Swedes also call themselves non-religious or atheist, I would suggest that the numbers are not nearly as close as they appear.

In other comparative research I have carried out on the depiction of death in children's literature (Epstein 2021), the role of religion may be decisive. Not having a strong religious faith and thus not believing that there is a life after this one seems to have made Swedish writers more realistic and practical in regard to accepting and writing about death. They do not rely on euphemism, and they seem to accept mortality and the realities of life. Swedish children's books talk about how sad it is to lose someone you love and explore different ways of mourning. The opposite is true in English; there is more euphemism and more discussion of heaven, with the implication being that there is a life after death and that everyone will be together again one day. My argument in regard to this is that religious beliefs have shaped views about death and thus the writing and illustration of death for children in literature. It is possible that there is something similar going on here. For example, non-religious people may have fewer religious or cultural ideas about shame or fewer fixed ideas about male versus female roles; it is also possible that they are more willing to discuss and consider such things. Women may therefore feel more able to breastfeed in public or to generally use their bodies as they choose. On the other hand, some religious people may feel pressure from their religion to breastfeed; certainly there are Christian symbols and paintings showing Mary breastfeeding Jesus, and the influence of Mary on ideas about the good mother was discussed previously in this book. Interestingly, though, one study found that Catholic countries had a negative correlation with breastfeeding (Bernard et al. 2016, n.p.), and perhaps this links back to shame about the body. Without further research into religious people's attitudes regarding breastfeeding in these two cultures, I cannot say definitively whether this plays a role here, but I suspect it may, not least based on my own and other scholars' research findings.

Political Differences

Another possible demographic difference is in regard to politics. In a report that analysed general elections in the United Kingdom between 1918 and 2019, Lukas Audickas, Richard Cracknell and Philip Loft found that out of 28 general elections, the Conservative Party had won 18 times (64%) and the Labour Party 10 times (36%); there are other parties, but they have never won the general election and are in some ways just slightly different versions of the main two parties. In other words, the Conservative Party has been predominant over the past century, and they are not conservative in name only; they tend to have more traditional, old-fashioned, capitalistic and nationalistic values, and the political and cultural mores that they espouse will certainly both reflect and affect societal opinions. It may be that during their time in power – years that have seen, for example, Section 28, which prohibited the 'promotion' of homosexuality, and the Brexit vote, among many other rulings, referendums and decisions – they have contributed to an attitude that women's breasts are for pleasure and not to feed babies.

For instance, it is the more conservative, right-wing newspapers/tabloids, such as the *Daily Mirror* or the *Sun*, that traditionally featured 'page 3 girls', or a photo of a topless woman on the third page of the newspaper.[6] That is, a daily newspaper ostensibly about the news found it newsworthy to sexualise women on a regular basis. If the breast is viewed as being for sexual objectification and pleasure, then it is arguably less likely to be seen in a maternal and/or nourishing role; depicting the breast in a child's mouth might then somewhat understandably startle, disgust, surprise or bring humour to the public, especially men (cf. Prorokova 2018, 137).

Sweden has a number of parties, but they too can mostly be divided into left-wing or right-wing, and they sometimes form coalitions. I could not find a simple report like the one referenced earlier for the United Kingdom, but I could find a table of statistics for national elections in Sweden between 1910 and 2014 (Anonymous n.d.b). The right-wing Moderaterna (Moderates) and Folkpartiet (Folk Party) won many of the elections early on in the twentieth century. As the website for the Socialdemokraterna (Social Democrats) party notes, 1938 was the first time a left-wing party won a general election in Sweden. They lost their power in 1976 but regained it in 1982. The right-wing coalition ruled between 1991 and 1994, and then again from 2006 until 2014. In the most recent election, 2018, there was a hung parliament, but the Social Democrats remained in power. While this all might sound confusing, it is clear that the left-wing Socialdemokraterna have been in power for much of the twentieth century and for some of the twenty-first (1938–76, 1982–91, 1994–2006, 2014–present). Their policies, which include the influential welfare state approach, were concerned from the 1930s onwards with issues such as health care, dental care, support for single mothers, care for families and similar (Anonymous 2020f, n.p.). This is in clear contrast to some of the more conservative policies in other countries, including the United Kingdom and

---

6. Many women, including members of parliament, campaigned against 'page 3 girls', and were successful in 2015 in getting this feature removed from publications (O'Carroll, Sweney and Greenslade 2015, n.p.).

also the United States[7] in the past years, which is perhaps what has made many people derogatively call Sweden socialist.

In other words, the left-wing government has had a major influence in Sweden, while the right-wing one has done so in the United Kingdom. Indeed, such influence has spread beyond the respective countries. In a recent article on Sweden's 'feminist foreign policy,' it is stated, 'Sweden's focus on sexual and reproductive care in the midst of a crisis [i.e. the coronavirus pandemic] is an example of its feminist foreign policy – an approach, first adopted in 2014, that places women and girls at the center of almost every diplomatic decision the government makes, with the ultimate aim of advancing gender equality around the world' (Gupta 2020, n.p.) Gupta goes on to note other feminist policy decisions that the Swedish government has made and continues to make, such as 'denounc[ing] Saudi Arabia's track record on women's rights in 2015 […] [and] potentially severing a trade relationship with a big buyer of Swedish goods and arms' and being 'the only country in the world that allocated almost 90 percent of its aid money for organizations focused on gender equality' (ibid.). In other words, the Swedish people have elected a left-wing government – although it was close in the most recent election – and this government institutes female-friendly policies at home and abroad.

Palmer writes that 'Scandinavia is the only region where political leaders have accepted the link between meeting the real needs of babies and general prosperity' ([1988] 2009, 164). She adds that the Scandinavian societies:

> have become more economically stable because women's talents and skills are incorporated into every aspect of society while, at the same time, a period of close physical contact between a mother and her child is politically supported. These countries have quotas for women in parliament. Their systems were not devised because of a sentimental

---

7. As noted, my focus here is the United Kingdom, but it is useful to mention how divided the United States is and how close recent elections there have been, which have been between two main parties, one more conservative and one more liberal. And it has followed that the conservative governments have enacted more conservative policies and have allowed people with more conservative views (views that are often described as 'family first' and 'America first') more political clout. Indeed, one conservative US politician even suggested assaulting breastfeeding women. Republican Josh Moore proposed a bill in New Hampshire that would make it illegal for a woman to show her nipple in public. He wrote, 'If it's a woman's natural inclination to pull her nipple out in public and you support that […] than you should have no problem with a mans inclantion to stare at it and grab it. After all […] It's ALL relative and natural, right?' (Tea 2016, n.p., mistakes in original).

nostalgia for mum with her apron, but because secure early childhoods are as vital for prosperity as a clean water supply. ([1988] 2009, 338)

I will say more about the connection to maternity leave later.

Of course, there is no way for me – as a literary critic, not a sociologist – to know whether Sweden valued women first and thus elected politicians that seemed to as well or whether it is the influence of the politicians and their policies that has made Sweden seemingly more supportive of breastfeeding or if, as with so many things, it is tightly connected, with one influencing the other. However, the political differences between the United Kingdom and Sweden are of great interest here, I would suggest.

Beyond the political parties, it is also useful to consider something Bryan Turner has written about the body and capitalism: 'What contemporary capitalism does require is the security of production, a technology of consumption and the commercial legitimation of desire. The differentiation of bodies by sex is increasingly irrelevant to these three conditions' ([1984] 1996, 59). This would suggest that the specific things that a (usually) female body can do, such as nurturing, birthing and feeding a baby, may no longer be seen as important or relevant, or as female-specific. Both English- and Swedish-speaking cultures are arguably capitalist; however, although Jon Henschen notes that Sweden redistributes wealth differently (2018, n.p.), one might expect to see similar treatment of female bodies and their specific capabilities in the two corpuses of texts, but this was not the case. So questions for further research would be to see if Turner's comment is in fact valid and also whether capitalism is the same across these cultures in terms of its approach, especially to the body.

The Influence of Formula-Milk Manufacturers and Advertising

I do not have the space in this book to explore the influence of manufacturers of artificial milk on society in the depth it deserves (see Palmer ([1988] 2009) for more on the politics of breastfeeding), but it is interesting to consider in brief. The International Code of Marketing of Breastmilk Substitutes 'is an international health policy framework to regulate the marketing of breastmilk substitutes in order to protect breastfeeding. It was published by the World Health Organization in 1981 and is an internationally agreed voluntary code of practice' (UNICEF 2020, n.p.). The code was developed in order to prevent commercial industries from negatively impacting on the health of mothers and babies. As UNICEF puts it on their website, 'The underlying basis for the Code is the belief that the *health of babies is so important* that the usual rules governing market competition and advertising should not apply to products intended for feeding babies. Therefore, all Governments should legislate to *prevent commercial interests from damaging breastfeeding rates and the health of their population*' (ibid.; emphasis original).

Interestingly, and perhaps not surprisingly given the analysis that has already been carried out in this book, the United Kingdom does not follow the entire code. While the United Kingdom has adopted some of it, the nation still allows advertising, and of course advertising influences the choices that families make and how people feel about themselves (cf. Strinati [1995] 2003, 177). Here is some clarification of the situation:

> These regulations only cover infant formula intended for babies *under six months* old; they do not cover any food, and do not cover the numerous products for babies older than six months. This loophole allows *widespread advertising* on television, in print media, online and via billboards. By using similar branding for all their products companies can in effect advertise all their products while still staying within the UK law. In addition, *the monitoring and enforcement of the UK legislation is very weak* which means that companies are rarely prosecuted for breaking the law. (UNICEF 2020, n.p.; emphasis original)

Even though organisations such as Baby Milk Action work hard to point out unethical behaviours of formula manufacturers, it is still common to see, for instance, artificial milk placed on the ends of aisles in grocery stores, where there is much footfall, or for them to be marketed with promotional offers or for manufacturers to make untrue or unproven claims about their products.

I would add that point 6 of the code is 'No words or pictures idealizing artificial feeding, including pictures of infants, on the products' (UNICEF 2020). While I know that literature is generally not a product produced by the artificial milk industry for the purposes of marketing – although Pollister found that some formula companies sponsor the making of TV shows (2012, 225) – I feel that many of the literary texts discussed in this chapter do 'idealis[e] artificial feeding' in both their words and images. I personally would love to see an even stricter code, one that more countries agree to and that does not allow for idealisation in advertising, literature, films, TV shows and other forms of media. Why not apply the code across society, including the publishing industry? Why not discourage or even forbid the idealisation of artificial milk in the media?

In comparison to the UK, Sweden has been following the code in its entirety since the 1980s (Erlandsson and Wiberg 2013, 15). In regard to the code, UNICEF writes:

The formula milk industry spends millions of pounds every year on advertising and marketing its products, *encouraging mothers not to breastfeed* or to stop breastfeeding early, and to use an array of different, expensive formula milks, as soon as possible and for as long as possible. In addition, parents are then urged to use costly, processed baby food, often before six months of age, the recommended age for starting solids. There is no evidence that more expensive formula milks or baby foods are beneficial to a baby's health. Most of these are unnecessary, and *can be harmful*. Where these products differ from most others is that such advertising can damage the *short and long-term health* of our children by *undermining breastfeeding and misleading parents* who bottle feed about what milk to use. (2020, n.p.; emphasis original)

Sweden's government, and thereby Swedish society, seems to accept this view, while the United Kingdom does not, at least not in its entirety. Why does the United Kingdom not prioritise the health of parents and their children? It is not too cynical to state that this is surely due to the bottom line. When artificial milk producers earn money, they can make the claim that they are contributing to society through employment and taxes, but it ought to be clear by now that those contributions do not stack up against the increased health costs, the sick or dead babies, the pollution, the additional sick days taken off work or school, the lower IQs, the erosion of women's belief in themselves and all the many other negative effects that formula milk is known to have. Additionally, if childcare, including breastfeeding, were given a monetary value, it would become clear that women's work offers much more to society than multinationals that live off stirring up consumers' fears.

As Soldavini and Taillie note, 165 out of 199 countries in the world have adopted the code, either fully or partially, but the United States is not among them (2017, n.p). Given the close relationship between the United States and the United Kingdom and the fact that a shared language also means that books in English can easily be read and are read in both countries, one could also speculate that cultural attitudes and commercial interests might be shared across the Atlantic (the so-called special relationship the two nations have). Political perspectives on the importance of a strong economy – and prioritising the economy over health – may mean that authors and publishers writing in English see formula advertised and used every day, and this affects how they write about feeding infants and children. This is beyond the scope of my work here, but as many researchers have pointed out, adopting stricter guidelines would save lives (e.g. Piwoz and Huffman 2015), and thus the code is very important. It may impact culture more widely, including the writing of literature.

Attitudes towards Women, Children and Families

The earlier section on political differences began to tease out societal differences in regard to attitudes towards women and children and thus also towards families. There are many topics that belong in this category that surely influence perspectives on different genders and on the raising of children, which in turn will affect how people view breastfeeding and write about it in literature, and I will refer some of them, although I will not explore them all in depth because this book unfortunately cannot be a full sociological comparison of the two countries. Examples of important subjects here are women's role(s) in a given society, women's rights, attitudes towards women's bodies and feminism.

In regard to feminism, the term has become a loaded one, and there are undoubtedly many people who agree with the feminist ideal of equality for everyone but who would not call themselves feminists. However, it is still interesting to note that a YouGov poll found that under 30% of people in the United Kingdom identify as feminist, while 56% identify as either not a feminist or actively an anti-feminist (YouGov 2010, n.p.), and a more recent poll suggests that only around one-third of young women in particular in the United Kingdom identify as feminists (Scharff 2019, n.p.). On the other hand, in Sweden, almost 50% of the population identify as feminists, with over 70% agreeing that the issue of equality of opportunity influences which political party they vote for (Marteleur 2014, n.p.). And, as noted earlier, Sweden has a feminist approach to foreign policy, but not only that, it claims to have the world's first feminist government. This means that 'equality is crucial for the government's priorities – in regard to decisions and the allocation of resources. A feminist government ensures that the perspective on equality is part of the formulation of policy in a broad sense, both nationally and internationally' (Anonymous 2020b, n.p.). The Swedish government's website goes on to detail all the ways in which their feminist perspectives influence their policy decisions. Feminism, it seems clear, runs through Swedish society, into the highest reaches of government.

One obvious issue related to breastfeeding and feminist politics is parental leave. In the United Kingdom, the person giving birth can take a maximum of 52 weeks of maternity leave, of which only 39 weeks are paid. The first six weeks are at 90% of the person's usual salary, while the following 33 weeks are at statutory maternity pay, which is currently £151.20, or 90% of their weekly salary, whichever is lower (Anonymous 2020c, n.p.). Some employers choose to increase the amount their employees get and/or allow the person to use paid annual leave for extra time off, but as is clear from these facts, there are many people who will be unable to take more than six or so weeks off work, due to the need to earn money. This will impact on their ability to breastfeed and to form a breastfeeding relationship with their child; as in the United States, it may lead to more women choosing to pump rather than feed at the breast, and this has other effects on breastfeeding dyads.[8]

On the other hand, in Sweden, a two-parent family gets 480 days (around 68 weeks) of parental leave; they can divide it more or less how they like, although at least 90 days are expected to be taken by the non-birthing parent (Anonymous 2020d, n.p.). A single parent would get the entire 480 days. The rules around how much payment you get are very complicated in Sweden, but currently, around 390 of those days (around 55 weeks) are at 80% of the person's income – although people can choose to take less of that money and instead spend more time with the child at home up until the child's eighth birthday – and 90 days are at a lower level, around 180 kronor (approximately £16) per day (i.e. around £80 per week) (Anonymous 2020h, n.p.). Even a cursory look at these numbers shows that parents in Sweden get more parental leave and more financial support for being at home. Having more time at home with the baby allows for more time to breastfeed, more time to solve any breastfeeding challenges and less stress around needing to leave the baby and possibly having to express milk. Sweden is 'ranked by unicef as the world's most family-friendly country and 17th for maternity leave' (Bryant 2020, n.p.).

Related to being family-friendly, supportive of women and breastfeeding-friendly is the issue of bodies in public. In both the United Kingdom and Sweden, it is legal to breastfeed anywhere in public, as long as it is safe to do so (e.g. it would not be advisable to breastfeed near open tubs of poison). In the United Kingdom, a woman cannot be asked to stop breastfeeding, she does not have to cover herself or her baby while breastfeeding and she

---

8. It is well known that 'the US is the only OECD [Organisation for Economic Co-operation and Development, a group of 38 countries] country without a national statutory paid maternity, paternity or parental leave. The Family and Medical Leave Act (FMLA) enables some employees to take up to 12 weeks unpaid maternity leave but only 60% of workers are eligible' (Bryant 2020, n.p.). The United States has a strong pumping culture, where women return to work quickly after birth and continue to express milk for their baby, but this requires an understanding employer, a private place to pump, breaks for expressing and a place to store the pumped milk, which is not something everyone has. It also requires the purchase of expensive pumps, bottles and other supplies, some of which are produced by companies that also produce artificial milk. One would imagine there would be more American novels or short stories featuring pumping, but this did not appear in my corpus frequently.

cannot be discriminated against while breastfeeding (see, e.g., Burbidge and Williams 2016, n.p.). Somewhat surprisingly, in Sweden, on the other hand, though breastfeeding is legal everywhere, it is not illegal to ask someone to stop (Sahamies et al. 2016). There have been several high-profile incidents in the United Kingdom where women have been told not to breastfeed in public, such as the Victoria and Albert Museum or at Claridge's, both in London (Brech 2017 and Tran 2014, respectively). Given all the evidence that suggests that Sweden was more supportive of families, I assumed that I would not be able to find any such cases of people asking women there to stop breastfeeding in public; however, I was proven wrong (Sahamies et al. 2016; Sahamies 2018). I even discovered that there is a movement, Amningsuppropet (The Breastfeeding Appeal) which aims to change the law in Sweden, so that it would become illegal to ask someone to stop breastfeeding.

So while in general it seems that Sweden has more positive attitudes towards women and families and provides more support, financially and practically, such as through longer parental leaves, it is obvious that no country is perfect. In general, though, I would suggest that having an explicitly feminist government and a larger proportion of people who call themselves feminists means that there will be better provision and more positive attitudes towards women and families in Sweden. This, then, would affect the breastfeeding relationship of the mother-and-child dyad and the way breastfeeding is perceived in society. I am aware some people find the term 'feminist' troubling, even if they agree with the ideals of feminism, and while I happily embrace the word myself, I could sum all this up as saying that we need more policies that are woman-positive and family-friendly, policies that offer genuine support rather than just throwing around the phrase 'family values' and implying women should stay at home, serving the family and being unrecognised and unsupported for doing so.

Reading Habits

Another consideration in this overview of sociological and cultural factors is how much people read and whether reading habits have any influence on what gets published.

According to statistics, 190,900,000 books were sold in the United Kingdom in 2018 (Johnson 2020, n.p.). Since the UK population is 66,000,000, this is approximately 2.9 books per person. Interestingly, Cooke reports that only 51% of adults read a book in 2018; her article claims that the average person bought nine books during the year, but clearly only some people read some of these works (Cooke 2019, n.p.), as there is a large gap between 2.9 and 9 books per person. Cooke also reports that the voracious readers tend to be 65 and older, while Johnson notes that the most read genre is crime fiction (2020, n.p.). Perhaps people are buying crime novels for older pensioners to read. It may also be that people buy books but do not end up reading them.

The annual statistics from Sweden, on the other hand, tell a different story: 51,819 books were sold in Sweden in 2019 (Wikberg 2019, 25). On first glance, given the population of 10,000,000, this looks like just 0.005 of a book per person, which is significantly smaller than the United Kingdom's 2.9 books per person. However, a study of media habits in Sweden shows that 39% of Swedish people between 9 and 79 years old read (or listen to an e-book) every day, and 60% read every week (von Friesen 2019, n.p.). These figures are quite different from the mere 51% of the British population who read over the course of an entire year. According to this study, the most prolific readers in Sweden are people between 9 and 14, and 61% of them read every single day. The most read genre in Sweden is literary fiction.

So there seems to be some discrepancy and much to unpack here. People in the United Kingdom buy lots of books, but do not read them, or else only a small swathe of society reads them, whereas Swedes read much more often but buy fewer books. The study in Sweden commented that 51% of those who had read a book the previous week had purchased it, while 22% had borrowed it from a library and 11% had received it as a gift. Using libraries may be more common in Sweden, where books can be quite expensive,[9] while in the United Kingdom, libraries have been closing down. A recent report shows that 800 libraries in the United Kingdom have closed in the past decade, since the Conservative political party instituted its dubious policy of 'austerity' (Flood 2019, n.p.).[10] So although there is a very popular 'bokrea', or 'book sale', every February in Sweden, when books are deeply discounted and when more books are sold than at Christmas (Anonymous n.d.a, n.p., and Anonymous 2019a), I would suggest that more Swedes use the libraries than people do in the United Kingdom, which explains their more extensive reading habits while also clarifying how, relatively speaking, so few books are purchased when so many are read.

Furthermore, as noted, the statistics suggest that in the United Kingdom, it is primarily older people who read regularly and that their preference is for crime fiction, while in Sweden, young people read more voraciously, although

---

9. Picturebooks, for instance, are primarily published in hardcover and can therefore be quite pricey.
10. This means many librarians have lost their jobs, and some libraries have replaced paid staff with volunteers (Anonymous 2016b, n.p.). The earlier discussion regarding breastfeeding helplines is applicable here, in that it is problematic when unpaid volunteers are used in professional roles; this has the effect of devaluing the work that is done. Volunteers are often excellent, educated, passionate breastfeeding counsellors or library workers, among other roles, but the question is why people are not paid to carry out such vital roles.

a great majority of people read or are read to every day, and literary fiction is the preferred type of writing.

How this relates to the depiction of breastfeeding in literature is, I would propose, as follows. First of all, literary fiction would probably be more likely to feature breastfeeding than crime fiction; this seems true from my corpus, but also from the plots of such works. A further study would need to confirm this, however. Also, related to this, women's stories, including books about parenthood, may be viewed as tales that are of general human interest, rather than a specific category or genre that only females would read. Second, a wider range of people in Sweden read regularly, especially young people, and young children are more likely to read, or be read, representations of their life, which might include babies and breastfeeding. In Sweden, approximately 30% of parents report reading to their children between the ages of 0 and 9 every day (Anonymous 2019b, n.p.), while the equivalent figure in the United Kingdom is 15% (Peat 2018, n.p.). Young children may be getting a sibling and may be read books about a pregnant parent or about life with a new baby, or they may simply be exposed to books about family life, which could include breastfeeding. A third point here is that adults in their 20s, 30s or 40s might read literary fiction about parenthood, which again would include breastfeeding, while in the United Kingdom, senior citizens are mostly reading crime fiction, which is not likely to focus on parenthood as a theme.

While further research would need to confirm some of these ideas, and while it is, as noted before with the other subjects analysed here, hard to know to what extent book-purchasing or book-reading habits influence what is written about and how, it is possible that given the apparently larger interest in reading in Sweden by a wider variety of readers, breastfeeding is more likely to be depicted in Swedish texts.[11]

Writing Habits

As one last topic to explore here, we can move on from reading habits to writing habits. Further research could look into, among other matters, the gender of people writing, editing and publishing literature in the United Kingdom versus in Sweden, while here I will focus on the gender of characters and also explore taboo subjects.

---

11. I would note that the coronavirus lockdown may change some of this, as people might turn more to reading, but how that will affect the depiction of breastfeeding remains to be seen.

Gender of Characters

I only want to briefly discuss the subject of writing habits in the respective countries, but another possible reason for the disparity between English-language and Swedish-language works may be the numbers of books that features female characters. It has been shown that English-language books feature boys, men and male animals more often than girls, women and female animals (see, e.g., McCabe et al. 2011, 209). The McCabe et al. study finds that males in English books appear twice as often as females, although, perhaps strangely, the ratio is even worse when it comes to animals, with many more male animals than female ones (ibid.). If, on the other hand, girls, women and female animals are included more often in Swedish works, then that could also be a reason why more female characters are depicted breastfeeding their young. This would, in turn, also reflect wider cultural as well as literary differences. If females are seen as worthy of being main characters in literature, then the things that females do, including breastfeeding, would also be viewed as relevant and of interest. As McCabe et al. write,

> The messages conveyed through representation of males and females in books contribute to children's ideas of what it means to be a boy, girl, man, or woman. The disparities we find point to the symbolic annihilation of women and girls, and particularly female animals, in twentieth-century children's literature, suggesting to children that these characters are less important than their male counterparts. (2011, 218)

Indeed, Swedish writing does not appear to privilege males in the same way; Warnqvist notes that females are the majority in regard to characters in children's and young adult literature in Sweden (2017, n.p.), with an analysis of young adult literature saying that 'girls dominate young adult books – 72 percent of the protagonists were female in 2017' (Svenska Barnboksinstitutet 2020a, b, n.p.). More research into literature for adults would have to be carried out to see if the figure is similar, but certainly it appears that Swedish authors are more likely to write about females and thus also about topics connected to females.

Taboo

Also in regard to writing habits and subjects, some topics may not be deemed appropriate or acceptable in particular cultures or for specific groups of readers. As Alvstad writes, 'Societies and cultures differ to a certain degree in their norms and taboos concerning the typically sensitive areas of nakedness, sexuality and gender roles, entailing that these issues are susceptible to change in translation' (2018, n.p.). Although I do not argue, in terms of literature for adults, that breastmilk is itself a taboo, there certainly is a societal disgust around breastfeeding in English-language works and, as already noted in Chapter 2, it appears as though there may be a taboo on featuring the female body in works for children in English. This stems from the conflation of nakedness with nudity and a generalised discomfort with seeing breasts, particularly in a non-sexualised way. It is also possible that this taboo extends to adult literature in English, in that a society that does not support women and families as much as some other cultures and that tends to see women's bodies as sexualised objects may feel discomfort or even repulsion when seeing depictions of breastfeeding in literature, particularly if they are positive portrayals. More research would need to be done in order to understand which topics, if any, are in fact taboo in Sweden and the United Kingdom/United States, and how this impacts literature.

Conclusion

As noted multiple times in this book, there is much more research that could be carried out in regard to the depiction of the female body in literature for adults and children – for example, into the impact of culture on writing and publishing, the gender of protagonists in books, taboos in literature, the effects of feminist (or anti-feminist) politics on society and the publishing industry, reader responses to literature, breastfeeding support in culture, which jobs are paid versus volunteer, how women's work is valued or not and many other subjects – but as a start towards understanding the cultural differences between these cultures, and thus between the bodies of literature, it seems clear that the United Kingdom and Sweden have different perspectives, experiences and ideas about breastfeeding in society and in literature.

In some sense, I feel that there is a vicious – or virtuous – circle here (like the circuit of culture discussed earlier in this book); perhaps it is better described as a feedback loop between perspectives on women and the breastfeeding culture, but it is hard to figure out which came first. A country with a more feminist outlook and more protections for women and children is, I would argue, more likely to support breastfeeding. This in turn perhaps leads to a country where breastfeeding is more normalised and thus seen in literature more, in terms of both positive descriptions and imagery in books. If young people see breastfeeding in society and read about it in literature, they may grow up to view it as the biological and cultural norm, and they will be likely to believe that women have the right to use their bodies as they like. This will impact society, so there will be more protection of women's rights, more paid parental leave, more support for breastfeeding, more respect for the work women do and so forth. And thus around the virtuous circle we go. On the other hand, a country that respects and protects women and children less may be more likely to sexualise women's bodies and to believe that women's breasts should not be employed in breastfeeding. If children and young people grow up seeing bottles in books and reading about how awful breastfeeding is, they may choose to bottle-feed. And thus we have the vicious circle.

In short, this quick exploration of some of the differences between the United Kingdom and Sweden supports what seems like an obvious idea that society impacts how people write and what they write about and what gets published. I would suggest that this can be changed, both through political and social movements and through what we might term a 'literary revolution'. If more people dare to write about and depict breastfeeding in words and images aimed at both adults and children, then it is likely that breastfeeding will eventually be seen as the cultural norm and as more important and more deserving of support and respect, and thereby more people may choose to breastfeed in the future. An increase of feminist perspectives and policies would benefit many fields, including publishing and health care.

CONCLUSION

My analysis of English-language literature for adults and children in the foregoing chapters suggests that contemporary society in the United Kingdom, and also to a certain extent in the United States and possibly other English-speaking countries, considers breastfeeding to be challenging in part because it employs the breasts in a non-sexual – albeit potentially sensual – way. Modern views of women and women's bodies insist upon the sexualisation of the breasts, making girls and women feel as though their breasts specifically, and their bodies more generally, are meant to be visible when it suits men and brings them pleasure, but invisible when those same bodies are used to nourish babies. The naked female body is always nude, but whether that nudity is considered sexy and titillating and acceptable or shameful and disgusting and inappropriate depends upon the situation. Besides the issue of nudity when it comes to the female body, my findings suggest that the work women do is undervalued or perhaps wholly unvalued, by society, and this includes breastfeeding. The situation is quite different in Swedish literature, with breastfeeding much more normalised and depicted more realistically. I wish to emphasise these things with the aim of effecting change in society, which would have the outcome of improving women's lives and influencing politics and culture.

Summary of Findings

In this book, I started with an analysis of what breastfeeding is and how breasts are viewed in English-speaking cultures, suggesting that there is a dichotomy between the mother and the sex object, with the latter currently preferred by society.

My exploration of literature began with a focus on works intended for children. Here, I found a stark difference between picturebooks in English and those in Swedish. In English, more books feature bottles than breasts, and this reflects the bottle-feeding norm in society. Out of those that do depict breasts, they tend to be one of two types. The first kind is the new baby-themed book, which is an 'issue' book that seems to be meant to help an older child get used to the idea of what life with a baby sibling might be like. The second kind is the breastfeeding-positive book, which is aimed at families that breastfeed and want to see families like their own depicted in words and images. Often, they do not have plots per se but rather focus on breastfeeding relationships, frequently showing breastfeeding taking place in different settings.

In Swedish, however, it is easier to find breastfeeding in picturebooks, where it is often treated in an unproblematised way, reflecting the societal breastfeeding norm in Sweden. While some picturebooks are the new baby type, instead of only exploring the practical aspect of having a new sibling, they also usually explore emotions, such as jealousy of the new baby, thereby taking children's feelings seriously. Swedish picturebooks also often show more of the breast, rather than keeping it covered, as tends to be the case in English-language original picturebooks. The translations to English are more along the same lines as the Swedish works in this regard, although they usually fall into the breastfeeding-positive type in terms of storyline.

What is true for both countries is that diversity is mostly absent. The picturebooks overwhelmingly show White faces, although of course skin colour does not necessarily reveal what ethnicity someone is. They also tend to show one male parent and one female one, and although it is obvious to many adult readers that one or both parents could be bisexual or trans, it seems to me that they would probably be read as a heterosexual, cisgender couple and that most children would interpret them this way, unless they themselves were more familiar with diverse family set-ups. On the whole, I found very few picturebooks that discussed in words or showed in images any significant diversity regarding (dis)ability, class, race, religion, sexuality, gender identity or family make-up.

When I turned to look at literature for adults, I again found a difference between English and Swedish texts. The English-language works repeatedly emphasise a limited number of tropes regarding breastfeeding. These tropes include the idea that breastfeeding is painful and often simply does not work, for reasons that range from low supply to trouble latching; the concept that formula is the answer to any breastfeeding difficulties (rather than getting support from a friend or a professional); the feeling that breastfeeding interferes with women's lives and with women's relationships with their male partners; the worry that breastfeeding may keep the father from connecting with his child due to the closeness of the dyad; the opinion that breastfeeding is disgusting, shameful or wrong and should not take place publicly; and the belief that breasts cannot be, or should not be, both sexual and nurturing. The few positive depictions of breastfeeding that I discovered in English were more often from works aimed at young adults (adults naturally could read these books as well), although I found only a few such portrayals. What was lacking were matter-of-fact or positive portrayals; people finding solutions to breastfeeding concerns and getting support from others; and variation among the breastfeeding experiences, such as preterm babies, tandem-feeding of a baby and an older child or multiples, or breastfeeding toddlers or older children, among other things.

Swedish-language fiction for adults, on the other hand, shows an awareness of some of these same negative tropes but is more likely to challenge them. Instead of simply repeating the tropes, Swedish literature portrays characters thinking about them, critiquing these societal voices and judgements, and attempting to find their own way with breastfeeding. Breastfeeding is generally more normalised in Swedish literature, with both the positive aspects and the more difficult ones depicted in a realistic way. The texts even make it clear that motherhood, including breastfeeding, is a worthy and important subject for literary fiction. Women's work is valued, including the literally creative work of making and raising a child.

Both Swedish and English literature engage with the concept of the good mother, and although both include characters who are struggling with the stress that comes with the pressure to be good, Swedish texts are more likely to explore the emotional impact that this has on women. In English, I found that harsh judgements of mothers seem to be accepted more readily instead of contested.

In terms of diversity, the situation for adult literature is the same as that for children's literature. That is, I found only a couple of specific references to non-White characters and to non-middle-class characters, though there was more class variation in Swedish. Other aspects of diversity were missing, such as sexuality, gender identity, religion and (dis)ability. I wished I had come across instances in literature of trans men chestfeeding, disabled people feeding their babies, people of different ethnicities and religions breastfeeding, and so forth. There was a yawning absence in literature that seems important to rectify.

Moving on from the specific literary examples, I then tried to figure out what might be behind these differing depictions of breastfeeding, so I explored a variety of facts and ideas about the United Kingdom and Sweden. Sweden has higher breastfeeding rates, and it also seems as though Swedish people are more likely to request support with breastfeeding, so then it follows rather naturally that Swedish literature would treat breastfeeding as the cultural norm that it is, but without ignoring any challenges that could arise.

Information about ethnic differences did not seem particularly useful at this stage, but religious differences might play a role. English-speaking cultures are more Christian, in terms of actual practice, than Sweden, which may suggest that a more traditional, conservative view of women and their bodies could mean that women feel unable to breastfeed in public; this is somewhat odd, perhaps, because I had the hypothesis that those who are Christian might look to Mary, the mother of Jesus, as the ultimate pure and good mother and may want to emulate her, including breastfeeding. Mary was seldom referenced in the works, but it is still possible that conservative Christian beliefs in culture could impact people's writing.

The term 'conservative' may also be relevant when it comes to politics. The United Kingdom is more right-leaning than Sweden and does not have the feminist approach to policy that Sweden does. A greater concern with the treatment of women and with broadening societal views of women's roles might cause a country to be more open and positive about women using their bodies as they wish, which could include breastfeeding. Generally, Sweden appears to have more generous policies and more positive attitudes towards women, families and breastfeeding; this includes longer maternity leaves at higher rates of pay as well as adherence to the WHO code. Being respectful, supportive and woman-friendly allows women in a given society to see themselves as the subjects of their own lives, instead of as objects in the lives of women.

Furthermore, it turns out that people in Sweden at varying ages are more liable to read literary fiction, whereas in the United Kingdom, the greatest readers are older people, who prefer crime fiction. And perhaps it is related to this that more books seem to feature female protagonists than male in Sweden. Such reading and writing habits might also reflect a desire to see women's lives and family sagas in literature and to view women's stories as being of general human interest, rather than something that should be relegated to a genre such as 'chick lit'.

Certainly, further research is required in general regarding these differences, but it seems to me that there could be an interplay between these factors that is behind the greater acceptance of breastfeeding in Swedish-language literature. Charlotte Young, writing specifically about the United Kingdom, states:

> In our society most mothers do not breastfeed past the first few weeks, and many mothers don't know anyone who has breastfed without problems or for very long. Those who do establish breastfeeding and continue for several months or longer can feel self-conscious in public, and as if they need to cover up or go somewhere private. In this situation is it surprising that many mothers do not breastfeed their babies for as long as they initially intend? The odds are stacked against them. What's more, breastfeeding is an emotive subject, because breasts are attached to a person. (2016, 10–11)

Breastfeeding is emotive for so many reasons, many discussed here already: it links to ideas about good mothering; it reflects feelings about what a woman's body is for; it is about more than nutrition; it forms a bond between mother and child; it can challenge the patriarchy; it prioritises women and children over men; and more. And Young's larger point – that people do not breastfeed as long as they intend to or want to – is reflected in English-language literature, where it is almost exclusively small babies who are breastfed. Few books depict breastfeeding in a positive manner. Perhaps some authors have had their own negative experiences with breastfeeding, as well as having internalised societal opinions about their bodies, and this has impacted how they write about breastfeeding.

If the 'odds are stacked against' women in the United Kingdom and yet this seems, from my analysis, to be different in Sweden, perhaps that means it is possible to change the situation.

Women's Power

Breastfeeding is one way women can control their own bodies and shape their interactions with their children. Encouraging women not to do it takes power away from them, whether by promoting artificial milk, suggesting formula as an easy solution, reminding women that they are or should be sexual beings who should satisfy their men, not giving women paid maternity leave so they can stay home with their children or any of the other multitude of ways that artificial milk is endorsed and prioritised by society. Seeing women as primarily or only sexual makes women into passive objects who are subjugated by the patriarchy.

Cindy A. Stearns refers to the contradictions around women's bodies when it comes to breastfeeding when she writes, 'Breastfeeding, like being pregnant, is a state in which the body is in some ways a public good and thus open for public comment. However, unlike pregnancy and childbirth, the expression of breastfeeding is a continuous activity that requires the ongoing participation of another person' (1999, 308). Breastfeeding is both public and private, although whether it should be 'open to public comment' is highly debatable, as it is a personal decision, although one heavily influenced by the time and place someone lives in and the people they have around them. It is the second part of Stearns's remark that is perhaps easier to dismiss in contemporary society; breastfeeding is an ongoing choice, an act in which both mother and child participate, and thus it is something that makes a woman active. If women being active is not considered a desirable quality, then breastfeeding would not be a valued activity.

We must begin to value breastfeeding and what women do (cf. Francis et al. 2002, 161–64). As Blaffer Hrdy comments, as mammals were evolving, breastfeeding would have been seen differently and would have been highly valued: 'Lactation was a caretaking adaptation linked to a specific sex as never before [and it] would make the individuals who produced milk an even more valuable, even more limited resource, than egg producers already were' (1999, 140). Humans usually produce just one young at a time and must invest enormous amounts of time and energy into them, and so this would, one might imagine, make the lactating parent hugely appreciated and valued. Some might balk at the idea that men and women are different and that women[1] contribute something unique through gestating and feeding children, but I suggest this is something to honour, appreciate, value and support.

And yet, as Palmer puts it, 'the feeding of a baby does provoke something far stronger than sexuality. It is a demonstration of power that is exclusively female and perhaps it is unacceptable for a woman who has claimed the supposedly male power to show she can have both' ([1988] 2009, 148). Indeed, patriarchy and sexism are threatened by female power, and so in turn they threaten breastfeeding and the mother–child relationship (c.f. Francis et al. 2002, 20) because, among other issues, it suggests that in order to succeed in our society, women must be like men, must claim 'male power', as Palmer says. To be like men, women should, for instance, not take long maternity leaves with their children and instead should return to work and focus on their careers. This makes breastfeeding, or even expressing breastmilk, tricky. Then, of course, there is the idea that women should return to how they were before they had a child as quickly as possible, in regard to both their physical appearance and their way of life, almost pretending that the baby does not exist, instead of giving themselves time to recover from pregnancy and birth and to adjust to their new role as mother.

There are a number of other challenges or pressures women face, throughout their careers, their pregnancies and their years with young children, many of which have been mentioned throughout this book, such as practical and emotional labour at home without much help, lack of education around breastfeeding and the risks of not doing it, subsidised formula milk, the marketing of formula, being separated from their babies and being encouraged to make their babies 'independent', 'neglect of the mother's health and nutrition' (Francis et al. 2002, 36), hospital practices, opinions about breastfeeding in public, 'unbalanced reports of breast milk pollution which formula manufacturers can seize on to excite mothers' and health workers' fears' (Francis et al. 2002, 39), heavy workloads, the idea that they must work long hours, shame or fear and much more.

---

1. And, of course, some trans men. As noted, though, I want to fight against the downgrading of women and women's contributions, so here I am emphasising that it is usually women who produce and birth and breastfeed children.

Palmer writes:

> There is no shortage of breastmilk. If all existing, supportive policies were fully implemented, breastfeeding rates could be doubled within a short time. No other production process is so easy to switch on and off. Women who stop breastfeeding because their confidence has been crushed through misinformation and inept care, or because they are denied access to their babies, have had their entitlement destroyed. Constraints in health systems, ignorance, commercial misinformation and greed, inhumane and unimaginative working systems, distorted cultural values and political blindness all come together to destroy the entitlement of women to sustain their children's health and lives, and protect their own bodies. ([1988] 2009, 340)

All this is to say that we do not value women's work and women's abilities, including breastfeeding, and this is the clear message we see in society and in literature. Western society values work and productivity, often to our detriment (e.g. Williams 2021), but only in certain circumstances; the work of pregnancy, labour (yes, literally labour), breastfeeding and parenting is not recognised, venerated or – if we must monetise such things – valued in terms of its economic contributions to the world. Instead of expecting women to be like men or to pretend they do not have children, perhaps it is time to get rid of rigid gender roles, different standards for different groups of people[2] and firm ideas about what 'success' means and to allow more flexibility about how to shape a life. If, as Palmer points out, new policies were put in place or existing policies were enacted, more women would breastfeed, again taking control over their lives and their bodies. They would have more self-esteem and be more empowered.

Some might understandably question why we should insist on the importance of this sort of work when, in our current circumstances, it does not offer women true power in our society. I would contend that breastfeeding is one important means for women to take power over their own bodies and to fight against prevailing societal values about what matters in life. Women fully controlling their own bodies and valuing the work they do, such as breastfeeding and childcare, would force a shift in society, because it would mean no longer accepting a devaluation. This could have many beneficial effects, not least for the individual women and their families. It might also mean, for example,

---

2. For instance, the idea that a man who leaves work early to pick up his children from school is a 'good', 'involved' father who is 'babysitting' his own offspring and doing his wife a favour, while a woman who leaves work early for the sake of her children is considered to be lacking in dedication to her job. These double standards continue to be common today, in the twenty-first century.

that employers and governments accept that women have to receive an extensive and well-remunerated maternity leave, in part so they can establish breastfeeding. It might mean the development of training in breastfeeding knowledge for health professionals or the start of paid roles that support breastfeeding dyads. It could even mean that individual organisations, or even society as a whole, might come to recognise that a nine-to-five job five days a week is not the way to create a happy, satisfied population and that earning more money is not all there is to life; perhaps work or school three or four days a week and/or fewer hours a day would allow more time for hobbies, for relaxation, for volunteering, for families and friends. Boosting breastfeeding could make for a happier population that cares for each other and for the world, and it could encourage new perspectives on everything, including parenting, GDP and climate change, among many other vital subjects.

The Importance of Portrayals in Literature

Women saying they choose to breastfeed and that this is a vital contribution to their society is one step. Likewise, writing and illustrating the stories of women and children who breastfeed would influence readers, who would come to realise that women's work does matter.

In some of my earlier research on the depictions of LGBTQ+ characters in children's and young adult literature (Epstein 2013), I discussed how media depictions are powerful in part because they can challenge and break down stereotypes and can help educate readers. We can learn about and connect to other people and other lives in part through literature. Books matter; they can, of course, be pleasurable and they often are, but they are also educational, offering messages about and critiques of people, concepts and society at large. This all applies to portrayals of breasts and breastfeeding in literature as well.

In the introduction to this book, I mentioned the concept of the circuit of culture (Hall et al. [1997] 2013, xviii), and elsewhere in the book, I called it a virtuous or vicious cycle. Regardless of the term employed, the fact is that reality influences representation, which influences reality, which influences representation and so on. If a society supports and normalises breastfeeding, then it will be featured in media as simply one, often positive and perhaps sometimes neutral, aspect of life; in turn, the media depictions will encourage people to recognise breastfeeding as the biological and cultural norm. The acceptance and the depiction feed into one another, with each increasing the other over time. This is the virtuous cycle. The opposite is also true: if breastfeeding is not normalised by a society, it will seldom be seen in a positive way in media. In turn, negative depictions or an absence of portrayals will help ensure that breastfeeding remains othered, undervalued, denigrated and discouraged by society. This is the vicious cycle. I strongly suggest that in English-speaking countries, we need a move towards the virtuous cycle. Seeing breastfeeding in literature could be a hugely important intervention.

In her analysis of breastfeeding in the media, Kathryn Pollister remarks that this matters because of the 'parasocial relationships formed between audience and characters' (2012, 222). Characters in books or television or in films seem real and can be friends or role models, so seeing them breastfeed can inspire people who are already parents or who intend to have children and can also educate other people, whether they plan to parent or not or have already parented. Pollister discusses how 'embodied knowledge', or seeing breastfeeding in person or in the media, helps people decide to breastfeed and to persevere with it (2012, 225). This would include portrayals in literature, in films, on TV, in advertisements and throughout the media. Charlotte Young confirms that ' "normal" is what we see every day around us, and what the majority of people do influences social acceptability' (2016, 13). What is normal in English-language literature is not breastfeeding. In Swedish-language literature, what is normal is breastfeeding.

In a long quote, Young writes:

Most of the infant feeding we see in society uses formula and bottles. Children play at feeding their dolls, popular TV shows, celebrities, adverts, magazines and news features all present imager that reinforces the bottle-feeding message. Gradually the concept of bottle feeding being linked with positive emotions has developed.

A 2016 study examining how infant feeding was portrayed in British women's magazines looked at the content of five of the bestselling women's weekly magazines of a four-month period. There was only one visual representation of breastfeeding, compared with 11 of bottle-feeding. The magazines also reported numerous barriers to breastfeeding, including concerns about adverse health consequences. The authors concluded:

An improvement in visual representations of and factual information about breastfeeding may be helpful in redefining social norms about infant feeding.

We can add this to what we know about babies and breastfeeding. As breastfeeding triggers the release of hormones associated with love and connected, it's well documented that breastfeeding is bonding. Given the culture around us, many of us mentally extrapolate this information to assume that feeding a baby is bonding, whether it's by breast or bottle. (2016, 90–91; italics original)

We internalise the messages we read, see and hear. Based on the explorations of literature in this book, the obvious question is: is it time to change that message?

Greta Gaard writes, 'Where are the literary and cultural texts depicting breastfeeding outside of oppressive institutional and cultural contexts? Where are the examples of free mothers of all races, classes, and species able to choose whether, where, and how long to breastfeed their own offspring? Perhaps those conditions have to yet to exist, and those narratives have yet to be written' (2013, 17). I would say there is definitely space for narratives that show pain during breastfeeding or the choice to use formula instead, for example, but there is also plenty of space for narratives that depict breastfeeding in a more positive, supportive, diverse and encouraging way.

Expecting the Breast

So, to close this book, I must say that, echoing Gaard, the narratives we need 'have yet to be written' but can and should be written. There is room in literature for women's stories and specifically for stories that include breastfeeding. And in a larger sense, we can change the narrative of society. Breastfeeding does not have to be painful or difficult or intrusive or disgusting, and so it should not be depicted only that way. Breastfeeding can be supported by society; women can get help with it. Breasts do not have to be solely sexual; they can be sexual, sensual and nurturing. Women can reject the male gaze and instead focus on their own gaze, or their children's gaze, or the exchanged look between a breastfeeding dyad as they feed. Women can reject a gaze altogether, if they like. Women do not have to feel pressured by societal ideals that are impossible to achieve, such as returning to work two weeks after giving birth or working long hours and giving all their time and energy to their employer or acting as though they do not have children. Women also do not have to hide at home or in a toilet to breastfeed; they can do it wherever and whenever they desire. They can breastfeed for as long as they and their child like. Women of all backgrounds, in short, can use their bodies as they wish, and this should be at the centre of policy and culture; it is important to value and it is worthy of being a subject in literature.

Women can expect and demand more; we can, in fact, expect and demand the breast and the best. Women are not passive members of society, but active ones, who can claim and create more power and more space.

It is time to rewrite the narrative regarding breasts and breastfeeding in our society.

REFERENCES

Ahlberg, Janet, and Allan Ahlberg. [1982] 2012. *The Baby's Catalogue*. London: Penguin.
Albertalli, Becky. 2015. *Simon vs. the Homo Sapiens Agenda*. New York: Penguin.
Alico, Leanne. 2016. 'Starbucks signs up with NCT to support Breastfeeding Campaign'. *Parent Herald*. 7 March. Available at: http://www.parentherald.com/articles/25090/20160307/starbucks-pro-breastfeeding.htm.
Alvstad, Cecilia. 2018. 'Children's Literature'. *The Routledge Handbook of Literary Translation*, edited by Kelly Washbourne and Ben van Wyke. London: Routledge, 159–80.
American Library Association. 2021. 'Top 10 Most Challenged Books Lists'. Available at: http://www.ala.org/advocacy/bbooks/frequentlychallengedbooks/top10.
Anderson, Lena. 2015. *Kanin-bad* (Rabbit-Bath). Stockholm: Rabén & Sjögren.
Andersson, Maria. 2015. 'Från stork till spermabank: Sexualupplysningslitteratur för barn 1965-2014' (From the Stork to the Sperm Bank: Sexual Education Literature for Children from 1965–2014). *Samlaren* 136: 5–37. Available at: https://uu.diva-portal.org/smash/get/diva2:908939/FULLTEXT01.pdf.
Anonymous. [1992] 2005. *The New Baby*. London: Usborne.
———. 2009. *My New Baby*. Swindon, England: Child's Play.
———. 2015. 'Just Five Percent of Swedes Are Regular Church Goers'. *The Local*. Available at: https://www.thelocal.se/20150413/swedes-least-religious-in-western-world.
———. 2016a. 'A Gallup Poll in 2016 Found That 18% of Swedes Self Report as Atheist and 55% as Non-Religious'. *Gallup*. Available at: http://gallup.com.pk/wp-content/uploads/2017/04/Global-Report-on-Religion-2.pdf.
———. 2016b. 'Libraries Lose a Quarter of Staff as Hundreds Close'. 29 March. Available at: https://www.bbc.co.uk/news/uk-england-35707956.
———. 2018. 'Statistik om amning 2017' (Breastfeeding Statistics 2017). *Socialstyrelsen*. Available at: https://www.socialstyrelsen.se/statistik-och-data/statistik/statistikamnen/amning/.
———. 2019a. 'Bokreans betydelse för bokbranschen i dag' (Book Sale's Meaning for the Book Industry Today). *Dagens Nyheter*. 25 February. Available at: https://www.dn.se/kultur-noje/bocker/bokreans-betydelse-for-bokbranschen-i-dag/.
———. 2019b. 'Föräldrar högläser mer sällan böcker för sina barn – och bokstunderna blir allt kortare' (Parents Read Aloud to Their Children More Seldom – and Those Times Are Ever Shorters). *Nextory*. 30 October. Available at: http://www.mynewsdesk.com/se/nextory/pressreleases/foeraeldrar-hoeglaeser-mer-saellan-boecker-foer-sina-barn-och-bokstunderna-blir-allt-kortare-2937049.
———. 2020a. 'Breastfeeding Report Card: United States'. *CDC*. Available at: https://www.cdc.gov/breastfeeding/data/reportcard.htm#:~:text=Among%20infants%20born%20in%202015,were%20breastfeeding%20at%2012%20months.

———. 2020b. 'Feministisk regering' (Feminist Government). *Regeringskansliet*. Available at: https://www.regeringen.se/regeringens-politik/feministisk-regering/.

———. 2020c. 'Statutory Maternity Pay and Leave: Employer Guide'. UK Government. Available at: https://www.gov.uk/employers-maternity-pay-leave#:~:text=Statutory%20Maternity%20Leave,as%20'Additional%20Maternity%20Leave'.&text=Employees%20must%20take%20at%20least,'re%20a%20factory%20worker.

———. 2020d. 'Föräldraledighet' (Parental Leave). *Babyhjälp*. Available at: https://www.babyhjalp.se/ledighet/.

———. 2020e. 'Hur många i Sverige är födda i ett annat land?' (How Many in Sweden Were Born in Another Country?). Available at: https://www.migrationsinfo.se/fragor-och-svar/hur-manga-utrikes-fodda-sverige/.

———. 2020f. 'Socialdemokraterna' (Social Democrats). *Socialdemokraterna* website (Social Democrats website). Available at: https://www.socialdemokraterna.se/vart-parti/om-partiet/var-historia#0.

———. 2020g. 'UK Demographics'. *Index Mundi*. Available at: https://www.indexmundi.com/united_kingdom/#Demographics.

———. 2020h. 'Föräldrapenning' (Parental Pay). *Babyhjälp*. Available at: https://www.babyhjalp.se/foraldrapenning.

———. 2021. 'Keira Knightley Rules Out Sex Scenes Directed by Men'. *BBC*. 26 January. Available at: https://www.bbc.co.uk/news/entertainment-arts-55795237.

———. n.d.a. 'Bokrean' (The Book Sale). Available at: https://sv.wikipedia.org/wiki/Bokrean#:~:text=Bokrean%20%C3%A4r%20ett%20%C3%A5rligt%20evenemang,datum%20i%20slutet%20av%20februari.&text=D%C3%A4remot%20inneb%C3%A4r%20inte%20rean%20l%C3%A4ngre,saluf%C3%B6r%20dem%20efter%20reans%20slut.

———. n.d.b. 'Historisk statistik över valåren 1910–2014. Procentuell fördelning av giltiga valsedlar efter parti och typ av val' (Historic Statistics for Election Years 1910–2014. Distribution by Percentage of Valid Ballots by Party and Type of Election'). *SCB*. Available at: https://www.scb.se/hitta-statistik/statistik-efter-amne/demokrati/allmanna-val/allmanna-val-valresultat/pong/tabell-och-diagram/historisk-valstatistik/historisk-statistik-over-valaren-19102014.-procentuell-fordelning-av-giltiga-valsedlar-efter-parti-och-typ-av-val/.

———. n.d.c. 'UK Census'. Available at: https://www.ethnicity-facts-figures.service.gov.uk/uk-population-by-ethnicity/national-and-regional-populations/population-of-england-and-wales/latest.

AskDrSears. 2020. '7 Benefits of Attachment Parenting'. Available at: https://www.askdrsears.com/topics/parenting/attachment-parenting/7-benefits-ap.

Atkins-Boyce, Kendra. 2016. 'Getting in Touch with the "Touched Out" Feeling'. *La Leche League USA*. Available at: https://lllusa.org/getting-in-touch-with-the-touched-out-feeling-2/.

Atkinson, Kate. 1995. *Behind the Scenes at the Museum*. London: Black Swan.

———. 2000. *Emotionally Weird*. London: Transworld.

———. 2002. *Not the End of the World*. London: Transworld.

———. 2010. *When Will There Be Good News?* London: Doubleday.

———. 2013. *Life after Life*. London: Transworld.

Audickas, Lukas, Richard Cracknell and Philip Loft. 2020. 'UK Election Statistics: 1918–2019: A Century of Elections'. *Parliament*. Available at: https://commonslibrary.parliament.uk/research-briefings/cbp-7529/.

REFERENCES

Ayuyang, Rina. 2018. *Blame it on the Boogie*. Montreal: Drawn and Quarterly.
Baby Milk Action. n.d. Home page. Available at: https://www.babymilkaction.org/.
Barker, J. n.d. 'Can You Spot the Tah-Tahs? Great Boobs in Advertising'. *InventorSpot*. Available at: http://inventorspot.com/articles/spot_jumblies_boobs_advertising_36987.
Barthes, Roland. [1970] 1991. *S/Z*, translated by Richard Miller. London: Farrar, Straus & Giroux.
Bartlett, Alison. 2010. 'Sex in the Seventies: 1970s Maternal Advice Manuals on Breastfeeding'. In *Mother-Texts: Narratives and Counter-Narratives*, edited by Julie Kelso and Marie Porter, 179–88. Newcastle: Cambridge Scholars.
Bauknecht, Sara. 2018. 'What's Right (and What Could Go Wrong) with Gap's New Breastfeeding Ad'. *Pittsburgh Post-Gazette*. 28 February. Available at: https://www.post-gazette.com/life/fashion/2018/02/28/What-s-right-and-what-could-go-wrong-with-Gap-s-breastfeeding-ad/stories/201802280119.
Baumslag, Naomi, and Dia L. Michels. 1995. *Milk, Money, and Madness: The Culture and Politics of Breastfeeding*. Mapusa, India: Other India Press.
Beauvais, Clémentine. 2017. *Piglettes*. London: Pushkin.
Bernard, Jonathan Y., Emmanuel Cohen and Michael S. Kramer. 2016. 'Breast Feeding Initiation Rate across Western Countries: Does Religion Matter? An Ecological Study'. *BMJ Global Health* 1, 4. Available at: https://gh.bmj.com/content/1/4/e000151.
Bernhard, Emery, and Durga Bernhard. 1996. *A Ride on Mother's Back*. London: Harcourt.
Blackall, Molly. 2021. ' "Stop the Breast Pest": MP's "Horror" at Being Photographed while Breastfeeding'. *Guardian*. 1 May. Available at: https://www.theguardian.com/lifeandstyle/2021/may/01/labour-mp-stella-creasy-horror-photographed-while-breastfeeding-prompts-campaign.
Blakemore, Erin. 2016. 'The Cultural Expectations of Breastfeeding'. *Jstor Daily*. Available at: http://daily.jstor.org/its-time-academics-pay-attention-to-breastfeeding/?utm_source=marketing&utm_medium=social&utm_campaign=twittermorning.
Breastfeeding Network. 2019. 'Breastfeeding with a Disability'. Available at: https://www.breastfeedingnetwork.org.uk/breastfeeding-with-a-disability/.
Brech, Anna. 2017. 'V&A Museum "Very Sorry" after Breastfeeding Woman Told to Cover Up'. *Grazia*. 7 August. Available at: https://graziadaily.co.uk/life/real-life/victoria-albert-museum-apologises-breastfeeding-mum-cover-woman-sexism/.
Broomé, Elisabet, and Cecilia Nordstrand Alin. 2005. *Hej lillebror* (Hi Little Brother). Stockholm: Opal.
Brown, Amy. 2016. *Breastfeeding Uncovered*. London: Pinter and Martin.
———. 2018. 'Baby Bottle Propping Isn't Just Dangerous – It's a Sign of a Broken Society'. *The Conversation*. Available at: https://theconversation.com/baby-bottle-propping-isnt-just-dangerous-its-a-sign-of-a-broken-society-94055.
———. 2019. *Why Breastfeeding Grief and Trauma Matter*. London: Pinter and Martin.
Brown, Amy, and Natalie Shenker. 2020. 'Breastfeeding Support during Covid-19'. Available at: https://www.breastfeedingnetwork.org.uk/wp-content/uploads/2020/08/BFN-Summary-COVID.pdf.
Brown, Anthony. [1990] 2008. *Changes*. London: Walker.
Bryant, Miranda. 2020. 'Maternity Leave: US Policy Is Worst on List of the World's Richest Countries'. *Guardian*. 27 January. Available at: https://www.theguardian.com/us-news/2020/jan/27/maternity-leave-us-policy-worst-worlds-richest-countries#:~:text=0%20weeks%20total-,The%20US%20is%20the%20only%20OECD%20country%20without%20a%20national,60%25%20of%20workers%20are%20eligible.

Burbidge, Anna. 2015. 'Breastfeeding: How the Biological Norm became perceived as a Modern Day Pressure'. *La Leche League*. Available at: https://www.laleche.org.uk/news/breastfeeding-how-biological-norm-became-perceived-modern-day-pressure.

Burbidge, Anna, and Eva Williams. 2016. 'Breastfeeding in Public Spaces'. *La Leche League*. Available at: https://www.laleche.org.uk/breastfeeding-public-spaces/#:~:text=It%20is%20entirely%20legal%20to,places%20anywhere%20in%20the%20UK.&text=Service%20providers%20dealing%20directly%20with,woman%20because%20she%20is%20breastfeeding.

Burt, Vivien K., Sonya Rasminsky and Robin Berman. 2016. 'Doctor Says: When It Comes to Breastfeeding, Your Health and Happiness Matter as Much as Your Baby's'. *Washington Post*. Available at: https://www.washingtonpost.com/news/parenting/wp/2016/03/03/doctor-says-when-it-comes-to-breastfeeding-your-health-and-happiness-matter-as-much-as-your-babys/.

Bury, Liz. 2013. 'Norfolk & Norwich Millennium Tops List of Most Popular UK Libraries'. *Guardian*. Available at: https://www.theguardian.com/books/2013/dec/11/norfolk-norwich-library-most-popular-top-20.

Calaf, Mònica. 2011. *You, Me and the Breast*, illustrated by Mikel Fuentes. London: Pinter and Martin.

Centre for Literacy in Primary Education. 2018. 'Reflecting Realities – a Survey of Ethnic Representation within UK Children's Literature 2017'. Available at: https://clpe.org.uk/library-and-resources/research/reflecting-realities-survey-ethnic-representation-within-uk-children.

Cleary, Beverly. 1999. *Ramona's World*. New York: Harper.

Cook, Emma. 2016. 'Poetry, Breastfeeding and Sex'. *Guardian*. 13 February. Available at: https://www.theguardian.com/lifeandstyle/2016/feb/13/poetry-breastfeeding-and-sex.

Cooke, Kirsty. 2019. '51% of UK Adults Read a Book in the Last Year'. *Kantar*. 6 March. Available at: https://uk.kantar.com/consumer/leisure/2019/51-of-uk-adults-read-a-book-in-the-last-year/#:~:text=Are%20we%20reading%20digital%20books,to%20Kantar%20Worldpanel%20purchase%20data.

Dahle, Gro. 2017. *Sesam Sesam* (Sesame Sesame), illustarted by Kaia Dahle Nyhus. Oslo: Cappelen Damm.

Damour, Lisa. 2019. *Under Pressure*. London: Atlantic.

Daniel, Carolyn. 2006. *Voracious Children*. New York: Routledge.

Davidson, Willing. 2018. 'Karen Russell on the Diabolical Side of Parenthood'. *New Yorker*. Available at: https://www.newyorker.com/books/this-week-in-fiction/karen-russell-on-the-diabolical-side-of-parenthood.

de Boitiz, Victoria. 2011. *The Mystery of the Breast*. Illustrated by by Afra. London: Pinter and Martin.

Dettwyler, Katherine A. 1999. 'Natural Age of Weaning'. Available at: https://www.researchgate.net/publication/265185534_A_Natural_Age_of_Weaning.

Dickens, Charles. [1850] 2008. *David Copperfield*. Oxford: Oxford University Press.

Douglas, Mary. [1966] 1994. *Purity and Danger*. London: Routledge.

Downham, Jenny. 2015. *Unbecoming*. Oxford: David Fickling.

Durdin, Kimberley. 2019. 'It's Black Breastfeeding Week – Here's Why It Matters'. *Mother*. Available at: https://www.mothermag.com/black-breastfeeding-week/#:~:text=According%20to%20Kimberly%20Sears%20Allers,the%20black%20community%20around%20lactation.&text=Black%20babies%20are%20dying%20at,the%20rate%20of%20white%20babies.

Eidelman, Arthur I. 2006. 'The Talmud and Human Lactation: The Cultural Basis for Increased Frequency and Duration of Breastfeeding among Orthodox Jewish Women'. *Breastfeeding Medicine* 11, 36–40. Available at: https://pubmed.ncbi.nlm.nih.gov/17661559/.

Elliott, Rebecca. 2014. *Mr Super Poopy Pants*. Oxford: Lion Hudson.

Enright, Anne. 2011. *The Forgotten Waltz*. Bath: Thorndike.

Epstein, B. J. 2012. *Translating Expressive Language in Children's Literature*. Bern: Peter Lang.

———. 2013. *Are the Kids All Right? Representations of LGBTQ Characters in Children's and Young Adult Literature*. Bristol: Hammer On Press.

———. 2014. 'The Case of the Missing Bisexuals: Bisexuality in Books for Young Readers'. *Journal of Bisexuality* 14, 110–125.

———. 2017. 'Breast versus Bottle: The Feeding of Babies in English and Swedish Picturebooks'. *Barnboken – Journal of Children's Literature Research*, 40. Available at: https://doi.org/10.14811/clr.v40i0.269.

———. 2021. 'Heaven Forbid: An Analysis of the Portrayal of Death in English-Language Picturebooks, with Comparison to Swedish and Norwegian-Language Ones'. *Norsk Barneboksinstitutt* (the Norwegian Children's Books Institute). Available at: https://barnebokinstituttet.no/faglitteratur-om-barnelitteratur/heaven-forbid/.

Erlandsson, Eskil, and Mats Wiberg. 2013. 'Lagrådsremiss: Marknadsföring av modersmjölksersättning och tillskottsnäring' (Proposal: Marketing of Mother's Milk Substitutes and Substitutes). Available at: https://www.regeringen.se/49bb8e/contentassets/859e628b2a01487494f5d62a5d63ce7e/marknadsforing-av-modersmjolkersattning-och-tillskottsnaring.

Evans, Diana. 2018. *Ordinary People*. London: Chatto and Windus.

Flood, Alison. 2017. 'Usborne Apologises for Puberty Book That Says Breasts Exist to Make Girls "Look Grown-Up and Attractive"'. Available at: https://www.theguardian.com/books/2017/aug/29/usborne-apologises-puberty-book-childrens-publisher.

———. 2019. 'Britain Has Closed Almost 800 Libraries since 2010, Figures Show'. Available at: https://www.theguardian.com/books/2019/dec/06/britain-has-closed-almost-800-libraries-since-2010-figures-show#:~:text=Almost%20800%20libraries%20have%20closed,in%202010%2C%20new%20figures%20reveal.&text=The%20closure%20of%20almost%20a,decline%20in%20spend%2C%20said%20Cipfa.

———. 2020. 'Children's Books Eight Times as Likely to Feature Animal Main Characters as BAME People'. Available at: https://www.theguardian.com/books/2020/nov/11/childrens-books-eight-times-as-likely-to-feature-animal-main-characters-than-bame-people.

Foss, Katherine A. 2018. '"That's Not a Beer Bong; It's a Breast Pump!": Representations of Breastfeeding in Prime-Time Fictional Television'. In *Breastfeeding and Culture: Discourses and Representation*, edited by Ann Marie A. Short, Abigail L. Palko and Dionne Irving, 93–111. Ontario: Demeter.

Francis, Solveig, Selma James, Phoebe Jones Schellenberg and Nina Lopez-Jones. 2002. *The Milk of Human Kindness: Defending Breastfeeding from the Global Market and the AIDS Industry*. London: Crossroads.

Fried, Dana. 2017. 'My First Time Breastfeeding My Daughter'. *The Stranger*. Available at: https://www.thestranger.com/queer-issue-2017/2017/06/21/25225867/my-first-time-breastfeeding-my-daughter.

Gaard, Greta. 2013. 'Literary Milk: Breastfeeding across Race, Class, and Species in Contemporary U.S. Fiction'. *Journal of Ecocriticism* 51, 1–18.

Gallagher, James. 2016. 'BBC Reports the UK Is the Worst in the World'. Available at: http://www.bbc.co.uk/news/health-35438049?SThisFB.

Garbes, Angela. 2018. *Like a Mother*. New York: HarperWave.

Garton Scanlon, Liz. 2015. *All the World*, illustrated by Marla Frazee. New York City: Little Simon.

Gledhill, Christine, and Vicky Ball. [1997] 2013. 'Genre and Gender: The Case of Soap Opera'. In *Representation*, edited by Stuart Hall, Jessica Evans and Sean Nixon, 335–84. London: Sage.

Gray, Emma. 2012. 'Breasts in Advertising: 10 Boob-Centric Ads'. *Huffington Post*. 6 June. Available at: https://www.huffingtonpost.co.uk/entry/breasts-in-advertising-10-boob-centric-ads_n_1572077?ri18n=true&guccounter=1&guce_referrer=aHR0cHM6Ly9j b25zZW50LnlhaG9vLmNvbS8&guce_referrer_sig=AQAAABVEX2Bxfgf32Sh0DI PuokwvFyxOtcCb1HHCdcQqwgDXLgNmmUEa69ZOrUb380pGIXb5zNyhBGa kQ0cAqohpPW-ZKIXoiFsWnz7KNLps_eazN_gkIv59ceBNBUFhkDmn5RFKFa-59UIv_9qnyGM6u6sa2kLif67C_91FOW3PbjBj.

Grayson, Jennifer. 2016. *Unlatched*. New York: Harper.

Green, Jen, and Mike Gordon. 2000. *I'm Still Important!* London: Hodder.

Gupta, Alisha Haridasani. 2020. 'Feminist Foreign Policy'. *New York Times, In Her Words* newsletter, July 21.

Hall, Stuart, Jessica Evans and Sean Nixon, eds. [1997] 2013. *Representation*. 2nd edition. London: Sage.

Halls, Stacey. 2018. *The Familiars*. London: Zaffre.

Haraway, Donna. 1989. *Primate Visions: Gender, Race, and Nature in the World of Modern Science*. New York: Routledge.

Harries, Victoria, and Amy Brown. 2017. 'The Association between Use of Infant Parenting Books That Promote Strict Routines, and Maternal Depression, Self-Efficacy, and Parenting Confidence'. *Early Child Development and Care* 189(8), 1339–50. Available at: https://www.tandfonline.com/doi/abs/10.1080/03004430.2017.1378 650?journalCode=gecd20&.

Hausman, Bernice L. 2003. *Mother's Milk*. London: Routledge.

Hawwas, A. W. 1988. 'Breast Feeding as Seen by Islam'. *Popular Science* 8: 55–58. Available at: https://pubmed.ncbi.nlm.nih.gov/12315539/#:~:text=PIP%3A%20Islamic%20 law%20requires%20mothers,to%20breast%20feed%20her%20infants.

Hedderwick, Mairi. 2007. *Katie Morag and the Dancing Class*. London: Red Fox.

Henschen, Jon. 2018. 'Is Sweden Socialist? No, but …'. *Foundation for Economic Education*. 5 March. Available at: https://fee.org/articles/is-sweden-socialist-no-but/.

Hess, Cynthia Tanima Ahmed, and Jeff Hayes. 2020. 'Providing Unpaid Household and Care Work in the United States: Uncovering Inequality'. *Institute for Women's Policy Research*. Available at: https://iwpr.org/wp-content/uploads/2020/01/IWPR-Provid ing-Unpaid-Household-and-Care-Work-in-the-United-States-Uncovering-Inequal ity.pdf.

Hinde, Katie. 2015. 'When to Wean'. *Mammals Suck … Milk*. Available at: https:// mammalssuck.blogspot.com/2015/01/when-to-wean.html#:~:text=Baby%20 mammals%20are%20able%20to,they%20produce%20the%20enzyme%20lact ase.&text=However%2C%20the%20end%20of%20any,being%20studied%20Swal low%202003.

Holden, Lynn. 2000. *Encyclopedia of Taboos*. Oxford: ABC-CLIO.

Holmes, Lucy-Anne. 2019. *Don't Hold My Head Down*. London: Unbound.

Hookway, Lyndsey. 2016. 'An Exploration of Common Infant Behaviour Misinterpretations That Can Lead to a Perception of Low Milk Supply'. *Community Practitioner*. Available at: https://www.communitypractitioner.co.uk/resources/2016/01/exploration-common-infant-behaviour-misinterpretations-can-lead-perception-low.
Hrdy, Sarah Blaffer. 1999. *Mother Nature*. London: Chatto and Windus.
Isaacs, Elizabeth B., Bruce R. Fischl, Brian T. Quinn, Wui K. Chong, David G. Gadian and Alan Lucas. 2010. 'Impact of Breast Milk on IQ, Brain Size and White Matter Development'. *Pediatric Research* 674, 357–62. Available at: https://www.ncbi.nlm.nih.gov/pmc/articles/PMC2939272/.
Jacobus, Mary. 1995. *First Things*. New York: Routledge.
Johnson, Joseph. 2020. 'Number of Books Sold in the UK from 2009 to 2018'. *Statista*. 5 March. Available at: https://www.statista.com/statistics/261278/number-of-books-sold-in-the-uk/.
Johnston, Elizabeth. 2018. 'Big Mother: Breastfeeding Rhetoric and the Panopticon in Popular Culture, 1700 to Present'. In *Breastfeeding and Culture: Discourses and Representation*, edited by Ann Marie A. Short, Abigail L. Palko and Dionne Irving, 15–32. Ontario: Demeter.
Jolly, Richard. 1995. 'Foreword'. In *Milk, Money, and Madness: The Culture and Politics of Breastfeeding*, edited by Naomi Baumslag and Dia L. Michels. Mapusa, India: Other India Press.
Klam, Matthew. 2020. 'The Liver'. *New Yorker*. 16 March, 72–79.
Krapu-Kallio, Solja. 2016. *Du ska få gröt och en lillasyster* (You'll Get Porridge and a Little Sister), illustrated by Anna Bengtsson. Stockholm: Alfabeta.
Kümmerling-Meibauer, Bettina, ed. 2018. *The Routledge Companion to Picturebooks*. London: Routledge.
Lancet. 2016. 'Breastfeeding: Achieving the New Normal', *Lancet* 387(10017), 404. 30 January. Available at: http://www.thelancet.com/journals/lancet/article/PIIS0140-67361600210-5/fulltext.
Lancet. n.d. *The Lancet* breastfeeding series. Available at: http://www.thelancet.com/series/breastfeeding.
Lancy, David. 2008. *The Anthropology of Childhood: Cherubs, Chattel, Changelings*. Cambridge: Cambridge University Press.
Landry, Susan H., Karen E. Smith and Paul R. Smith. 2003. 'The Importance of Parenting during Early Childhood for School-Age Development'. *Developmental Neuropsychology* 24(2–3), 559–91. Available at: https://pubmed.ncbi.nlm.nih.gov/14561562/.
Laskey, Kathryn. 2004. *Love That Baby*. London: Walker.
Lawrence, Claire. 2020. 'I Was Turned on by Breastfeeding – am I a Freak?' *Today's Parent*. 20 April. Available at: https://www.todaysparent.com/family/womens-health/i-was-turned-on-by-breastfeeding-am-i-a-freak/
Lee, Ellie, Jennie Bristow, Charlotte Faircloth and Jan Macvarish. 2014. *Parenting Culture Studies*. London: Palgrave.
Lee, Ellie. 2014. 'Introduction'. In *Parenting Culture Studies*, edited by Ellie Lee, Jennie Bristow, Charlotte Faircloth and Jan Macvarish, 1–22. London: Palgrave.
Lesnik-Oberstein, Karín, ed. 2006. *The Last Taboo*. Manchester: Manchester University Press.
LeVine, Robert A., and Sarah LeVine. 2016. *Do Parents Matter?* New York: PublicAffairs.
Lister, Kate. 2020. *The Curious History of Sex*. London: Unbound.
Lowery, Annie. 2019. 'Pumping Milk and Nursing Are Not the Same'. *Atlantic*. 24 July. Available at: https://www.theatlantic.com/ideas/archive/2019/07/exclusive-pumping-research/594580/.

Luscombe, Belinda. 2016. 'Why Do We Have the Breastfeeding Wars? Two Words: Maternity Leave'. *Time*. 29 January. Available at: http://time.com/4199721/why-do-we-have-the-breastfeeding-wars-two-words-maternity-leave/.

Maher, Vanessa, ed. [1992] 1995. *The Anthropology of Breast-Feeding: Natural Law or Social Construct*. Oxford: Oxford University Press.

Marteleur, Maria. 2014. 'Allt fler kallar sig feminister' (Ever More Call Themselves Feminists). *Sveriges Television*. 22 August. Available at: https://www.svt.se/nyheter/inrikes/allt-fler-feminister.

Martinson, Moa. 1933/2019. *Kvinnor och Äppelträd* (Women and Apple Trees). Stockholm: Modernista.

Martucci, Jessica, and Anne Barnhill. 2016. 'Unintended Consequences of Invoking the "Natural" in Breastfeeding Promotion'. *Pediatrics* 137, 4. Available at: https://pediatrics.aappublications.org/content/137/4/e20154154.

McCabe, Janice, Daniel Tope, Emily Fairchild, Liz Grauerholz and Benice A. Pescosolido. 2011. 'Gender in Twentieth-Century Children's Books: Patterns of Disparity in Titles and Central Characters'. *Gender and Society* 252, 197–226.

Messac, Luke. 2018. 'Women's Unpaid Work Must Be Included in GDP Calculations: Lessons from History'. *The Conversation*. 20 June. Available at: https://theconversation.com/womens-unpaid-work-must-be-included-in-gdp-calculations-lessons-from-history-98110.

Meyers, Susan. 2001. *Everywhere Babies*, illustrated by Marla Frazee. London: Houghton Mifflin Harcourt.

Miller, Alyson. 2014. 'Unsuited to Age Group: The Scandals of Children's Literature'. *College Literature* 41(2), 120–40.

Miller, Isabel. 1969/2005. *Patience and Sarah*. Vancouver, CA: Arsenal Pulp.

Mishan, Ligaya. 2009. 'First Contact: A Talk with Ursula K. LeGuin'. *New Yorker*. Available at: https://www.newyorker.com/books/book-club/first-contact-a-talk-with-ursula-k-le-guin.

Moberg, Kerstin Uvnäs. 2019. *Why Oxytocin Matters*. London: Pinter and Martin.

Moebius, William. 2009. 'Picturebook Codes'. In *Children's Literature: Approaches and Territories*, edited by Janet Maybin and Nicola J. Watson. Houndmills, England: Palgrave Macmillan.

Mulvey, Laura. [1975] 2009. *Visual and Other Pleasures*. 2nd edition. London: Palgrave.

Narančić Kovač, Smiljana. 2018. 'Picturebooks and Narratology'. In *The Routledge Companion to Picturebooks*, edited by Bettina Kümmerling-Meibauer, 409–19. London: Routledge.

National Childbirth Trust. 2021. 'What Can I Do to Help Support My Partner With Breastfeeding?' Available at: https://www.nct.org.uk/baby-toddler/feeding/tips-for-dads-and-partners/how-can-dads-and-partners-support-breastfeeding.

Nära Förlag's Facebook page. n.d. Available at: https://www.facebook.com/naraforlag/.

Nicholls, Sally. [2012] 2013. *All Fall Down*. London: Marion Lloyd Books.

———. 2013. *Close Your Pretty Eyes*. London: Scholastic.

Nodelman, Perry. 1984. 'Of Nakedness and Children's Books'. *Children's Literature Association Quarterly* 9(1), 25–50.

———. 1988. *Words about Pictures*. Athens: University of Georgia Press.

NSPCC. n.d. 'Pants'. Available at: https://www.nspcc.org.uk/keeping-children-safe/support-for-parents/underwear-rule/.

O'Carroll, Lisa, Mark Sweney and Roy Greenslade. 2015. 'Page 3: The Sun Calls Time on Topless Models After 44 Years'. *Guardian*. 20 January. Available at: https://www.theguardian.com/media/2015/jan/19/has-the-sun-axed-page-3-topless-pictures.

O'Farrell, Maggie. 2016. *This Must Be the Place*. London: Tinder.
Office of National Statistics. 2016. 'Unpaid Work Calculator'. Available at: https://www.ons.gov.uk/visualisations/dvc376/index.html.
op de Beeck, Natalie. 2018. 'Picture-Text Relationships in Picturebooks'. In *The Routledge Companion to Picturebooks*, edited by Bettina Kümmerling-Meibauer, 19–27. London: Routledge.
Palmer, Gabrielle. 1988/2009. *The Politics of Breastfeeding*. London: Pinter and Martin.
Peat, Jack. 2018. 'Only 30% of Parents Read Stories to Their Children Every Day, Poll Claims'. *The Independent*. 31 August. Available at: https://www.independent.co.uk/lifestyle/health-and-families/parents-reading-children-books-uk-roald-dahl-mcdonalds-damian-hinds-a8516436.html.
Pelenius, Linda. 2012. *Lillasyster är ett monster* (Little Sister Is a Monster). Stockholm: Berghs.
Perez, Caroline Criado. 2019. *Invisible Women*. London: Chatto & Windus.
Perry, Whitney. 2021. 'This Nike Maternity Ad Featuring Pregnant and Breastfeeding Athletes Is So Empowering'. *Glamour*. 14 March. Available at: https://www.glamour.com/story/this-nike-maternity-ad-featuring-pregnant-and-breastfeeding-athletes-is-so-empowering.
Piwoz, Ellen G., and Sandra L. Huffman. 2015. 'The Impact of Marketing of Breast-Milk Substitutes on WHO-Recommended Breastfeeding Practices'. *Food and Nutrition Bulletin* 364, 373–86. Available at: https://pubmed.ncbi.nlm.nih.gov/26314734/.
Pollister, Kathryn. 2012. 'And Now, the Breast of the Story: Realistic Portrayals of Breastfeeding in Contemporary Television'. In *Mediating Moms: Mothers in Popular Culture*, edited by Elizabeth Podnieks, 221–35. Montréal: Publication Information.
Prorokova, Tatiana. 2018. 'Gender, Psychology, and Breastfeeding as "Perverse": From A Clockwork Orange to Game of Thrones'. In *Breastfeeding and Culture: Discourses and Representation*, edited by Ann Marie A. Short, Abigail L. Palko and Dionne Irving, 134–48. Ontario: Demeter.
Pullman, Philip. 2017. *The Book of Dust*. London: Penguin Random House Children's and David Fickling Books.
Rahill, Elske. 2017. *White Ink*. London: Head of Zeus.
———. 2019. *An Unravelling*. London: Head of Zeus.
Ramqvist, Karolina. 2015. *Den vita staden* (The White City). Stockholm: Norstedts.
———. 2019. *Björnkvinnan* (The Bear Woman). Stockholm: Norstedts.
Rao, Aliya Hamid. 2019. 'Even Breadwinning Wives Don't Get Equality at Home'. *Atlantic*. 12 May. Available at: https://www.theatlantic.com/family/archive/2019/05/breadwinning-wives-gender-inequality/589237/.
Renfrew, Mary, Chloe Fisher and Suzanne Arms. 2004. *Bestfeeding: Why Breastfeeding Is Best for You and Your Baby*. 3rd edition. Berkeley, CA: Celestial Arts.
Russell, Karen. 2018. 'Orange World'. *New Yorker*. Available at: https://www.newyorker.com/magazine/2018/06/04/orange-world.
Ruta, Matilda. 2016. *Ninna och syskongrodden* (Ninna and the Sibling Sprout). Stockholm: Natur och Kultur.
Sahamies, Kicki, Johanna Persenius Svensk, Sabina Bähr, Johanna Lindh, Angelica Lundgren Bielinski, M Anna Kohlén, Ewa Agami and Vaya Perera. 2016. 'Lagstifta om skydd för ammande på offentlig plats' (Legislate for Protection of Breastfeeding in Public). *Dagens Nyheter*. 11 March. Available at: https://www.dn.se/asikt/lagstifta-om-skydd-for-ammande-pa-offentlig-plats/.

Sahamies, Kicki. 2018. 'Lagstifta mot trakasserier av ammande kvinnor' (Legislate Against Harassment of Breastfeeding Women'. *Dagens Nyheter*. 15 June. Available at: https://www.dn.se/asikt/infor-lag-som-skyddar-ammande-kvinnor-fran-ofredande/.

Sánchez, Cristina L., Javier Cubero, Javier Sánchez Alarcón and Belén Chanclón. 2009. 'The Possible Role of Human Milk Nucleotides as Sleep Inducers'. *Nutritional Neuroscience* 121, 2–8.

Sandberg, Kristina. 2010. *Att Föda Ett Barn* (To Birth a Child). Stockholm: Norstedts.

———. 2012. *Sörja för De Sina* (Grieving for Their Own). Stockholm: Norstedts.

———. 2014. *Liv Till Varje Pris* (Life at Any Cost). Stockholm: Norstedts.

Sansom, C. J. 2018. *Tombland*. London: Mantle.

Scharff, Christina. 2019. 'Why So Many Young Women Don't Call Themselves Feminist'. *BBC*. 6 February. Available at: https://www.bbc.co.uk/news/uk-politics-47006912.

Short, Ann Marie A. 2018a. 'Introduction: Contextualizing Breastfeeding and Culture: Discourses and Representation'. In *Breastfeeding and Culture: Discourses and Representation*, edited by Ann Marie A. Short, Abigail L. Palko and Dionne Irving, 1–12. Ontario: Demeter.

———. 2018b. '"In This Whole Story, That's the Shocking Detail?"': Extended Breastfeeding in Emma Donoghue's Room'. In *Breastfeeding and Culture: Discourses and Representation*, edited by Ann Marie A. Short, Abigail L. Palko and Dionne Irving, 149–64. Ontario: Demeter.

Short, Ann Marie A., Abigail L. Palko and Dionne Irving. 2018. *Breastfeeding and Culture: Discourses and Representation*. Ontario: Demeter.

Silverberg, Cory. 2013. *What Makes a Baby*, illustrated by Fiona Smyth. Berkeley, CA: Seven Stories.

Smith, Philip, and Alexander Riley. [2001] 2009. *Cultural Theory*. 2nd edition. Oxford: Blackwell.

Soldavini, Jessica, and Lindsey Smith Taillie. 2017. 'Recommendations for Adopting the International Code of Marketing of Breast-Milk Substitutes into United States Policy'. *Journal of Human Lactation* 333, 582–87. Available at: ncbi.nlm.nih.gov/pmc/articles/PMC5515674/.

Stark, Ulf. 2007. *En stjärna vid namn Ajax* (A Star Called Ajax), illustrated by Stina Wirsén. Stockholm: Bonnier Carlsen.

———. 2016. *Lillasyster* (Little Sister), illustrated by Charlotte Ramel. Stockholm: Lilla Piratförlaget.

Stearns, Cindy A. 1999. 'Breastfeeding and the Good Maternal Body'. *Gender and Society* 13, 308–25.

Stoneley, Ellie. 2015. *Milky Moments*, illustrated by Jessica D'Alton Goode. London: Pinter and Martin.

Strinati, Dominic. [1995] 2003. *An Introduction to Theories of Popular Culture*. 2nd edition. London: Routledge.

Struwe, Hanna Zetterberg. 2008. *Nejlika och lilla lillasyster* (Nejlika and Little, Little Sister), illustrated by Anna-Karin Garhamn. Stockholm: Rabén och Sjögren.

Sunderland, Margot. 2016. *What Every Parent Needs to Know*. 2nd edition. London: DK.

Svenska Barnboksinstitutet. 2020a. '2019 Book Tasting', translated by B. J. Epstein. Available at: https://www.barnboksinstitutet.se/wp-content/uploads/2020/09/Bp_eng-2019.pdf.

———. 2020b. '25 Years of the Book Tasting 1993–2017 and Summary 2017–2018', translated by B. J. Epstein. Available at: https://www.barnboksinstitutet.se/wp-content/uploads/2020/06/Bp_eng-2020.pdf.

Tanrikulu, Hacer, Daniela Neri, Aileen Robertson and Melissa Mialon. 2020. 'Corporate Political Activity of the Baby Food Industry: The Example of Nestlé in the United States of America'. *International Breastfeeding Journal*, 15. Available at: https://internationalbreastfeedingjournal.biomedcentral.com/articles/10.1186/s13006-020-00268-x.

Tea, Kristine. 2016. 'Lawmaker Suggests Sexually Assaulting Breastfeeding Moms'. *Mothering*. 19 February. Available at: http://www.mothering.com/articles/lawmaker-suggests-sexually-assaulting-breastfeeding-moms/.

Therén, Ida. 2014. *Rida ryggen* (Ride on Back), illustrated by Z. Keller. Stockholm: Nära förlag.

———. 2016. *Alltid tillsammans* (Always Together), illustrated by Nathalie Ruejas. Stockholm: Nära förlag.

Thomson, Rupert. 2018. *Never Anyone but You*. London: Corsair.

Thore, Maria Nilsson, and Annika Thore. 2014. *Leka tittut!* (Play Peekaboo!). Stockholm: Bonnier Carlsen.

Tran, Mark. 2014. 'Claridge's Hotel Criticised after Telling Breastfeeding Woman to Cover Up'. *Guardian*. 2 December. Available at: http://www.theguardian.com/lifeandstyle/2014/dec/02/claridges-hotel-breastfeeding-woman-cover-up.

Tremain, Rose. 2016. *The Gustav Sonata*. London: Vintage.

Trias, Elisenda Isabel Serrano, and Rosa Ma Masvidal. 2003. 'La lactància en els llibres per a nens i nenes de 0 a 6 anys English summary'. *Pediatr Catalana* 63, 314–18.

Tsiang, Sarah. 2011. *Dogs Don't Eat Jam*. Cardiff: Firefly.

Tupera, Tupera. 2017. *What Does Baby Want?* London: Phaidon.

Turner, Bryan S. [1984] 1996. *The Body and Society*. 2nd edition. London: Sage.

UNICEF. 2020. The International Code of Marketing of Breastmilk Substitutes. Available at: https://www.unicef.org.uk/babyfriendly/baby-friendly-resources/international-code-marketing-breastmilk-substitutes-resources/the-code/.

Uzon, Jorge. 2010. *Hello, Baby!* Toronto: Groundwood Books.

van Esterik, Penny. 1989. *Motherpower and Infant Feeding*. London: Zed Books.

Vargas-Silva, Carlos, and Cinzia Rienzo. 2020. 'Migrants in the UK: An Overview'. *The Migration Observatory*. Available at: https://migrationobservatory.ox.ac.uk/resources/briefings/migrants-in-the-uk-an-overview/#:~:text=to%20the%20UK.-,In%202018%2C%20people%20born%20outside%20the%20UK%20made%20up%20an,in%202018%20Figure%201.

Von Friesen, Anna. 2019. 'Mediebarometern 2018 om bokläsning: 11 procent prenumererar på en streamingtjänst för böcker' (Media Barometer 2018 about Book Reading: 11 Percent Subscribe to a Streaming Service for Books). *Boktugg*. 24 May. Available at: https://www.boktugg.se/2019/05/24/mediebarometern-2018-om-boklasning-11-procent-prenumererar-pa-en-streamingtjanst-for-bocker/.

Wagner, Tamara S. 2019. '"Nature's Founts": Breastmilk in Victorian Popular Culture'. *Victorian Review* 45(1), 18–22. Available at: doi:10.1353/vcr.2019.0026.

Wambach, Karen, and Jan Riordan. 2016. Breastfeeding and Human Lactation. 5th edition. Burlington, MA: Jones and Bartlett.

Warnqvist, Åsa. 2017. 'Flickans århundrade?: generationsskiftet i den svenska barn- och ungdomslitteraturen under 2000-talet' (The Century of the Girl?: The Generation Shift in Swedish Literature for Children and Young Adults in the 21st Century). *Konstellationer: festskrift till Anna Williams* (*Constellations: A Festschrift for Anna Williams*), 145–58. Möklinta, Sweden.

Weiss, Elizabeth. 2014. 'Selling the Myth of the Ideal Mother'. *New Yorker*. 8 May. Available at: https://www.newyorker.com/business/currency/selling-the-myth-of-the-ideal-mother.

Wiessinger, Diane, Diana West and Teresa Pitman. 2010. *The Womanly Art of Breastfeeding*. 8th edition. London: Pinter and Martin.

Wikberg, Erik. 2019. 'Bokförsäljningsstatistiken' (Book Sales Statistics). Svenska bokhandlareföreningen och svenska förläggareföreningen. Available at: https://www.forlaggare.se/sites/default/files/bokfors_statistik_helar_2019_ny.pdf.

Williams, Carolyn D. 2006. '"That Wonderful Phænomenon": Female Body Hair and English Literary Tradition'. In *The Last Taboo*, edited by Karín Lesnik-Oberstein, 103–25. Manchester: Manchester University Press.

Williams, Zoe. 2021. 'Burnt Out: Is the Exhausting Cult of Productivity Finally Over?' *Guardian*. 22 April. Available at: https://www.theguardian.com/money/2021/apr/22/burnt-out-is-the-exhausting-cult-of-productivity-finally-over?fbclid=IwAR2yGJmgvLT6rLeG2z3M8meIF13vUdD9qbSu1NPIeFnI0zRQOAMG_PAMCeY.

Winnicott, D. W. 1973. *The Child, the Family, and the Outside World*. New York: Penguin.

Winstanley, Nicola. 2011. *Cinnamon Baby*, illustrated by Janice Nadeau. Toronto: Kids Can.

Wolde, Gunilla. 1975/1998. *Emma och lillebror* (Emma and Little Brother). Stockholm: Natur och Kultur.

Wolitzer, Meg. 2003. *The Wife*. London: Vintage.

Wordley, Biana. 2019. 'The Brilliant New Ad Normalising Breastfeeding'. *Essentialbaby*. 2 October. Available at: http://www.essentialbaby.com.au/baby/breastfeeding/the-brilliant-new-ad-normalising-breastfeeding-20191001-h1ijbi.

YouGov. 2010. 'Equality for Women Survey'. Available at: https://web.archive.org/web/20171125131915/http://d25d2506sfb94s.cloudfront.net/today_uk_import/YG-Archives-Pol-YouGov-EqualityWomen-011010.pdf.

Young, Charlotte. 2016. *Why Breastfeeding Matters*. London: Pinter and Martin.

INDEX

Note: Page numbers with an "n" denote notes.

Adidas ad 4
advertising, influence of 4, 115–18
Afra 38
Ahlberg, Allan 42
Ahlberg, Janet 42
Albertalli, Becky 86
Alin, Cecilia Nordstrand 48
All Fall Down 85–86
All the World 34–35
Alltid tillsammans 47–48, 55, 81
Alvstad, Cecilia 123–14
Amningshjälpen (Breastfeeding Help), Sweden 63, 108
anatomy 2, 9, 108
Anderson, Lena 52n14
Andersson, Maria 49
areola 34, 36, 37–38, 40, 50, 51, 52
artificial milk. *See* formula milk
Atkinson, Kate 65, 72, 73, 75, 81, 84, 90
Att föda ett barn 100
Audickas, Lukas 112
Ayuyang, Rina 89

Baby Milk Action 64, 116
Baby's Catalogue, The 42
babywearing 18, 32, 46
Ball, Vicky 6n6
bare breasts 1–2, 36, 40, 48, 51, 74
Bauknecht, Sara 4–5
Beauvais, Clémentine 74n8, 87n12
Behind the Scenes at the Museum 72–73, 75–77
Bengtsson, Anna 49
Berger, John 51
Bernhard, Durga 36

Bernhard, Emery 36
Big Bang Theory, The 3n3
biphobia 54
bisexuals 54, 128
Björnkvinnan 104
Blakemore, Erin 13
Blame It on the Boogie 89
body 25–28. *See also* women's bodies
   as a set of social practices 26
   societal view of 26
Body and Society, The 25
Book of Dust, The 78–79, 80
bottle-feeding 4, 6, 21, 22, 32–33, 36, 41–44, 49–50, 56. *See also* formula milk
breastfeeding
   academic study of 2–5
   breast as norm 19n6
   breastfeeding wars 13
   as caring work 23–24
   on children's television 3
   as comforting and peaceful 104
   cost of 24
   as cultural norm 50
   devil metaphor 60–61, 77, 78
   as disgusting, shameful or wrong 17, 73–80, 128
   diversity, lack of 53–55, 92–96
   as a duty 14
   and economy 14
   as an emotional impediment 68–73
   evolutionary importance 18–19
   and father–child relationship 128
   and good mothering 87–92
   health benefits 19, 24–25

breastfeeding (cont.)
  health considerations 22–23
  interfering with other relationships 71–72, 81, 128
  and liberation 21–22
  monetisation 4, 24
  naturalness 90
  neutral breastfeeding 83–84
  normalisation of 103–5, 129, 135
  not breastfeeding as failure 89–90
  of older child 96
  as painful and difficult 63–67, 128
  and parent–child bond 27, 130–31
  positive breastfeeding 84–87
  as primitive activity 93
  psychoanalytical approach 19n5
  in public 74–75, 80
  and racial hierarchy 22
  rate of 129
  reasons for becoming less common 20
  reduction in rate of 13–14
  right to feed in public 3
  and self-worth 24
  versus sexual attractiveness 81–83
  as taboo 50–53
  on TV shows 3
  in United States 17–18
  in Victorian fiction 61n2
breastfeeding-positive book 128
breasts 29, 50–51, 136
  depiction in society 86–87
  ownership of 17, 26
  sexual aspect 27, 56
  sexualisation of 14–18, 127
Broomé, Elisabet 48
Brown, Amy 3, 11, 18, 21, 23, 23n12, 39, 42, 73, 90, 109n5

Calaf, Mònica 37, 39
Catalan-language children's books 37
Centre for Literacy in Primary Education (CLPE), UK 54
chestfeeding 9, 10, 10n9, 31, 39, 129
Christianity 56, 86, 88n14, 111–12, 129–30
Cinnamon Baby 35–36
circuit of culture 8, 9, 124–25, 134–35
Cleary, Beverly 30n2

Clockwork Orange, A 3n3
Close Your Pretty Eyes 84–85
combination-feeding 32, 41, 42, 43, 92
Conservative Party, UK 112–13
Cooke, Kristy 120–21
Covid-19 pandemic 109nn4–5
Cracknell, Richard 112
Criado Perez, Caroline 15
culture 6n6, 7–8, 17, 124
  circuit of 8, 9, 124–25, 134–35
  myth 103

Dahle, Gro 29n1
Daily Mirror 113
Damour, Lisa 16
Daniel, Carolyn 73n6, 87, 91
David Copperfield 61n2
de Boitiz, Victoria 38
Den vita staden 104–5
Desperate Housewives 3n3
Dickens, Charles 61n2
disability, and breastfeeding 54, 128, 129
diversity, lack of 53–55, 92–96, 128, 129
Dogs Don't Eat Jam 34
Donoghue, Emma 94, 95
Douglas, Mary 80
Downham, Jenny 65, 66, 92
Du ska få gröt och en lillasyster 49

Elliot, Rebecca 42
Emma och lillebror 45
Emotionally Weird 72, 85
Encyclopedia of Taboos 50
English-language books 8, 41
  children books, depiction of breastfeeding in 30
  discretion 33–41
  diversity, lack of 53–55, 128
  literature for adults and young adults 59, 63–67, 128–29
  picturebooks 32–33, 41–44, 127
  prevalence of bottle in 32–33
Enright, Anne 64
ER 3n3
ethnicities 39, 93, 110–11, 128, 129
Evans, Diana 69
Evans, Jessica 7, 8
Everywhere Babies 41–42

Familiars, The 83–84
feminism 2, 11, 21, 56–57, 118, 120, 124
Flood, Alison 81, 91, 91n16, 111, 121
Folkpartiet (Folk Party), Sweden 113
Forgotten Waltz, The 64
formula milk 19, 20–21, 43, 65, 87–88n13, 128. *See also* bottle-feeding
  compared with breastmilk 22–23
  influence of manufacturers of 115–18
Foss, Katherine A. 64, 66, 67, 74, 75, 82, 90–91, 93, 94, 96
Frazee, Marla 34, 41
Fuentes, Mikel 37

Gaard, Greta 4, 21, 24, 54, 106, 136
Game of Thrones, A 3n3
Gap ad 4–5
Garbes, Angela 16
Garhamn, Anna-Karin 45
gender 9–10
  identity 129
  roles 133
genitals, depiction of 52–53
Gledhill, Christine 6n6
Goode, Jessica D'Alton 38
good-enough mother 103
good mother/mothering 24, 60–61, 87–92, 94n19, 100–103, 105, 129, 130
Gordon, Mike 42
Grayson, Jennifer 20, 50
Green, Jen 42
Guatemala, carrying of babies in 36
Gupta, Alisha Haridasani 114
Gustav Sonata, The 65–66, 81–82, 88

Hall, Stuart 7, 8
Halls, Stacey 84
Hamidi, Yamina 63, 109
Haraway, Donna 9n8
Hausman, Bernice L. 17–18, 22, 23
Hedderwick, Mairi 40
Hej lillebror 48
Hello, Baby! 35
heterosexuals 1, 24, 29n1, 48, 54, 59, 87, 97, 128
Holden, Lynn 50
Holmes, Lucy-Anne 16
Hrdy, Sarah Blaffer 17, 18–19, 21, 131–32

implied reader 35n4
I'm Still Important! 42
industrialisation, impact on breastfeeding 20
internalised gaze 96–97, 107
International Code of Marketing of Breastmilk Substitutes 64, 108, 115–17

Jacobus, Mary 19n5, 92
Johnson, Joseph 120–21
Johnstone, Elizabeth 10

Kanin-bad 52n14
Katie Morag and the Dancing Class 40
Keller, Z. 46
Kempe, Mats 100n23
Knightley, Keira 15n3
Krapu-Kallio, Solja 49
Kvinnor och Äppleträd 98–99

Labour Party, UK 112
La Leche League 14
Lambert, Felicity 108, 109
Laskey, Kathryn 41
left-wing politics 112–14
LeGuin, Ursula K. 79–80
Leka tittut! 52n14
Lesnik-Oberstein, Karín 2n1
LeVine, Robert A. 17
LeVine, Sarah 17
LeVine and LeVine 56
LGBTQ+ literature 40n9, 67n5
Life after Life 73–74, 90
Lillasyster är ett monster 49
Lister, Kate 2n1
literary fiction 121–22
Liv till varje pris 101
Loft, Philip 112
Love That Baby 41
Lowery, Annie 42

Maj trilogy 100–103
male gaze 97, 107
Married … with Children 75
Martinson, Moa 98
Mary, the mother of Jesus 92, 112, 130
maternity leaves 13, 20, 118, 131, 132, 134

McCabe, Janice 123
media, depiction of breastfeeding in 2, 3–5, 8, 11–12, 16, 21, 27, 64, 82, 97, 116, 121, 134–35
medicalisation, impact on breastfeeding 20–21
#MeToo movement 15n4
Meyers, Susan 41
Milky Moments 38–39, 56
Miller, Isabel 86
Mister Rogers' Neighborhood 3
Moberg, Kerstin Uvnäs 17
Moderaterna (Moderates), Sweden 113
Moore, Josh 114n7
Mr Super Poopy Pants 42
Mulvey, Laura 97
Mummel. En ny människa 49
My New Baby 34
Mystery of the Breast, The 38

Nadeau, Janice 35
naked versus nude 50–53, 80, 127
Nära Förlag 46
Narančić Kovač, Smiljana 35n4
National Breastfeeding Helpline, UK 23n11, 108
National Childbirth Trust 49
Nejlika och lilla lillasyster 45–46
neutral breastfeeding 83–84
Never Anyone but You 77n9
New Baby, The 42
new baby-themed book 34, 42–43, 127
Nicholls, Sally 84, 85
Nike ad 4
Ninna och syskongrodden 46
nipples 38, 40, 51, 64
Nixon, Sean 7, 8
Nodelman, Perry 29, 33, 51, 53, 56
non-breastfeeding families 43
Not the End of the World 81
nursing 9
nutrition 12, 19, 22, 61, 95, 130, 132
Nyhus, Kaia Dahle 29n1

O'Farrell, Maggie 73, 92
Office of National Statistics (ONS) 24
older child, breastfeeding of 127, 129

op de Beeck, Natalie 5n5
'Orange World,' 59–60
Ordinary People 69
oxytocin 17, 66

Palmer, Gabrielle 19, 20, 22–23, 50, 51, 55, 90, 114, 132, 133
Papua New Guinea, carrying of babies in 36
parent–child bond 27, 130–31
parenting books 11
Patience and Sarah 86–87
patriarchy 7, 83, 96–97, 131, 132
Pelenius, Linda 49
performance poetry 5n5
picturebooks 5n5, 29, 39
    discretion 33–41
    English-language picturebooks 32–33, 41–44, 127
    nudity in 29–30
    Swedish-language picturebooks 44–50, 127, 128
    Swedish vs English 30
Pienkowski, Jan 51
Piglettes 74n8
Pinter and Martin 37, 38
plays 5n5
Pollister, Kathryn 3–4, 64, 93, 116, 135
portrayals in literature, importance of 134–36
positive breastfeeding 84–87
premature baby 94n19
pro-breastfeeding books 43
Prorokova, Tatiana 3n3, 82–83, 97
puberty 91n16
Pullman, Philip 78, 79, 80, 82

queer movement 25

race 53–54, 93, 96, 111, 128
Rahill, Elske 69, 71–72, 77–78, 84
Ramona's World 30n2
Ramqvist, Karolina 63, 99, 103–4, 105
reading habits 130
religion, and breastfeeding 55, 128, 129–30
Rida ryggen 46–47
Ride on Mother's Back, A 36
right-wing politics 112–14
Riley, Alexander 7, 26

INDEX

Room 94–96
Ruejas, Nathalie 47
Russell, Karen 59, 62, 77, 78, 93
Ruta, Matilda 46

Sandberg, Kristina 63, 99, 100, 100n23, 101, 102, 103, 105, 106
Sansom, C. J. 88, 89n15
Scandinavian societies 114–15
Scanlon, Liz Garton 34
Sesame Street 3
Sesam Sesam 29n1
sexism 9, 97, 132
sexual attractiveness, versus breastfeeding 81–83
sexuality 54, 128, 129
Shenker, Natalie 109n5
Short, Ann Marie A. 3, 4, 57, 94, 95, 96
sibling feeling towards new babies 34, 48
Silverberg, Cory 29n1
Simon vs. the Homo Sapiens Agenda 86
single parents 39, 54, 113, 119
Smith, Philip 7, 26
Smyth, Fiona 29n1
soap opera 6n6
Socialdemokraterna (Social Democrats), Sweden 113
Soldavini, Jessica 117
Sörja för de sina 100
Stearns, Cindy A. 74, 81, 83, 87, 89, 131
Stoneley, Ellie 38, 39, 55
Strinati, Dominic 6–7, 26–27
Struwe, Hanna Zetterberg 45
Sun 113
Sweden and United Kingdom, comparison between 124–25
  attitudes towards women, children and families 118–20, 130
  breastfeeding support services 108–10
  ethnic differences 110–11
  gender of characters, in writing 123
  influence of formula-milk manufacturers and advertising 115–18
  political differences 112–15, 130
  reading habits 120–22
  religious differences 111–12
  taboo, in writing 123–24
  writing habits 122–24

Swedish-language books 8, 56, 97–99, 105–6
  children's book 30
  diversity, lack of 92–96, 129
  fiction for adults 59, 128, 129
  picturebooks 44–50, 127, 128

Taillie, Lindsey Smith 117
tandem-feeding 55, 94, 129
television programmes/shows 64, 75, 82, 91, 94, 96
Therén, Ida 46, 47, 55
This Must Be the Place 73
Thomson, Rupert 77n9
Thore, Annika 52n14
Thore, Maria Nilsson 52n14
Time magazine 13
Tombland 88–89
trans parent 10n9, 39, 128, 129, 132n1
Tremain, Rose 65, 81, 88
Trias, Elisenda Isabel Serrano 37
Tsiang, Sarah 34
Tupera, Tupera 40
Turner, Bryan S. 25, 26, 80, 97

Unbecoming 65, 66, 92–93
UNICEF 115–17
United Kingdom and Sweden, comparison between. *See* Sweden and United Kingdom, comparison between
United States 127
  breastfeeding rate in 14, 108n2
  child mortality rate in 19
  children's books in 52
  Family and Medical Leave Act (FMLA) 119n8
  formula-feeding in 20, 22, 42
  political differences 114
  pumping culture in 108n2, 119n8
Unlatched 20
Unravelling, An 70–71, 78, 84
Usborne 91n16
Uzon, Jorge 35

van Esterik, Penny 21, 23, 56
Vestin, Frances 49
Victorian fiction, breastfeeding in 61n2
Vogel, Saskia 63, 104n26

Wagner, Tamara S. 61n2
Warnqvist, Åsa 123
weaning 3, 38n7, 55, 64, 71, 94, 95–96
Weiss, Elizabeth 103
What Does Baby Want? 40–41, 48, 56, 81
What Makes a Baby 29n1
When Will There Be Good News? 65
White Ink 69–70, 77–78
Wiessinger, Diane 33
Wife, The 68–69
Williams, Carolyn D. 2n1
Winnicott, D. W. 103
Winstanley, Nicola 35
Wolde, Gunilla 45
Wolitzer, Meg 68, 72
women
  fiction of 6n6
  maternity leave 13, 20, 118, 131, 132, 134
  power of 131–34
  practical and emotional labour at home 132
  pressure to earn money 20
  sex, as a domestic labour 27
  social roles 10
  work and abilities, valuing of 132–33
women's bodies 1–2, 10, 14–15, 25, 62, 130, 131
  depiction in literature 2
  shame and confusion feeling about 17
  societal perspective 26
World Health Organization 13, 130
writing habits 130

You, Me and the Breast 37–38, 56
Young, Charlotte 4, 17, 19n6, 130–31, 135
young adult (YA) novels 85–87

www.ingramcontent.com/pod-product-compliance
Lightning Source LLC
Chambersburg PA
CBHW021144230426
43667CB00005B/245